HISTORICAL COLLECTIONS
of
COSHOCTON COUNTY
OHIO

A Complete Panorama of the County, from the
Time of the Earliest Known Occupants
of the Territory unto the
Present Time

1764–1876

*Entered According to Act of Congress in the Year
1876, in the Office of the Librarian of Congress
by*

William E. Hunt

HERITAGE BOOKS
2010

HERITAGE BOOKS
AN IMPRINT OF HERITAGE BOOKS, INC.

Books, CDs, and more—Worldwide

For our listing of thousands of titles see our website
at
www.HeritageBooks.com

A Facsimile Reprint
Published 2010 by
HERITAGE BOOKS, INC.
Publishing Division
100 Railroad Ave. #104
Westminster, Maryland 21157

Copyright © 1993 Heritage Books, Inc.

Originally published
Cincinnati
Robert Clarke & Co., Printers
1876

— Publisher's Notice —
In reprints such as this, it is often not possible to remove blemishes from the original. We feel the contents of this book warrant its reissue despite these blemishes and hope you will agree and read it with pleasure.

International Standard Book Numbers
Paperbound: 978-1-55613-875-1
Clothbound: 978-0-7884-8314-1

PREFACE.

The tastes of the preparer of this volume disposed him to undertake it; a residence in Coshocton of twenty years, and peculiar relations and associations of favorable sort, gave him, as friends claimed, at least a certain fitness to do it; and the Centennial year seemed to be the proper occasion. Amid ill-health and other hindrances wholly unanticipated when the work was begun, the book has been written. If it does not meet all expectations, it is hoped it will not disappoint any reasonable ones. It could scarcely be expected that a work of the sort should be entirely free from errors, but great care has been taken to make it at least correct as far as it goes. Of course, in the line of personal history, regard must be had to the limits and scope of the work. It only purports to be a panorama—not a series of finished portraits, with every shadow and light. Mere mention of every person and thing not amiss in such a volume would indefinitely extend it and add to cost. To those who have kindly assisted in its preparation, I shall ever feel grateful; and I can confidently say that if there had been on the part of some others such help as those kind friends rendered, and as a little public spirit, local fame and denominational interest might well prompt, the book would be a better one. As it is, I respectfully submit it as at least an honest endeavor to put in convenient and permanent form something of the record of a locality of classic (American) interest, and to trace the steps whereby we have reached our present position as a county.

WM. E. HUNT.

CORRECTIONS AND ADDITIONS.

Page 7, read capital for capitol.
" 17, county for country.
" 26, Joseph W. for John G.
" 30, Hesket for Herkett.
" 35, Micajah for Michael.
" 41, Weatherwax for Weatherwat.
" 42, Ireland for Pennsylvania and Eastern Ohio.
" 59, through for though, and insert in third paragraph after railroads, "have been projected."
" 78, Hagerstown, Md., for Fayette county, Pa.
" 79, strike out statement that C. C. Leonard was in partnership with J. D. Nicholas.
" 81, read James for Jones
" 89, Hailstorm for Snowball.
" 99, Assignee's for Sheriff's.
" 104, McNary for McNarry.
" 105, read E. T. Dudley.
" 108, Brelsford for Bretsford.
" 114, Joseph for Isaac.
" 123, William K. for Wm. N.
" 134, $13,835 for 10,885.
" 138, Thompson for Thomas.
" 240, found for founded.
" 257, 1837 for 1857.
" 261, in notice of Charles S. Barnes, whence for when.

To list of earliest settlers in Perry township, add Joseph Mills, coming in 1823, and dying in his 87th year, in 1876; and the father of J. S. McVey, of Walhonding, long resident in the township.

To the list of Jefferson township, add Henry Metham, father of Col. Pren Metham, settling in 1814.

To the list of families on page 30, add the Williams family.

To list of Physicians on page 118, add J. R. Gamble, of New Castle, removing from county in 1876.

To list of Building Association Directors, page 112, add H. N. Shaw and Wm. Ward.

CONTENTS.

CHAPTER I.
Territorial Limits and Subdivisions of the County—Date of Organization of County—Names and Date of Organization of Townships, Villages, etc.. 1–5

CHAPTER II.
Indian Occupancy, and Early Military Expeditions—The Pre-Historic Race—The French Rule—The Delawares—Their Towns in Coshocton County—Netawatwees, or King Newcomer—Killbuck, White Eyes, etc., etc.—Boquet's Expedition—The Coshocton Campaign—The Revolutionary War—The Character of Indians, and subsequent whereabouts....... 6–15

CHAPTER III.
Notes on Settlement of County and Growth in Population...... 16–22

CHAPTER IV.
Notices of the Earliest Settlers, and other Points of Interest pertaining to each Township.. 23–34

CHAPTER V.
Same Subject continued.. 35–48

CHAPTER VI.
Advancement of County in Wealth, Matters of Taxation, etc... 49–51

CHAPTER VII.
Something about Roads, Ferries, Bridges, Canals, Steamboats, and Rail Roads.. 52–59

CHAPTER VIII.
County Buildings and County Officers—Complete lists of latter. 60–68

CHAPTER IX.
Relations to State and National Government—Members of the Legislature, Congress, etc... 69–71

CHAPTER X.
The Courts and the Bar.. 72–82

(v)

vi   *Contents.*

CHAPTER XI.

PAGES.

Notes on Agricultural Affairs—Extent of this interest—Corn, Wheat, etc.—Hogs, Fine Cattle, Blooded Horses, etc.—County Agricultural Society—County Fairs, etc............... 83–94

CHAPTER XII.

Notes on Manufacturing and Mining. 95–107

CHAPTER XIII.

Notes on Merchandizing, Banking, Tavern-keeping—Transportation Business, etc.. 108–115

CHAPTER XIV.

Physicians—Health Items—Medical Remedies of the Pioneers. 116–122

CHAPTER XV.

Newspapers—Coshocton County Authoresses, etc.................. 123–127

CHAPTER XVI.

School Matters.. 128–138

CHAPTER XVII.

Military Affairs... 139–150

CHAPTER XVIII.

County Bible Society—S. S. Association—Temperance Movements—Secret Orders.. 151–158

CHAPTER XIX.

Miscellaneous Matters—1. The Pre-Historic Race. 2. Ancient Burial Grounds. 3. Meaning of the names Muskingum, Tuscarawas, and Walhonding. 4. Prose Legend of the Walhonding. 5. Heckwelder's Famous Ride. 6. Temperance Crusade among the Indians. 7. The Gnadenhutten Massacre. 8. Curious Stories Touching Captives Reclaimed by Boquet. 9. Description of the Hunting-Shirt. 10. The Houses and Furniture of the Pioneers in Coshocton County. 11. Louis Philippe at Coshocton. 12. How to Raise a Large Family. 13. Indian Stories. 14. Backwoods Sports 159–177

CHAPTER XX.

Miscellaneous Matters—1. The Killing of Cartmill, the Post Boy. 2. Shocking Murders in Coshocton County. 3. Colored People in Coshocton County. 4. Fires in Roscoe—An Incident and a Joke. 5. A Bundle of First Things. 6. Relics and Curiosities in Personal Possession. 7. Coshocton Wags in Early Days. 8. The Treasury Robbery. 9. Humors of the Crusade... 178–191

CHAPTER XXI.

The Churches—General Statements—Detailed Accounts of the Baptist, Christian, Catholic, and Lutheran Churches...... 192–204

CHAPTER XXII.

The Churches—Detailed Accounts of the Methodist Episcopal, Methodist (Protestant), Presbyterian, United Presbyterian, Protestant Episcopal, Christian Union Churches, etc.......... 205–231

CHAPTER XXIII.

Brief Biographical Sketches—Charles Williams. Thomas L. Rue. James Renfrew. Abraham Sells. Dr. Samuel Lee. James Robinson. Thomas Darling. Benjamin Ricketts. John Carhart. James Le Retilley. Thomas Johnson. Joseph Burns. John Burns. John Johnson. Wm. K. Johnson. Robert Hay. John Elliott. Taliaffero Vickers. Wm. Brown. Alexander Renfrew. Eli Nichols. Nathaniel Conklin. G. W. Silliman. Robert M. Lamb. David Spangler. Peter Humrickhouse. Arnold Medberry. Matthew Scott. John Lockard. Sharon Williams. Isaac Darling. Matthew Trimble. William Pancake. Reuben Whittaker. James W. Pigman. Samuel Brillhart. Matthew Ferguson. John C. Tidball. Joseph B. Crowley. Clark Johns. C. C. Nichols. Wm. B. Glover. Joel Clark Glover. Thomas Carroll, Jr. Robert S. McCormick. Asa G. Dimmock. M. C. McFarland. Samuel Ketchum. Samuel Morrison. John Morgan. Charles S. Barnes. Wm. Henderson. Geo. Darling. Samuel Squire. Nicholas Bassett. W. H. Vickers. Thompson Carnahan....................... 232–264

[*Many scores of sketches, scarcely less brief than many of these, will be found in other parts of this work.*]

HISTORICAL COLLECTIONS

OF

COSHOCTON COUNTY.

CHAPTER I.

TERRITORIAL LIMITS AND SUBDIVISIONS OF THE COUNTRY.

THE territory embraced in what is now the State of Ohio (and even a large territory adjacent *) was at one time divided into only three counties — viz.: Washington, Hamilton, and Wayne. The boundaries of Washington county, as constituted in 1788, were as follows: "Beginning on the bank of the Ohio river, where the western boundary line of Pennsylvania crosses it, and running with that line to Lake Erie; thence along the southern shore of said lake to the mouth of the Cuyahoga river; thence up said river to the portage between it and the Tuscarawas branch of the Muskingum river; thence down that branch to the forks at the crossing above Fort Laurens (near the present town of Bolivar); thence with a line to be drawn westerly to the portage of that branch of the Big Miami on which the fort stood that was taken by the French in 1752, until it meets the road from the Lower Shawneetown to Sandusky; thence south to the Scioto river; thence with that river to its mouth, and thence up the Ohio river to the place of beginning."

Out of this territory nearly thirty counties as they now exist have been erected. The northern central part of Washington county was, in 1804, erected into Muskingum

---

* Including parts of what are now the States of Indiana and Illinois, and most of Michigan and Wisconsin.

county, and in 1811, by the Legislature then in session at
Zanesville, the northern part of Muskingum county was
set off under the name of Coshocton* county; Guernsey,
Tuscarawas, Knox, and Licking having all been previously
organized. As originally constituted, Coshocton county
embraced a considerable part of what is now Holmes, extending to the Greenville treaty line, six miles north of
Millersburg; but that county having been organized in 1824,
the limits of Coshocton county were fixed as they now are.
Prior to the adoption of the present State Constitution,
in 1851, there was considerable agitation about a new
county to be formed out of parts of Guernsey, Tuscarawas,
and Coshocton, with New Comerstown as the county-seat.
There was also a movement contemplating a county, with
Walhonding as the county-seat. But that instrument rendered such movements hopeless. The territory embraced
in Coshocton county is part of that designated as United
States Military Land District—so called from the fact that
Congress, in 1798, appropriated it to satisfy certain claims of
the officers and soldiers of the Revolutionary War. These
lands were surveyed into townships five miles square, and
these again into quarter townships, containing four thousand acres, and subsequently some of these into forty
lots, of one hundred acres each, for the accommodation
of soldiers or others holding warrants for that number of
acres. What land was not required for the satisfaction of
the military warrants was subsequently sold by act of Congress, under the designation of Congress land. Twenty-
two and a fraction of these original townships were embraced within the limits of Coshocton county as finally
fixed in 1824. Owing to the inconvenience arising from
the intermediate rivers, part of Tuscarawas township was
attached to the one west of it.† As the population of the

---

* The name is unquestionably a modification of the name of the old
Indian town at the forks of the Muskingum—*Goschachgunk*—as somewhat variously spelled according to sound by the old chroniclers in
different languages. Different and quite contradictory definitions of
the name have been given.

† After the Ohio canal was made, and before the bridges were built.

townships warranted, they were named (having been previously designated as yet in all conveyances by numbers), and elections for justices of the peace and other officers ordered by the county authorities.

The townships first organized were Tuscarawas, Washington, New Castle, and Franklin, in 1811. The territory adjacent embraced in originally surveyed townships was connected with these for purposes of government and taxation, and afterward set off and organized as population might require. Oxford was thus set off in the fall of 1811, and Linton in 1812. Perry township was organized in 1817; the election for officers was appointed to be held in April, at the house of Elias James. Mill Creek was organized in July of the same year, and the election held at the house of John P. Wilson. Pike was organized in August, 1818, the election being at the house of James Bryan. The next township organized was White Eyes, in 1823; then followed Tiverton and Monroe and Keene the next year. Bedford was organized in 1825, and Bethlehem and Jefferson in 1826; Crawford, Virginia, and Jackson in 1828, and Clark in 1829. Adams township was organized in 1832, and Lafayette (the last) in 1835.

There are in the county at this writing one incorporated village—Coshocton—and the following other villages, viz.: Roscoe, Warsaw, West Carlisle, West Bedford, Jacobsport, New Castle, Walhonding, East Union, Keene, New Bedford, Bakersville, Chili, Canal Lewisville, Spring Mountain, New Princeton, West Lafayette, Linton Mills, Mohawk Village, Plainfield, Evansburg, Orange, Bloomfield, Moscow, and Avondale.

Coshocton was laid out in 1802, by Ebenezer Buckingham and John Matthews, who called it Tuscarawas. In 1811 it became the county seat, and its name was changed to Coshocton. At that time a number of blocks of town lots at the southern end were vacated and laid out into what were designated as south out-lots, answering to those called east out-lots, being east of the present Fifth street. The town plat embraced a territory about three-quarters of a mile square. The first addition to the town plat was

Lamb's—a strip of several subdivided acres on the northeast, in 1837. For more than thirty years there was no further addition. Then, just east of Lamb's, Dr. S. H. Lee's addition was made. In 1869, the corporation limits were extended so as to include these additions; also the ground of the Agricultural Society, still further east, subdivided at a later day, and that included in John Burt's subdivision and Rickett's subdivision, together with adjoining tracts, making the village plat embrace territory a mile and a half square. The first subdivision was the "county commissioners'." The original proprietors of the town donated the square south of the present public square to "the public;" but when the town was made a county seat, on petition of the proprietors, and subject to the approval of the lot-holders of the town, the Legislature authorized the county commissioners to subdivide that square and sell the lots, and use the proceeds for the erection of public buildings.* The next subdivision was De La Mater's; and the principal ones of later date are James M. Burt's, Williams', John Burt's, Spangler's, Johnson's, Triplett's, Agricultural Society's, Steel Works, and Rickett's.

In 1808, a town called *New Castle* was laid out by Robert Giffin, but does not seem to have come to much. In 1830, John Clark laid out one called West Liberty; and the new town and the old name became one some time thereafter. In 1816, James Calder laid out Caldersburg. After the Ohio canal was built, Ransom and Swayne made an addition on the north, and the town thus extended was called *Roscoe*, after a then famous English author, Wm. Roscoe.

Thomas Johnson laid out the town of *Plainfield* in 1816.

---

*The ownership of the public square has been much discussed. Originally it was given to "the public." It was never given to the town nor formally to the county, but impliedly in 1811 to the latter. The commissioners have controlled it from that time on. They authorized certain citizens of the town to build a school house on the square; they also leased a piece of it to the Presbyterians, and proposed to lease another piece to the Methodists.

Territorial Limits and Subdivisions. 5

It has been of late supplanted by the adjoining village of *Jacobsport*, laid out by Jacob Waggoner in 1836.

West Bedford was laid out, in 1817, by Micajah Heaton. *Keene* was laid out, in 1820, by James Beal; Farwell's addition being made in 1839.

Wm. Brown and Wm. Henderson laid out *West Carlisle* in 1821, and John Gonser, *New Bedford*, in 1825. *Evansburg* was laid out, in 1830, by Isaac Evans; *Canal Lewisville*, in 1832, by Solomon Vail and T. Butler Lewis; *Warsaw*, in 1834, by Wm. Carhart—additions since by Eldridge and N. Buckalew; *Chili*, in 1834, by John and Samuel Fernsler; *Walhonding*, in 1841, by Wm. K. Johnson, G. W. Silliman, and T. S. Humrickhouse; *Bakersville*, in 1848, by John Baker; *West Lafayette*, in 1850, by Robert Shaw and Wm. Wheeler—Rue's and Ketchum's and James M. Burt's additions made since; and *Mohawk Village*, in 1859, by James and William Thompson.

The old-time chronicles tell of Lima, Newport, Maysville, Birmingham, Zeno, Providence, New Princeton, Cavallo, and Rochester; but these, and even others, never got beyond the infantile condition, and some of them are now entirely undiscernable by the eye.

CHAPTER II.

INDIAN OCCUPANCY, AND EARLY MILITARY EXPEDITIONS.

WHEN the English-speaking white man first came into the territory now embraced in Coshocton county, it was in the occupancy of the Delaware Indians. It is quite certain that just before them the Shawnee Indians were in the land, retiring, as the Delawares came in, to the more westerly and southerly regions. The French were then claiming dominion of all the Mississippi Valley, and the head of the Muskingum, as an interesting and favored locality, was not unknown to their soldiers, traders, and missionaries. Some have been pleased, without any very clear evidence, to believe that the famous French explorer La Salle, more than two hundred years ago, traversed these valleys.

Indefinitely before that period was the pre-historic race, who have left their traces in numerous mounds and circles and grave-yards, proving their number and power, and perplexing the men of subsequent times, concerning which things some statements and speculations will be found in another part of this volume.

The Delawares, crowded out by the white settlers about the Delaware river and in Eastern Pennsylvania—their Indian name means "People from the Sunrise"—found a home to their taste in the beautiful and fertile Tuscarawas, Walhonding, and Muskingum valleys.

Their language at least will abide in the land as long as the names just mentioned, and also those of White Eyes, Mohican, and Killbuck continue to be accepted as the designations of the rivers and creeks to which they are now attached. Within the limits of the county as now bounded, there were, a hundred years ago, at least five considerable Indian towns, the houses being built of bark and limbs and logs, and arranged in lines or on streets. One of these towns was called White Eyes (Koguethagachton) town, in the neighborhood of Lafayette. Two other towns were located—one three and the other ten miles up the Walhonding—and were called the Monsey towns, the more distant being occupied by a faction of the Delawares under control of Captain Pipe, who became disgusted with the generally peaceful and Christian policy of the nation, and seceded from it, desiring more indulgence for their base and bloody passions. The lower town was Wengimunds'.* The fourth town was Goschachgünk, occupying that part of the present town of Coshocton (a name said to be a modification of the name of the old Indian town) between Third street and the river. This was much the largest town, and for many years was the capitol of the Delaware nation, where the grand councils were held and whither the tribes assembled. It was the residence of Netawatwees, their great chief, and was often visited by the famous councilors, White Eyes and Killbuck (Gelelemend), as well as the big captains and braves of numerous tribes. The fifth town was situated about two miles below Coshocton on the east side of the Muskingum river (on the farms now in the possession of Samuel Moore and the Tingle heirs), and was called Lichtenau ("Pasture of Light"). It was occupied by Christian Indians under the direction of Rev. David Zeisberger (and afterward Rev. Wm. Edwards in conjunction with him), the famous Moravian missionary.

At the request of Netawatwees, Killbuck, and White Eyes, the town was established in close proximity to the capitol (which afterward was sometimes distinguished as "the heathen town"), in hope of its Christian influence thereupon. On the 12th of April, 1776, Zeisberger, with John Heckewelder as his assistant, at the head of eight families numbering thirty-five persons, encamped on the site of the future town, and began the next morning the work of felling the trees for the houses. The town grew rapidly; the mission work prospered greatly; a grandson

---

* There was also a small Shawnee town in Washington township on the Wakatomica.

of old Netawatwees and many of the head men at the capitol were baptised into the Christian faith, and became residents of the town. The place soon fitted the name, "a meadow beautiful by nature, and brightened by the light of grace." At one time the Christian Indians from all the Tuscarawas towns were gathered into Lichtenau to escape the evil influences and persecutions to which they were exposed through the machinations of evil-disposed white men, and, even worse, apostate and bloody-minded Indians. They remained for over a year, then returning to the Tuscarawas valley.

The Indian towns about the forks of the Muskingum were the objective points of two famous military expeditions. The first, both in order of time and importance, has been usually designated as "Boquet's Expedition."

The Indians of the Northwest having started on the war-path, General Gage, whose headquarters were at Boston, in the spring of 1764, directed Colonel Boquet to organize a corps of fifteen hundred men, and to enter the country of the Delawares and Shawnees at the same time that General Bradstreet was engaged in chastising the Wyandots and Ottawas of Lake Erie, who were then infesting Detroit. As a part of Colonel Boquet's force was composed of militia from Pennsylvania and Virginia, it was slow to assemble. On the 5th of August, the Pennsylvania quota rendezvoused at Carlisle, where three hundred of them deserted. The Virginia quota arrived at Fort Pitt on the 17th of September, and uniting with the provincial militia—a part of the Forty-second and Sixtieth regiments—the army moved from Fort Pitt on the 3d of October. When Colonel Boquet was at Fort Loudon in Pennsylvania, between Carlisle and Fort Pitt, urging forward the militia-levies, he received a dispatch from General Bradstreet notifying him of the peace effected at Sandusky. But the Ohio Indians, particularly the Shawnees of the Scioto river, and some of the Delawares of the Muskingum river, still continued their robberies and murders along the frontiers of Pennsylvania; and so Colonel Boquet determined to proceed with his division, notwithstanding the peace of Gen-

Early Military Expeditions.

eral Bradstreet, which did not include the Shawnees and Delawares. From Fort Pitt, Boquet proceeded westward along the Ohio and Little Beaver and across the highlands to the waters of Yellow creek, then to Sandy creek, and along it to a point near the present village of Bolivar. There he erected a stockade and completed his arrangements. The Indians being convinced that they could not succeed in any attempt against him, made a treaty of peace, engaging to restore all their white prisoners. The expedition then passed down the Tuscarawas on the north side, and encamped on the high ground between the rivers near the Indian town at the forks of the Muskingum, and, erecting a stockade, there awaited the arrival of the prisoners. On the 9th of November, two hundred and six captives had been delivered, and on the 18th, the army broke up its cantonment and marched for Fort Pitt, arriving there on the 28th of the same month.

The second expedition is commonly known as the "Coshocton Campaign." It was undertaken in the summer of 1780, and grew out of the deepened feeling of antipathy to the Indians because of some recent depredations and outrages committed upon settlers in Pennsylvania, Western Virginia, and Eastern Ohio. It was also understood that the Delawares, contrary to pledges, were joining the British.

The number of regulars and militia was about eight hundred, under the command of General Broadhead. It marched from Wheeling directly to the Tuscarawas valley. A part of the militia were anxious to go up the river and destroy the Moravian villages, which they regarded as at least shelters and half-way houses for Indian marauders, but they were restrained from executing their project by special exertions of General Broadhead and Colonel Shepherd. They kept on toward Coshocton, and observing some Indian scouts (one of whom was shot) a few miles therefrom, they made a forced march and surprised both Goschachgunk and Lichtenau, capturing, without firing a gun, all the Indians then in them. Among those captured in Lichtenau were several Christian Indians from Gnaden-

hutten. These were released promptly by the commander
of the expedition, and started in a canoe for their home, but
some of the militia followed after and fired at them. For-
saking their canoe, they took to the hills, and all except
one, who was wounded, reached their home in safety. Sixteen of the other prisoners, having been pointed out by
Pekilon, a friendly Delaware chief who was with the army
of Broadhead, were doomed to death by a council of war,
and having after dark been taken a little ways from the
town, were speedily dispatched with spear and tomahawk
and scalped. Having destroyed the towns, the army, at
eleven o'clock the next day, set out on its return. The
prisoners (twenty odd in number) were under guard of the
militia, and, after marching about half a mile, these commenced to use their knives and tomahawks, slaughtering
all of them, except a few women and children, who were
taken to Fort Pitt and subsequently exchanged for a like
number of white ones. Tradition locates the site of this
butchery near a spring about three-fourths of a mile east
of Coshocton, on a tract of land now owned by Mrs. S. H.
Collier.* Goschachgunk and Lichtenau were both subsequently rebuilt, to some extent, and became for some years
the home of more intense haters of the white race, by reason of the associations of the place. But the towns never

---

* Among the militia of this expedition was the famous Indian killer,
Lewis Wetzel, from Western Virginia. Just before the expedition set
out on its return, an Indian chief appeared on the opposite bank of the
river proposing "a talk." He was invited over by General Broadhead,
and assured of safety. But while he was talking, Wetzel slipped up
behind him, and, drawing a tomahawk which he had concealed in his
hunting-shirt, sunk it in the chief's skull, instantly killing him. Legends
of Wetzel's shrewdness and courage are abundant, and there is no
doubt he was one of the most successful trappers and hunters and Indian fighters of his time. He and his friends had suffered much at
the hands of the Indians. He moved, in 1795, to the frontier, on the
Mississippi, that he might trap the beaver and hunt the buffalo and
deer, and occasionally shoot an Indian. The exploit (not in some
lights very creditable, but showing his intense antipathy to the redskins) above mentioned was his only one performed in Coshocton
county as reported by his admirers.

again reached the proportions attained before the "Broadhead Campaign."

Usually, and as to the great mass of them, the Delaware Indians entertained very friendly feelings for the whites. In their old home in Pennsylvania, from the day of Wm. Penn's treaty down, they had received a treatment calculated to produce such feelings, and the influence of the Moravian missions among them was felt unto the same end. Far more Indian blood than white was shed about the forks of the Muskingum, and there is neither dark and bloody battlefield nor site of sickening family massacre within the limits of the county of Coshocton. The numerous bullets found in after times, in the plowed fields near Coshocton, were doubtless from the volleys fired by the expeditions, or from the rifles of the early settlers, with whom shooting at marks was a grand pastime. At one time seven hundred Indian warriors from the West encamped near the town, many with rifles. Accepting the idea of the poet, that "peace hath her victories as well as war," it may be claimed that one of the grandest of these was won at Goschachgunk, the Delaware capital. When the Revolutionary War broke out, it was a matter of the utmost importance to the colonists to secure at least the neutrality of the Indian tribes, and efforts were accordingly made. Two treaties were made at Pittsburg in successive years—1775 and 1776—binding to neutrality the Delawares, and some of the immediately adjacent nations.

At the opening of 1777, the hatchet sent from Detroit (the British headquarters), was accepted by the Shawnees, Wyandots, and Mingoes. Rumor had it that it was also to be sent to the Delawares, and if they declined it they were to be treated as common enemies, and at once attacked by the British and their Indian allies. The famous chief Cornstalk himself came to Goschachgunk, reporting that despite his efforts the Shawnees were for war; parties were already out, and ammunition was being forwarded for their use from Detroit. Even a portion of the Delawares had been already pledged to take up arms. At this crisis—so threatening to the colonists—a general council of the

Delawares met at the capitol, on the 9th of March, 1777. Some of the young warriors appeared with plumes and war paint. After earnest discussion and eloquent speeches, especially from White Eyes, it was resolved to decline the hatchet should it be offered. Three times during that summer it was tendered and as often declined. Despite the taunts of their own race—against even a faction of their own nation—rejecting bribes and spurning threats, the people stood, month after month, as a mighty wall of protection to the western colonists. Looking to the plainly discernible natural consequences of a different decision in that grand council, it is not without reason that the claim may be made, that one of the grandest victories for the colonists in the American Revolutionary war was won at the Delaware capitol, at the forks of the Muskingum. Subsequently, indeed, by the machinations of renegades like Simon Girty (who was several times at the capitol), and the taunts of the tribes, a part of the nation was led to join the British Indians; but these were too few, and it was too late to do the colonists much harm, especially with the wisest and bravest of the nation committed to peace and friendliness with the Americans. In 1778, the rightful authorities of the nation made a complete treaty of alliance with the commissioners of the United States, therein providing for carrying out a cherished project of White Eyes, that the Delaware nation should be represented in the Colonial Congress, and become, as a Christian Indian state, one of the United States. By the neighboring tribes the Delawares were often taunted with being unduly gentle—" women "—and were always remarked upon as having too many captives; making exertions to secure as such those commonly appointed by other Indians to the tomahawk or stake. On one occasion, as already noticed, at their principal village, there were turned over to Boquet's forces two hundred and six captives, of whom thirty-two men and fifty-eight women and children were from Virginia, and forty-nine men and sixty-eight women and children from Pennsylvania. These were not indeed all captured by the Delawares; but a large proportion was, and others of them would doubtless have been butchered but for the influence of the Delawares, who would sometimes arrange with the tribes further south and west for their captives. The legend of the Walhonding (White Woman), telling how the captive virgin wildly fled from the camp and threw herself from an uprearing and overhanging rock,* into the seething waters of the storm-swollen river, choosing death rather than captivity, is significant of the horrors attending captivity, even among the Delawares.† It is, however, most likely that she was a captive of the Monsey or Wolf tribe of Delawares, who were, perhaps, the worst representatives of the nation. Experience and tastes no doubt differed among the captives. It is said that some of the captives delivered to Boquet were compelled to go with him, and some escaped after the expedition started toward Fort Pitt, and returned to the free forest life. Simon Girty and two brothers were captured when young, and, having been adopted by the Indians, continued in their preference of Indian life. Despite all that has been said or may be claimed, it is no doubt true that even among the Delawares the savage nature was frequently displayed, especially when in the bad company of other tribes; and they were not without much blame at the mouths of the whites, for cruelties upon the hapless settlers, whose settlements to the east and south of them they invaded, and who, individually or in small hunting or scouting parties, might fall into their hands.

It can not be doubted that their treatment of Colonel Crawford out in the Wyandot country, when they bound him to a stake, fired numerous charges of powder into his flesh, cut and beat and burned, and by every possible torture put him to a lingering death, was Indian, fiendish. Yet it is to be remembered that the Delaware Indians

---

* Near the residence of Mrs. C. Denman, four miles northwest of Coshocton.

† See a very different legend in Chapter XIX.

doing these things were confessedly the more bloody-minded part that had turned away from those at the forks of the Muskingum and set up their lodges in the Wyandot country; that they were incited by the Shawnees and Wyandots, and regarded their work as a retaliation for the bloody massacre of the Christian Indians at Gnadenhütten, and other outrages that their race had suffered at the hands of those who were crowding them out of the land.

The great chief Netawatwees died about the opening of the Revolutionary war, and White Eyes in 1778.*

Killbuck ("deer-killer") was the successor of a chief having the same name, whose town was on Killbuck creek, between Millersburg and Wooster, and who died, a very old man, in the Wyandot country, and was often designated Killbuck, Jr. When baptized by the Moravian missionaries he took the name of William Henry. Less shrewd and eloquent, he was a worthy associate and successor of White Eyes. He was even more pronounced in his religious views and less wavering. Adhering to the fortunes of the Americans and Moravians, he at length (in 1810) died at Goshen, near New Philadelphia.

Killbuck, aided by the other Christian Indians, for a time still held the nation very much in hand; but by 1780 Captain Pipe got the ascendancy at Goschachgünk, and put the people on the side of the British, setting up a new town in the Seneca country. Killbuck and those who sided with him went over fully to the colonists, and left the forks, never to return. After the massacre at Gnadenhütten, the few remaining Delawares gradually retired to

---

* White Eyes (so called from the unusual proportion of white in his eyes) died near Fort Laurens, on the Tuscarawas, on the 10th of November, 1778, of small-pox. General McIntosh's colonial forces were at that time encamped near by. His death was a marked event of the time. His broad views and truly eloquent expression of them can not be questioned. His fair dealing with the whites, and his earnest and steadfast efforts for the civilization and christianization of his race ought not to be forgotten. A successor to the name—perhaps a degenerate son of this sire—was killed in what is now Columbiana county, in 1797, by a young man named Carpenter, whom he was, while under the influence of fire-water, assailing and threatening.

the West or were taken to Canada; and in 1795 their country, of which Coshocton county forms the central part, and in which was their capitol (removed from New Comerstown), became by treaty the possession of the United States. Until after the war of 1812, a few straggling members of the nation, especially the Guadenhütten ones, moved about in the country, hunting, disposing of pelts, or possibly visiting the graves of their ancestors. In 1819 there were eighty Delawares near Sandusky, Ohio, and two thousand three hundred in Northern Indiana. Fragments of the nation are yet recognized in Canada and in the Indian Territory, but its power was broken and the scepter had departed when it was turned away from its loved haunts in the Tuscarawas and Walholding valleys.*

* The sources of information for the foregoing chapter are mainly Doddridge's Notes, Howe's Historical Collections of Ohio, de Schweinitz's Life and Times of Zeisberger, and Mitchener's Ohio Annals; in which works those interested in Indian history and legends will find much to their taste. See also Chapter XIX, this volume.

CHAPTER III.

NOTES ON THE SETTLEMENT OF THE COUNTY* AND GROWTH OF POPULATION.

THE military expeditions mentioned in preceding chapter, besides accomplishing the immediate object for which they were undertaken, drew attention to the excellencies of the country. Wonderful stories about " the forks of the Muskingum " were told by the returning soldiers. The father of Geo. Beaver, of Keene township, was in Boquet's expedition. John Williams (brother of Charles) afterward settled in Mill Creek township, was in the Coshocton campaign; and among the earlier settlers were several whose relatives had been in Broadhead's forces. The first white man known to have come into the territory now embraced in Coshocton county, with the purpose of abiding in it, was Charles Williams. In the spring of the year 1800, having come up the Muskingum in a canoe, he passed on up the Walhonding to what is now known as the Denman land, long called " the Paraire " (four miles above Coshocton), and there raised that season a patch of corn, besides fishing, hunting, and prospecting. The next year he fixed upon the site of Coshocton as his home, and was there joined by his brothers-in-law, the Carpenters, and William and Samuel Morrison, who, after staying with him for the season, went on up into what is now Holmes county, in the Killbuck valley. The same year, 1801, a settlement was made in Oxford township by Isaac Evans and others, who are reputed as having raised some corn and picked their land the preceding year. The Robinson and Miller settlement in Franklin township was made about the same time. The Hardestys are reputed as having been in Washington township the same year. A little later the Millers and Thomas Wiggins were located in Lafayette township. Nicholas Miller, James Oglesby, Geo.

---

*See notices of early settlers by townships in next chapter.

McCullough, Andrew Craig, Isaac Hoagland, Benjamin Fry, and Barney Carr are repored as on the Lower Walhonding in 1805. In 1806, Philip Waggoner, Geo. Loose, John Wolf, and Geo. Leighninger settled in Oxford township, and the McLains were in Lafayette. In the same year the Darlings, the Butlers, John Bantham, and John Elder went to the Upper Walhonding valley. In 1807, Francis McGuire, who had been living above New Comerstown, moved down to the locality known as the McGuire settlement, above Canal Lewisville. Then came Moore, Workman, Neff, Lybarger, Thompson, the Bakers, Cantwell, and Whitten to Coshocton; and Meskimens, Johnston, and Harger to the Wills Creek region; and Mitchell, Markley, and Williams to the north of Coshocton; and Pigman, Chalfant, Norris, Slaughter, Woolford, Wright, Stafford, Meredith, John, and Severns into the western part of the country. No regular census of the country was taken until 1820. In 1810, Muskingum county, embracing the present Muskingum, Morgan, Coshocton, and part of Holmes, had only ten thousand population. A Scotch traveler, who spent the night at Coshocton in 1806, wrote of it as having a population of one hundred and forty; but it was doubtless not understated to him. Dr. S. Lee, who came to the place in 1811, found it a hamlet with a score or so of rude structures. Fifteen hundred would probably be a large statement as to population at the time the country was organized in April, 1811. Immediately after the organization, the immigration was large. The war of 1812, while temporarily checking the growth of the country, and especially the inflow of population, was yet an advantage, particularly in making the region known to the people to the East and South. Just at the close of the war there were in the county one hundred and thirty-eight resident landholders, owning tracts of land varying in size from thirty-five acres to four thousand and five acres. The list of these, and the townships as now named in which they resided, is as follows:

Tuscarawas—John D. Moore, Nicholas Miller, Henry

Miller, John Noble, Isaac Workman, and Charles Williams.

New Castle—David John, Thomas John, Obed Meredith, T. Hankins, John Wolf, Matthew Duncan, David and Martin Cox, and Robert Giffin.

Washington—Payne Clark, Mordecai Chalfant, Isaac Holloway, Peter Lash, Geo. Smith, and Frederick Woolford.

Franklin—O. Davidson, Valentine Johnston, Catharine Johnston, Michael Miller, Sr., Wm. Robinson, James Robinson, Benjamin Robinson, Jos. Scott, James Tanner, Wm. Taylor, Abraham Thompson, John Walmsly, and Jacob Jackson.

Oxford—Jacob Reed, David Douglas, Henry Evans, Isaac Evans, John Junkins, George Looze, John Mills, Wm. Mulvain, Jas. Mulvain, John Mulvain, Andrew McFarlane, Ezekiel McFarlane, Samuel McFarlane, Benjamin Norman, George Onspaugh, Wm. Peirpont, Geo. Stringer, Philip Wolf, Philip Waggoner's heirs, and James Welch.

Linton—Hugh Addy, Wm. Addy, Wm. Evans, James McCune, John McCune, James Meskimens, Joseph Scott, Geo. McCune, and Amos Stackhouse.

Pike—Daniel Ashcraft.

Keene—George Armory, Elizabeth Armory, and John Colver.

Tiverton—Isaac Draper.

Jefferson—Joseph Butler, Thomas Butler, and Robert Darling.

Virginia—Beal Adams, Patrick Miller, Joseph McCoy, Richard Tilton, and Joseph Wright.

Adams—David Mast.

Lafayette—Hugh Ballantine, Archibald Elson, William Johnston, George Miller, Sr., Francis McGuire, Thomas McLain, Elijah Nelson, Matthew Orr, Lewis Vail, and Jane Wiggins.

Bedford—James Craig, Ezra Horton, and Thomas Horton.

Bethlehem—Henry Crissman, Benjamin Fry, John Shaffer, John Thompson, Geo. Skinner, and Wm. Trimble.

A number of these landholders were heads of quite considerable families, and upon some of the large tracts were several tenants. A list of those who were croppers and hired men, and of those occupying town-lots, and of those who were on their lands under contract for purchase, is not accessible. It is, however, known that besides those whose names appear in this list, and their children, the following persons were residents of the county at that time, several of them having been so for a number of years preceding : Richard Fowler, Wm. Lockard, James Willis, Joseph Harris, C. P. Van Kirk, Peter Casey, Geo. Carpenter, Joseph Neff, Wm. and Sam'l Morrison, Jas. Jeffries, Dr. Sam'l Lee, Wright Warner, A. M. Church, Thos. L. Rue, Wm. Whitten, Thomas Means, Thomas Foster, Barney Carr, James Oglesby, Geo. Bible, John Bantham, Wm. Bird, Jas. Calder, Wm. Mitchell, Lewis Vail, Asher Hart, John Williams, Adam Johnston, John Dillon, Abel Cain, Joseph Vail, Rezin Baker, Israel Baker, John Baker, James Buckalew, Benjamin Burrell, Joseph Burrell, James Cantwell, Barney Cantwell, J. G. Pigman, J. W. Pigman, John Elder, Archibald Ellson, Samuel Clark, Ezekiel Parker, Andrew Lybarger, John Hershman, Peter Moore, the McLains, Wm. Biggs, Geo. and Levi Magness, Richard Hawk, Isaac Shambaugh, and Elijah Newcum.

At the October election, in 1814, there were one hundred and three electors in Tuscarawas township, which, however, embraced at that time not only the township proper on both sides of the river, but also all the territory north of the Tuscarawas, and east of the Walhonding rivers.

After the war the accession to the population was large, running through several years. In those years 1815–1820 came the progenitors of the since well-known Burns, Crowley, Ricketts, Sells, Mossman, Heslip, Renfrew, Boyd, Gault, Thompson, Roderick, Squires, James, Tipton, Powelson, Luke, Borden, Neldon, Ravenscraft, Norris, Winklepleck, McNabb, Slaughter, Mulford, Stafford, Cresap, and Lemert families. In 1818 there were 285 resident landholders.

The personal and family records of the period running from 1814 to 1820 (especially the earlier part of it) are full of stories of laborious efforts and wearying hardships in clearing and planting and building. The large inflow of population involved a great deal of exposure. The conveniences of life, even with those best supplied, were scarce. Sickness, incident to all new countries, abounded, especially was a form of congestive chills known as "the cold plague" very prevalent, carrying off many of the settlers and discouraging immigration. Milling facilities were still poor and remote. Corn meal and bacon afforded, in many cases, almost the whole support. Even whisky, the panacea of those days, was not yet plenty. Yet, despite all drawbacks, children were born and settlers came in, and in 1820 the census-taker found 7,086 inhabitants in Coshocton county.

From 1820 to 1830 there was apparently an increase of only a few over four thousand, making the population in the latter year 11,162. It must, however, be borne in mind that in that period, by the formation of Holmes county, a number of people, hitherto counted as of Coshocton county, were set over, and the limits of the county decreased. Still the immigration was not heavy, especially in the earlier part of the period. Reports of the sickliness of the river region and of the rough ways of the settlers had gone abroad. It may be stated in this connection that the advancement of the county in both population and wealth has been regarded by many as having been hindered in all its earlier stages by the fact of there having been a large number (thirty-three) of four-thousand-acre tracts taken up by military land warrants, and held mainly by non-residents, cultivated only by a few cabin tenants, if at all.

From 1830 to 1840 the population of the county was nearly doubled, there being in the latter year 21,590 inhabitants. This large increase was largely owing to the opening of the Ohio canal.

The immigration of that period was of a much more miscellaneous sort, and having almost nothing of the old Virginian and Marylander element, so prominent in the first settlement of the county. New York, Western Pennsylvania, Eastern Ohio, Germany, and Ireland were most largely represented.

The population of the county in 1850 was 25,674; in 1860, 25,032; and in 1870, 23,600. It will be seen by these figures that there was a decrease within the twenty years from 1850 to 1870.

The same condition of things has been noted in many other counties in Ohio, especially such as have hitherto been most largely agricultural. It is observed in this connection that the cities and larger towns of the State show the chief gains attributed to it. Thus, while Coshocton county lost during that time above noted, the town of Coshocton more than doubled its population, which in 1840 was 845, and in 1870, 1,757—being in 1875 about 2,800. The disposition to forsake the farm for the shop and store and office, the "go-west" fever, the readiness of forehanded farmers to purchase at good prices the small tracts adjoining their larger ones, the enlargement of the stock interest, the development of manufacturing interests, and even the casualties of war, have all had to do with this generally diminished population, especially in the rural districts, and the filling up of the cities and towns.

Appended will be found the population, as enumerated by the Federal census-takers, of the several townships for 1850, when the maximum population was attained, and also for 1870:

	1850.	1870.
Adams	1,419	1,113
Bedford	1,221	918
Bethlehem	822	850
Clarke	833	867
Crawford	1,552	1,245
Franklin	966	972
Jackson	2,037	1,767
Jefferson	929	1,059
Keene	1,078	787
Lafayette	1,040	920
Linton	1,592	1,600
Mill Creek	872	586
Monroe	760	832
New Castle	1,229	1,005
Oxford	1,112	1,140
Perry	1,340	932

Pike	1,080	773
Tiverton	842	804
Tuscarawas	1,593	2,725
Virginia	1,226	1,014
Washington	998	768
White Eyes	1,132	923

CHAPTER IV.

NOTICES OF SOME OF THE EARLIEST SETTLERS, AND OTHER MATTERS OF IN-
TEREST PERTAINING TO EACH TOWNSHIP.

TUSCARAWAS TOWNSHIP.

THE first "settlement" made in the county was in this township. Charles Williams,* a native of Maryland, residing for a time in Western Virginia, and yet later on the Lower Muskingum, came up the river in a canoe, and located on the site of Coshocton, early in the year 1801; having spent part of the preceding year in what is now Bethlehem township, but without definite purpose as to place of settlement. George Carpenter, a brother-in-law of Williams, and William and Samuel Morrison, came soon afterward, but, after stopping to help Williams raise a crop of corn, passed on up the Killbuck, becoming the earliest settlers in what is now Holmes county. Another brother-in-law of Williams, John Hibits, came a little later, and subsequently located in the Upper Walhonding valley. Several of the early residents were "croppers," and after a time picked up a piece of land and settled in some other township.

Nicholas Miller, from Virginia, came in about 1803—spent his long life in farming, dying at a good old age. John D. Moore (father of Commissioner Moore), also from Virginia, came a little later—was an easy-going, quiet farmer, dying many years since in the township. Peter Moore was a regular trapper and fisher. John Noble had a little farm near the ford, three miles below Coshocton; for a time kept a ferry there in later years. J. Fulton was from Maryland—lived on the place best known as the Ricketts farm, about a mile southeast of Coshocton. He had a mill (run by the water of a big spring), making more corn-meal and whisky than anything else, said to have

---

* See "Biographical Sketches."

been the first mill set up in Coshocton county. Among others recognized as very early settlers were J. Workman, from Virginia (the father of General Jesse Workman), a farmer; Joseph Neff, from same State, a tailor; Asa Hart, from New Jersey, a blacksmith; Andrew Lybarger (grandfather of Representative E. L. Lybarger), from Pennsylvania, a tanner; Wm. Whitten, a general business man, the first justice of the peace; Dr. Samuel Lee;* Thomas L. Rue;* Adam Johnson (a son-in-law of Charles Williams and the father of Matthew, Charles, and Wm. A. Johnson), the first county clerk and auditor; Wilson McGowan, from Mount Holly, New Jersey, a gentleman of the continental style, wearing a "queue," and flourishing a gold-headed cane; Alex. McGowan, a younger brother of the above, who set up as a physician of the Tompsonian school, but was chiefly occupied in public office, having been many years auditor, etc.; Cornelius Van Kirk (a very stalwart man), the first tax-collector and sheriff; James Cantwell, a farmer; Geo. McCullough, an Indian scout and hunter; James Winders and Geo. Arnold, corn-raisers, and, as reputed, general "whisky punishers."

These were all settled in the township before the county was organized, in 1811—many of them years before.

FRANKLIN TOWNSHIP.

The list of earliest settlers in Franklin township includes the names of James Robinson, Benjamin Robinson, John Robinson, Wm. J. Robinson, Michael Miller, Jacob Jackson, James Tanner, John Walmsley, William Taylor, Abraham Thompson, Joseph Scott, John G. Pigman, Obadiah Davidson, Valentine and Jane Johnson, Geo. Littick, Isaac Shanbaugh, Philip Hershman, and Lewis Roderick. One-half of the township was originally owned by Michael Miller, Sr., and the Robinsons, each having a four-thousand-acre tract. James Robinson, William Davidson, and John G. Pigman were men of more than the average (for their day) education and force of character. None of those taking part

---

* See "Biographical Sketches."

in the organization of the township are now living, but the descendants of many of them are still well known in the township. The earlier settlers were nearly all from Virginia.

The German element, for some years quite prominent in this township, first became noticeable about 1835. About 1840, there was a considerable immigration of French. Of later years, the Germans have been outnumbered by the French, the former having moved largely to the west. James Robinson, of this township, was a member of the Legislature, and also an associate judge of the county. G. A. McCleary has also been in the Legislature. Henry Schmeser has served as county commissioner. Isaac Shambaugh was the discoverer of the Wills creek oil springs. Louis Roderick was a preacher connected with the German Baptists (Dunkards). He held services mainly at the house of Philip Hershman for more than thirty years, and was well-known throughout the county. He died a few years since in Lafayette township at the advanced age of ninety-five years. Mrs. George A. McCleary is reputed as the first child born in the township. She was a daughter of James Tanner. Isaac Shambaugh is doubtless the oldest person now living in the township. He came from Virginia in 1816, and is nearly ninety. He was a soldier in the war of 1812, as was also Robert Hawk, of this township.

NEW CASTLE TOWNSHIP.

Robert Giffin was among the earliest settlers in New Castle township. He was, for a number of years, the largest landholder in it; but, after a time, sold out his interest there and became more largely identified with Knox county. Edith Hull, a very early tax-payer in the township, was Giffin's sister. They are reported as being from the State of Delaware.

Thomas Butler and Joseph Severns are reputed as having come into the township about 1806. They were both from Virginia—the south branch of the Potomac. They were connected with Robert Darling, and he and they removed to Ohio about the same time. Mr. Severns died in 1857, being about eighty years of age. A son, of same name, died near New Castle, in 1850. A grandson is now living near Coshocton. Samuel Severns, the oldest son of Joseph, yet living on the old farm on Severn's Ridge, in New Castle township, is, at this time, about eighty-four years old. Another son, William, has reached the good old age of seventy-five years. A son of Mr. Butler, James, is now living just over the line in Jefferson township, at the advanced age of eighty-three years; and another son, Felix, about sixty-seven years old, resides on the old home place. Few, if any, people have given character to the upper Walhonding valley beyond the Butlers. Both Joseph Severns and Thomas Butler were out in the war of 1812.

Martin and David Cox were early settlers, keeping the post-office, for the township, for many years, at Cox's Cross roads. John Eli owned the farm on which New Castle now stands, though the town was laid out by John Clark under the name of West Liberty. The Meredith family was one of the earliest and best known in this township. They were from Virginia. Squire Humphrey lived, at an early day, on the tract now owned by Loyd Nichols. M. Duncan made his mark, in early times, by building a large stone house, as also did the two Johns—David and Thomas—who were among the earliest, coming from New Jersey. John G. Pigman was a prominent settler in New Castle; but is reported more fully in Perry, within whose geographical limits, as ultimately fixed, he lived. John Wolf was another early settler.

The mother of Thomas Dwyer, of Coshocton, came into New Castle with her son-in-law (she then being a widow), Benjamin Farquhar, in 1808. They were from Maryland. Of Eli Nichols, long a prominent citizen of this township, mention is elsewhere made.

This township is the home of one of the professors of the occult sciences, Wm. Gorham, who claims to be able to discover hidden things, whether of the past or the future, and has sometimes created a sensation in the classic Owl Creek valley.

One of the noticeable people of New Castle township, some years ago, was one Walter Turner, an Englishman, who figured at a saw-mill in an effort to make the same water do duty several times—pumping it up again into the race after it had run over the wheel.

New Castle was one of the four townships organized before the county was organized (Tuscarawas, Washington, and Franklin being the others); and it is understood to have been named after New Castle in Delaware.

WASHINGTON TOWNSHIP.

The first settlers of this township were John Hardesty, Jacob Cray, Mordecai Chalfant, Peter Lash, Francis Stafford, Frederick Woolford, James Williams, Bradley Squires, and George Smith. These were all in before 1811. John Hardesty was from Maryland, and came into the territory afterward embraced in Washington township before the State of Ohio was admitted. He was a regular frontiersman, and kept moving with the tide of emigration westward while his years admitted. He died some years ago in St. Louis. Edmund Hardesty, also from Maryland, came into the township in 1811; died a few years ago in Illinois. Mordecai Chalfant came from Pennsylvania in 1808; was for some time an associate judge of the county. George Smith was from Virginia. Bradley Squires was from Vermont. Jacob Cray came from Wheeling, Va., in 1808; was a farmer; died about 1864. Thomas Hardesty, coming from Maryland about 1811, still lives in the township. Walter McBride, farmer and carpenter, came from Pennsylvania in 1814; he is now more than seventy years of age.

The township was named at its organization by Mordecai Chalfant. Through his influence, a small mill was built in 1810. In 1811 a school-house was erected, and also a church (M. E.), which still goes by the name of Chalfant's meeting-house.

OXFORD TOWNSHIP.

It is believed by some that the first settlement made in the county was made in this township. It would seem that, at all events, the same season that Charles Williams was raising his corn on "the prairie," Isaac and Henry Evans and Charles and Esaias Baker, all from Virginia, were raising a crop on the Tuscarawas, near Evansburg. Williams had come up the Muskingum, and the four above named had come down the Tuscarawas. The Bakers afterward went over into Linton township, and were among the very earliest settlers there. Isaac Evans brought his family in 1801, and remained in the township until his death. He was a captain in the war of 1812; was also one of the associate judges of the county. He built a mill, and was extensively engaged in farming. In 1806 Philip Waggoner, from near Carlisle, Pa., came in, and soon thereafter a brother-in-law, George Loose, and another named Philip Wolf, and still another, George Leigninger, all from Cumberland county, Pa. John Junkin, John Mills, and William and Joseph and John Mulvain, and Andrew and Ezekiel and Samuel McFarlin were all quite early settlers. Moses Morgan was an early settler, and well known as the keeper of the tavern at the forks of the road to Cadiz and New Philadelphia.

LINTON TOWNSHIP.

Among the earliest and best-known settlers in Linton township may be mentioned the following: The Addys, the Bakers, the McCunes, the Meskimens, the Heslips, Thomas Johnson, George Magness, the McLains, R. Fowler, and George Smith.

The Addys were from Delaware. One of the family (the mother of Rev. John Baker) is perhaps the oldest person now resident in the township, being in her eighty-eighth year. They came to Ohio in 1806. The Bakers were from Pennsylvania. Rezin (father of Rev. John and Lane) came into the county as early as 1802, and remained until his death, in 1842, in his sixty-second year. The family removed from Pennsylvania to Harrison county, and Rezin, just as he had fairly attained his majority, passed on out west, and hired out with John Fulton, living near Coshocton until he had earned enough to buy a farm in what is now known as the north bend of Will's creek, of which tract he took possession in 1808. His wife was in Harrison county, and she and two children were removed by death, he afterward marrying Miss Addy. Three other families bearing the name of Baker (Charles and Esaias and Basil), relatives of the above, came in at a very early day, and were recognized as of the " bone and sinew " of the township. The McCunes were also from Pennsylvania, and came in about 1806. The Meskimens were from Virginia (Potomac valley), and were originally quite large landholders. James Meskimens was a man of more than ordinary force, and was of the first board of county commissioners. Joseph Heslip, now living at an advanced age, in his youth had a passion for a life on the ocean wave. His father thought " the wilderness " would afford as much variety and spice, and prevailed upon him, after he had made a voyage or two, to settle upon a large tract, on part of which has since been built " the Linton mills " and the little circumjacent village. The elder Mr. Heslip was a minister, and was much observed in the neighborhood because of his regard for the Sabbath, in a day when the chief use made of it was to hunt and fish.

As early as 1808 Andrew Tairare built a little mill on Wills creek, about fifty rods above where the mill now stands, but a freshet soon swept it away. A few years later Mr. Loose built a mill near the mouth of Bacon run, making, with the volunteered help of the neighbors, a race some eighty rods long. But that was the day of hard toil. A walk of ten or twenty miles for a quarter of tea by a boy was nothing unusual, and a journey to Cambridge or Zanesville for a little flour was a common thing. Of Thomas Johnson an extended account is given in the " Biographical Sketches."

George Magness was from Maryland; was in the war of 1812. Of the McLains, mention is made in Lafayette. Fowler and Smith were from Virginia; both in war of 1812. These all died at an advanced age in the township, and are still represented therein by descendants.

Among the more prominent families of later date have been the Shafer, Sibley, Bassett, Love, Glenn, and Herkett.

PERRY TOWNSHIP.

Among the earliest settlers in Perry township who have attracted most attention were the following: Samuel Farquhar; came from Maryland with six sons and five daughters; lived to be over ninety years of age, and none of his children have died under eighty. They were Quakers in their religious views, farmers as to employment. John Pritchard, a Baptist preacher; Wm. Coulter, from Bedford, Pennsylvania, who did most of the surveying in the western part of the county, and, it is said, with "a grape-vine chain;" Joshua Cochran, originally from Dublin, Ireland, directly from Maryland, who had six sons and five daughters; also his sons-in-law, John and Solomon Smith, all coming in about 1814; Joseph W. Pigman, a famous Methodist Episcopal preacher, who was associate judge, and was also in the Legislature. He came from Cumberland, Maryland.

The first residents of the township to pay taxes on real estate were Andrew Billman, holding southwest quarter of section twenty, and Ann James, holding the northeast quarter of same section, and the southeast quarter of section twelve. That was in 1817. Several of those who at that time were non-resident tax-payers, as, for instance, John Berry, Samuel Farquhar, John Pritchard, and Peter Dillon, soon took possession of their lands.

William Dillon, father of Israel Dillon, the present clerk of the court, came from Greene county, Pennsylvania, to the township about 1815; entered and cleared a quarter section of land, continuing to occupy it until his death, in 1862, he being then sixty-eight years of age. He was a zealous Baptist.

Dr. E. G. Lee, the first physician in the towhship, came from Mount Vernon, and laid out a town called New Guilford. Calvin Hill, also from Mount Vernon, built a storeroom on one of the lots, and kept the first store. The next year David McHenry opened a hatter's shop.

Soon after New Guilford was laid out, John Conway, who owned the quarter section of land next east of that on which Guilford was located, started a town on his land, calling it Claysville. The rivalry between the towns was disastrous to both. After some years, they were consolidated under the name of East Union by act of the Legislature. The plat of New Guilford is now all used for farming purposes, having been practically vacated.

MILL CREEK TOWNSHIP.

Richard Babcock purchased a quarter section of land in this township, and settled on it in 1812 with his family. They came originally from Vermont, but had stopped for a time in Harrison county. Mr. Babcock was killed by a run-away team about 1823. His widow died a few years later. His youngest son resided upon the home farm until his death, in 1874. His grandson, Daniel, now lives upon the place.

Solomon Vail purchased and settled on a tract immediately south of Babcock, in 1815. He removed to Illinois, and there died. His widow still lives—probably the only one of the parents among the first settlers. Vail had a hand-mill, on which a few of the settlers did their own grinding. He afterward, assisted by his brother-in-law, built the first mill on the creek. It was a primitive affair, truly, grinding only Indian-corn, which was about all there was to grind for several years. The stones for the mill were hauled from Mansfield by Thomas Elliott, who was to receive for his labor a pair of shoes, which Vail, who was a sort of "jack of all trades," was to make for him.

In March, 1816, Moses Thompson, from Jefferson county, but originally from Ireland, took possession of his Mill creek "cabin," which he had built after the most approved "back-woods" style of the day. He died in 1862 on the same place. He was the first clerk of the township. His son S. T. Thompson resides near Keene. In 1817, there was quite a number of settlers came in. Henry Grimm (afterward associate judge), Thomas Moore, Joseph Beach, and John P. Wilson—these, as the former, came from

Eastern Ohio. With the exception of Babcocks and Mrs. Bible (whose father's name was Tipton), now eighty-five years old, none of the descendants of settlers prior to 1820 are now in the township. The Sheplons and the Mitchells came in somewhat later. The township is largely peopled by those coming from Jefferson and Harrison counties.

The township was originally very heavily timbered, and most of the early settlers were poor and had very hard work to get their lands. Wolves and other wild animals were numerous, and sheep could be raised only by the closest attention. Many of the people wore deer-skins, others linsey. Still, there, as elsewhere, those who made due exertion soon had enough to eat and wear. As to drink, as soon as grain was raised, whisky was at hand and freely dispensed. The first "gathering" of men without whisky was at the raising of John Shannon's barn, say about 1835.

The first school in the township was taught by David Grimm, son of Henry. The pupils came from remote points, and had nothing scarcely but bridle paths to come by. The first church built was the Protestant Episcopalian at the Knob. Among the earlier settlers of this township was John Williams. He was a brother of Colonel Charles Williams, and the father of Wm. G. Williams, a former county treasurer, and of Joseph Williams, now of Coshocton. He was in the Revolutionary War. At its close he settled near Wheeling; was in the Moravian campaign (the cruelties of which he always condemned); also was in the Coshocton campaign. He moved to Coshocton about 1812; came into Mill Creek about 1817, and there died in 1833, when about eighty years of age.

PIKE TOWNSHIP.

Daniel Ashcraft, from Pennsylvania, came to what is now Pike township, and entered the first quarter of land taken up in that township. His son, Jonathan Ashcraft, now eighty-four years of age, was the first man to plow a furrow in that township. He also had a saw-mill. Alexander Graham, also from Pennsylvania, came into Pike township in 1819. He died in July, 1844. One of his sons, William, still resides in the township, and is seventy-two years of age. Daniel Forker came into the township in 1824, from New Jersey. He worked at shoemaking for a number of years in the town of West Carlisle, and then bought a farm about three miles south of the town, where he still lives, being about eighty-four years of age. He served many years as justice of the peace, and also was county commissioner. Two of his sons, Samuel and Wm. R., have held the office of county auditor. John Rine came from Maryland about the year 1819, and is still living in the township, being over eighty years of age. He was a soldier of the war of 1812, and now a pensioner. Peter Ault, in 1814, came from Belmont county, Ohio. He died in 1844. He was a cooper. Augustine White, Joshua Lemert, Pierce Noland, and Payne Clark were all from Virginia. Clark came in in 1808, farmed extensively for several years, and then removed to Indiana. Lemert came in 1810, and was for years a prominent citizen of the township. His descendants are still well known in the region. White came in 1818; reared a large family; died in 1852. Noland came in 1814; was a farmer; died in 1834. Adam Gault came into the township in 1815; was from Pennsylvania; died in 1846. About 1817, Samuel Perkins, from Pennsylvania, entered the tract on which West Carlisle is now situated.

WHITE EYES TOWNSHIP.

The first freeholder in this township was John Henderson, who was in possession of four hundred and eighty acres of land in 1818. His brother, George, is understood to have been interested with him, and they were both occupants. They were from Beaver county, Pennsylvania. George died on his farm in White Eyes, at advanced years, in 1868.

In 1818, Michael Stonehocker settled in White Eyes. He was from Jefferson county, Ohio, not far from Smithfield. The next year Jacob Stonehocker, brother of Michael, and John M., the father of both Michael and Jacob, came to White Eyes. John M. died in a few years.

Michael removed to Powsheik county, Iowa, in 1865. Jacob died in White Eyes.

Michael Frock was born in Chester county, Pennsylvania, May 9, 1785. He married Elizabeth Seldenright, in 1807. In 1818, they came to White Eyes. He was the first justice of the peace of that township. His wife died in 1856, and himself in 1871.

Abner Kimball, from New Hampshire, settled in White Eyes in 1818; died in 1870.

John McPherson, from Virginia, was a resident of White Eyes from 1821 to 1834. He was a soldier in Anthony Wayne's army.

Robert Boyd, from county Donegal, Ireland, came to White Eyes in 1824. He died in a few years. His sons are yet well-known citizens of the neighborhood.

The Ravenscrafts were among the best known citizens of White Eyes for many years. They were freeholders in 1820. One of the family (William) was a Revolutionary soldier. James was county surveyor for some years. He died in the township about 1854.

John Carnahan came to White Eyes in 1826, and in the following year his father and the rest of the family, viz.: Adam, James, Ellanor, Andrew, Thompson, William, Nancy (now Mrs. Alex. Renfrew), Eliza, and Hugh. Most of these are still in the land. The family came originally from Westmoreland county, Pennsylvania. John, the first named, died November 21, 1869, being sixty-six years old. His wife (Sarah Marshall, of Jefferson county) died January 30, 1872, aged about seventy-three years.

George McCaskey, from Donegal county, Ireland, came to White Eyes in 1819, and remained on the same farm until his death, in 1871. He was eighty-six years of age. His wife died in 1862, in her eightieth year.

Wm. Himebaugh, long a resident of this township, was county auditor.

CHAPTER V.

SOME NOTICES OF THE PRINCIPAL EARLY SETTLERS, AND OTHER MATTERS OF INTEREST PERTAINING TO EACH TOWNSHIP.

THOMPSON has been a prominent name in the heraldry of Bedford township from the start. The name, familiar and in good repute in all that region, was among the first, if not the first, heard in the township as that of a settler. James Thompson, a native of New Jersey and a soldier in the Revolutionary War, settled near West Bedford, in 1808. Henry Haines and his bachelor brother, John, came in about the same time. They were from Bedford county, Pennsylvania; as also was Michael Heaton, who laid out the town of West Bedford. Heaton set up the first loom in the township, and for many years his own and his wife's fame was good in connection with "the fine linen," which was quite a thing in that day. Thomas and Edward Smith came in about the close of the war of 1812. The story was long current that the latter accompanied some American soldiers on their return home from Canada, where he had been in the British army.

The first resident land tax-payers were Ezra and Thomas Horton. They had some blooded-stock, and were well up in " the horse talk " of their day. Elias James still lives on the place in the township where he settled at a day giving him rank among " the earliest settlers," paying taxes on it since 1822, but occupying it at a still earlier day. The family was from Virginia. John McNabb entered, before much land was taken up in the township, the place now occupied by his son. So, likewise, did Thomas Norris, Sr. Daniel and James McCurdy, long known in the township, were among the pioneers. So, too, were Bennett Browner, Nathan Evans, Edward McCoy, Henry Rine, Wm. Richards, and Hugh Barrett.

The township got its name through the influence of the settlers who had come from Bedford, Pennsylvania.

VIRGINIA TOWNSHIP.

In Virginia township, as in some others, there were some who spent a single season taking a little tract by towahawk title, or beginning a little clearing, and then selling out their claims to some one coming along a few months later. The first settler, properly so called, in this township, was probably Joseph Tilton, coming in about 1804. He was from Maryland. Considerably beyond the four score, he still lives in the township. His descendants are, for the most part, in the west. Joseph Wright and Joseph McCoy came together into the township, December 24, 1806. Mr. Wright died, April 1, 1867, being eighty-seven years of age. Probably no one was more prominent in the township. His oldest son, Willis, is now a resident of Coshocton. Another son, Thomas, still lives in the old home township. Mr. McCoy, a number of years ago, was injured by a horse in his stable, and died from the effects of the injury, being in his eighty-seventh year. His children (one of them now eighty-two years of age), are well-known residents of Virginia or Jackson townships. Wm. Norris settled in Virginia township in 1808, and remained until his death, which occurred many years ago, at advanced years. One son, Daniel, died in 1875, aged eighty-one years. Another son, Samuel, still lives in the township, as also other descendants. These three families were all from the south branch of the Potomac, and were somewhat intermarried. Nancy Hays was a daughter of Norris—afterward married to Joseph McCoy. Mrs. Hays was a tax-paying landholder in 1814. Elisha Compton, now of Roscoe, married her daughter.

Henry Slaughter settled in Virginia township in 1812. He died in 1858, in his eighty-seventh year. Alex. Slaughter and Dr. Slaughter are his sons.

Beall Adams also came into Virginia in 1812, settling upon three hundred and twenty acres of land. He died, at advanced age, some years ago. Two of his sons are still in the township. John Graves—the father of Wesley, of

Jackson township, and also of Joseph—came into Virginia in 1814.

The descendants and successors of the early settlers, as they themselves did, have given their attention almost exclusively to agricultural affairs.

The township was called Virginia, in remembrance of the old home of most of the early settlers.

KEENE TOWNSHIP.

Geo. Bible is recognized by many as the first settler in what is now Keene township. He came from Virginia very early in the century; was a good example of the Daniel Boone type of pioneer; loved the solitude of the woods, and was happiest roaming them, with no companion save dog and rifle, or sitting by his cabin fire "far from the haunts of busy men." James Oglesby was a very early settler in the township, some say the earliest. He also came from Virginia, and is said to have traveled up the Muskingum and Walhonding rivers, in true Indian style, in a canoe. Bartholomew Thayer and Samuel Wiley were Revolutionary soldiers—taking up lands with their land warrants. Mr. Thayer and his wife were buried on their farm, near Keene. He died in 1826—about seventy years of age; she in 1825, at same age. A son, over ninety years of age, is reputed as still living at Elyria, O. Jesse Beal, the founder of the town of Keene, was from Nelson, Cheshire county, N. H. He died about 1835, being some forty-five years of age.

Adam Johnson (father of Dr. M. Johnson, of Roscoe) and Dr. Benjamin Hill were born in Cheshire county, N. H.; came to Keene about 1820. The doctor returned to New England and died, after burying his wife, who lies in the Keene burial-ground. Mr. Johnson was a good representative of Continental days; strong in body and mind; dignified in manner; wore a queue; had knowledge of the Latin language; was a student of the philosophies. James Pew was a soldier of 1812, still living in the township. The Farwells came in about 1825, from Cheshire county, N. H. Benton and Farwell built the first grist and saw-mill in the township. Robert Farwell kept hotel for many years in Keene. William Livingston was a justice of the peace, shrewd in judgment, but keeping such a docket that it was nicknamed "Bulwer's Novels." He died in 1840, aged seventy-two years. Andrew and Elisha Elliott and Henry Ramsey were well-known residents of Keene township, all immigrants from Ireland. Ramsey kept store in Keene about 1835. All three are dead.

Timothy Emerson was a citizen of Keene township from 1818 until 1873; came from Ashby, Mass. He reached the good old age of ninety-six; was a farmer; died October 30, 1873, just as arrangements were about being carried out for removal to Granville, where two children resided. He was greatly beloved—"a good man."

Jonas Child, Chancery Litchfield, Calvin Adams, Samuel Stone, and Jacob Emerson were early and active citizens of Keene township, and long dwelt in it. They were all from New England.

John Sprague, born in Cheshire county, N. H., in 1796, came to Keene in 1834; recently removed to Illinois.

It will be observed that many of the early settlers of Keene township were from Cheshire county, N. H., the county-seat of which is *Keene*, and hence the name of the township.

The oldest man now living in the township is doubtless John Crowley, a Virginian by birth, who came into the county about 1816. He is verging on to a century in years; was for some time sheriff, and held other offices, including that of member of the legislature.

John Daugherty lived fifty odd years on the farm near Keene, where he died about ten years ago. George Beaver is also a very old man, full of memories of the pioneer times.

The death of two "centenarians," Mr. Humphrey, aged one hundred and three, and Mr. Oglesby, about one hundred, is reported as having occurred in one day.

The claim is that Keene township can show the longest

roll of very old people. Still people do sometimes die even in Keene.

JACKSON TOWNSHIP.

The first resident tax-paying landowners in Jackson township were the Fosters (Samuel, William, David, Benjamin, Moses, and Andrew). The family was originally from Virginia, but came to Jackson township from Harrison county, Ohio, in 1816. The father died soon after the removal. David died some twenty years ago, and Samuel some two years. Moses and Andrew removed to the west a number of years ago. William still lives at advanced years where he first settled upon his marriage.

Barney and Thomas Cantwell were very early settlers in that part of Jackson township which originally belonged to Tuscarawas. The run just below Roscoe was long known as "Cantwell's run." Abel Cain was another very early settler.

About 1814 a man by the name of Sible built a small distillery on the farm just south of Roscoe, now owned by John G. Stewart. A little later he put up a little mill on Cantwell's run, about a third of a mile up. It was called a thunder-gust mill, as it only ran with full force after a heavy shower.

"Sible's corn-juice" was very popular in that day, and the business done by him and his neighbor, Samuel Brown, was enough to warrant the idea of a town, and doubtless led James Calder to lay out in that vicinity "Caldersburg."

Brown was from Massachusetts; first located, in 1814, at Rock run, three miles south of Coshocton. In 1816 he settled on a tract about a mile and a half west of Roscoe, and, after clearing a few acres and building a cabin, sold his claim to John Demoss. He then built a saw-mill on Cantwell's run, which had head of water enough to run the mill on an average three days in the week. For a number of years (until he united with the church) he depended on Sunday visitors to give him a lift in getting enough logs on the skids to keep the mill at work. The neighborly feeling, mellowed with a good supply of neighbor Sible's corn-juice, sweetened with neighbor Creig's maple-sugar (see below), was always equal to the demands thus made. Later in life Mr. Brown engaged in the making of brick. He remained in the vicinity until he died, in February, 1871, aged eighty-four years. He was for many years a useful and highly esteemed citizen.

About 1815 a man by the name of Creig bought forty acres of land, and built a cabin a little south of Robert Crawford's residence, on the tract now owned by Burns and Johnson. He was one of the most successful makers of maple-sugar, an article largely made, and in universal use in early days in Coshocton county for sweetening coffee, tea, whisky, etc. Mr. Creig died about 1826, and the family removed from the county.

Theophilus Phillips was from the State of New Jersey. He lived in Zanesville several years, and in 1815 entered and settled upon the farm now best known as the Dr. Roberts' farm, in the western part of Jackson township. In 1816 he sold this tract, and built a cabin in what is now Roscoe, and having lived in that a few years, he built, in 1821, the first brick house in the vicinity, using it for a tavern for a number of years. He moved to Indiana about 1845, and there died in 1858, being seventy-four years old. His daughter, Mrs. Hutchinson, is still living in Roscoe, understood to be the only person resident in Roscoe in the day of the opening of the "Phillips' tavern."

Reuben Hart was a brother-in-law of Phillips, also from New Jersey, and in 1816 occupied the farm next to Phillips, now known as the Wallace Sutton farm.

Wm. Starkey came from Virginia in the spring of 1815, worked for a time in Carhart's tannery, one mile north of Roscoe; afterward lived for a time in Coshocton, but is an old settler in Jackson.

John Demoss (father of Lewis Demoss, of Empire Mill) came from Virginia, and settled in Jackson township in 1817. He bought out Samuel Brown, as elsewhere stated, and lived on the tract until his death, March 4, 1840.

Abraham Randles and Thomas J. Ramphey came from Virginia, about 1817. They have both been dead many years. John Randles, son of Abraham, is supposed to be the oldest citizen now in the township that was born in it.

CLARK TOWNSHIP.

The earliest settlers in Clark township are understood to have been the following: Parker Buckalew, from Virginia, came in about 1817, settling in Killbuck valley; Isaac Hoagland, from Virginia, was here at a very early day; Abraham Miller, also a Virginian, came in about 1819; Andrew Weatherwat, a New Yorker, arrived about same date; Piatt Williamson, from Virginia.

These were all farmers, and encountered the hardships and perils in that line of work.

About 1820, Eli Fox, originally from the State of New Hampshire, but directly from Zanesville, built a mill on Killbuck, to which the settlers had to blaze paths. The mill was burned in 1829. Before it was built the people went to Knox county for flour, or got it at Zanesville, as well as other goods, which they received in exchange for logs cut on the banks of the Killbuck, and rafted down to that place.

John and William Craig, from Western Pennsylvania, fixed their stakes on Doughty's fork of Killbuck before 1820.

Joel Glover, from Jefferson county, long holding the important office of justice of the peace, and who (as well as his children) has " stood high " among his fellow-citizens, dates his location among the hills of Killbuck, 1829.

It is understood that the township was named in honor of old Samuel Clark, long a county commissioner, who was among the earliest and most highly esteemed citizens of the Killbuck valley.

JEFFERSON TOWNSHIP.

In 1818, the tax-paying landholders in Jefferson township were Joseph Butler, Thomas Butler, Robert Darling, Stephen Meredith, and Abner Meredith. They were all from Virginia. Darling and the Butlers came in 1806; the Merediths a little later. They and their descendants have been well known in the land. One of Darling's sons

(Thomas) was for years county commissioner. They were all farmers.

Henry Carr came from Virginia in 1805, and, after raising a few crops in the prairie in Bethlehem township, settled in Jefferson. He was the grandfather of ex-sheriff J. H. Carr.

Colonel Wm. Simmons, a Virginian, who had been a colonel in the Revolutionary War, received for his services " Simmons section," the southeast quarter of this township, and settled thereon about 1819. He died at a good old age, and was buried on his farm. The family was one of the few who brought a carriage with them to the county. A son, C. W. Simmons, was in the Legislature; now resides in Iowa at very advanced age. A daughter was married by General Wm. Carhart.

John Elder emigrated from Ireland to Virginia in 1804, and thence came with the Darlings to the Walhonding valley, in 1806. After making several other locations, he settled in Jefferson township about 1820. He died in 1851, on his farm, now occupied by his son, Cyrus Elder, a little west of Warsaw. He was a full-blooded, county Antrim, Presbyterian. He was twice married, and reared a large family, still prominent in the township. During the War of 1812, he spent some months in hauling supplies to the soldiers.

The Thompsons, Givens, and Moores have also long been among the well-known citizens of this township, and the two first named were very early settlers in it, coming from Pennsylvania or Eastern Ohio. The Tredaways have also been long in the land.

CRAWFORD TOWNSHIP.

The early settlers in Crawford township were almost, without exception, Pennsylvania Germans, and the leading element of the township is even yet of at least German descent; Protestant as to religious faith. Most of the tracts of land originally taken up were small, and it is the most densely populated—more inhabitants to the square mile—of any of the townships in the county. In 1822 the resident landholders were Philip and John Fernsler, George and William Gotshall, John and Jacob Luke, John Smith, Daniel Salsbury, John Albert, and William Stall. These were all in the township a little before that time, but then were tax-paying residents. The township was organized in 1828, and from 1830 to 1850 the inflow of population was very great, the township having in the latter year some 1,500 people in it. The Crawfords and Himebaughs and Lorentzs and Lowens and Everharts and Winklplecks and Doaks are reported as old and well-known families of this township. From 1850 to 1870 the population of Crawford fell off nearly three hundred, and it is said many of the old "first families" in point of settlement are now scarcely represented in it. The name of the township is said to have been given in honor of Associate Judge Crawford, who held a considerable tract of land in it, and was very popular.

MONROE TOWNSHIP.

Among the pioneers of Monroe were James Parker, William Tipton, Daniel and Jeremiah Fetrow, William Griffith, Thomas J. Northrup, William Bailey, Anthony Evans, and Jonas Stanberry.

The population has never been very distinctly marked as to nationality. In later years there was for a time a considerable inflow of Germans, but the tide, even in respect to these, soon ebbed rather than flowed. The modesty of the people, or the fact that there has actually been little of general interest in "the previous condition" of the early settlers or the movements of the township, makes these notices exceedingly brief. The capital of the township was originally designated *Van Buren*, but a change having been determined upon, the gallant citizens, it is said, conferred the honor of selecting the new name upon the wife of the principal of the academy (George Conant, now of Coshocton), and she, with an eye to natural fitness, called it *Spring Mountain*. The region may be called the highlands of the county, and the population likely to be drawn to it, as hitherto it has been, will be chiefly of the frugal and contented sort. It has furnished what indeed some of the more fertile and famous townships have not—a member of the legislature (Hon. E. L. Lybarger), to say nothing of the present auditor and of other county officers. Evidently the early settlers gave the township a good "send-off."

TIVERTON TOWNSHIP.

In 1817, the only settler who had got his name into the books as a resident land-owner in this township was Isaac Draper. He had indeed been in for some time before, as were a few others; but getting a name and a place in a new country even yet takes some time. "Tomahawk titles" were no longer recognized; but transfers of titles, and verifying of lines, etc., took time when nothing else did.

A few years later than Draper's entering, the following were in Tiverton: Thomas Borden, Wm. Humphrey, Matthew and William Hirt, Charles Ryan, James and John Conner, Wm. Durban, John Holt, and Isaac Thatcher.

Tiverton has always been a sparsely settled township— her people almost purely agricultural, frugal, hardy, boasting of the good health found in their highlands. Some of the early settlers came in from counties in Ohio, somewhat further east or south; but a very noticeable element was of New England or New York origin. Several of the older branches of the early settlers have paid the debt of nature—in almost every case attaining to a good old age, and passing away as quietly as they had lived; but the families of forty years ago in Tiverton are, in noticeable degree, the families of to-day.

When the Walhonding canal was being built, some expectation was indulged of Tiverton attaining quite a degree of commercial importance, and especially of its *Rochester* reaching prominence as a manufacturing point; but this failed with the failure to extend the canal.

BETHLEHEM TOWNSHIP.

When this township was organized, the honor of naming it was given to the then oldest resident of the region, who was Wm. Speaks, a Revolutionary soldier, and he named it Bethlehem.

Very early in the century, say about 1801, Wm. and Samuel Morrison, Ira Kimberly, and James Craig lived in what is now Bethlehem township. The first three were from Virginia. Craig, after a few years, moved to Coshocton, where he and all his family died, about 1814, of "Cold Plague." John Bantham and Henry Carr came to Bethlehem about 1806—the former from Virginia, the latter from near Baltimore, Md. The Burrells were early settlers in the township. Joseph Burrell died in the township in August, 1874, being about eighty-eight years of age. Benjamin Fry, occupying the land about "Fry's Ford," was also an early settler. Adam Markley, about 1808, came in with a large family—eight sons and four daughters. They were all farmers, and nearly all have been buried in this county. Barbara Markley, in her ninety-first year, and probably the oldest person now living in the township, is the widow of Wm. Markley. John Markley, killed by Geo. Arnold, at an election in Coshocton, in 1816, was of this family; also David Markley, now living at Lewisville.

Samuel Clark came from Virginia to Coshocton county about 1801, settling a few years later in Bethlehem, and there dying, a few years since, at a good old age. He was a justice of the peace during nearly all his active life; was also county commissioner several times. Gabriel Clark came about same time. Three sons of Samuel Clark (William, John, and Gabriel), with many descendants, are still living in the county.* Michael Hogle, John Merrihew, and David Ash settled in the township, April, 1814. They were all from Vermont. Michael Hogle raised a family of nineteen children; removed to Illinois in 1845, and died there in June, 1846.

The first mechanic (blacksmith) in the township was Albert Torrey, about 1814.

---

* William Clark died, April 14, 1876, of lung fever, at his home in the township. He had been for some time a justice of the peace. Was sixty-five years old.

The first school (in a log house) was taught by Charles Elliott, afterward the famous Methodist preacher, editor, and college president.

ADAMS TOWNSHIP.

One-half of this township was military land, and the other half Congress land. Much of the latter was entered after the township was organized, which was in 1832. Wm. Addy was the first tax-paying freeholder (in 1819). Among the earliest settlers were Robert Corbit; James Jones, who, while the region was yet a part of Oxford township, served as justice of the peace, and his brother Wm. Jones; Wm. Norris, from Virginia, whose distinction was that of having twenty-one children; Thomas Powell, an emigrant from England; John Baker, the founder of Bakersville, coming from New Jersey; another branch of the Norris family settled near Bakersville, and of a somewhat later date, but still in before the township was organized; the Campbells from Steubenville, and the Walters from Eastern Ohio. The first justice of the peace was Patrick Steele Campbell, who held the office until his death in 1850, Vincent DeWitt, and Leonard Hawk were early settlers, and the latter name is still represented in the township. The Mysers and Shannons, too, have long had a place "in the land."

LAFAYETTE TOWNSHIP.

Although Lafayette township was the last to be organized, the territory in it was among the first occupied. As early as 1801, Charles and Esaias Baker were raising corn on what is now known as the Colonel Andrew Ferguson farm. In 1802, George and Wendell Miller came out from Virginia, and continued to dwell in the township until they died at advanced years. Thomas Wiggins, also from Virginia, came in about the same time. In 1804, Francis McGuire, who had lived in the same locality (on the south branch of the Potomac, near Romney), whence the Millers and Wiggins had come, moved to the Tuscarawas valley above New Comerstown, and in 1807 came on down the valley to the locality in Lafayette township still known as the " McGuire settlement." The family were carried in a wagon which was driven along on the bank of the river, sometimes in it, and they afterward used the wagon-bed as their shelter and sleeping-place until a cabin could be built, which, in the want of help to any considerable extent from neighbors, took more time than in after years. Mr. McGuire died on the place thus taken up by him in 1853, being about seventy-six years of age.

In 1804, Seth McLain, also from Virginia, settled near the Bakers, putting up a cabin near the fine spring which now supplies Colonel Ferguson's house. After residing some ten years, the " settlers " discovered they were on the " Higby section " of military land, and moved over into Linton township, becoming thus early settlers therein. McLain married one of the Sells, whose connections had settled further up the river. His son James (father of Seth and Colonel R. W. McLain) died a couple of years ago, aged about seventy-five years. Thomas McLain came into Lafayette township in 1805, and remained until his death. A son (Isaac) is probably the oldest citizen now in the township, about seventy-two years of age.

Joseph C. Higbee, from Trenton, New Jersey, settled on his military section about 1820, and remained there until his death, about 1873, in the seventy-fourth year of his age. It is said his death was hastened, if not caused, by a violent abuse he received from some one who, it is believed, purposed robbery. His first wife was Miss Hackinson. One of his daughters was married to Rev. Mr. Southard, who was for a time a minister of Trinity Church, New York. Another is said to have married Mr. Hay, a lawyer, in Pittsburg. John Richmond, of Orange, married a daughter by the second wife. As illustrating " the style " of the man, the story was long current in the neighborhood, that, when he first came to the country, then in comparatively a wilderness condition, he brought with him six dozen ruffled shirts.

James M. Burt and Andrew Ferguson, long prominent citizens of the township, do not lay claim to being among the "old settlers," but they were in the neighborhood before it was organized.

CHAPTER VI.

ADVANCEMENT OF COUNTY IN WEALTH, TAXATION, ETC.

THE wealth of the first settlers of Coshocton county was almost wholly in their bold hearts and brawny arms. Some of them readily carried all their stuff in a small watercraft or on horseback. A few of them had in addition their broad, uncleared acres. Many of these were entered with land-warrants at nominal cost. Many acres were bought for from one to three dollars apiece. Even as late as 1830, the farm now occupied by J. W. Dwyer was bought at nine dollars an acre. It had, however, it is only fair to say, been sold for ten dollars, and the lower price above given was owing in part to the depression in lands on the east side of the river, in consequence of the canal having been built upon the other side. About the same time, some good lots in Coshocton were sold at sheriff's sale for from six to ten dollars. A few years later, after the bridges had been built, the land again changed hands at fifteen dollars per acre. Some of the early settlers spent the first season in bark or branch huts. The rifle and fishing-line secured much of the subsistence. It is claimed that old Michael Miller lived for weeks upon bear and deer meat, most of the time being even without corn-bread. For many years barter was the only kind of trade, and at first the skins of wild animals entered into it largely.* As late as 1825, the only surplus products of the county were ginseng, maple sugar, honey, bacon, and whisky. But lands were being cleared and improved, and appreciated every year. Do-

---

* Bear and deer meat occasionally graced the tables of the settlers as late as 1830. Bagnell and Retilley, of Roscoe, about that time traded for many a venison ham at twenty-five cents apiece. Still later, General Burns took a wolf-skin as pay for a marriage-license. Rattlesnakes were never quite so plenty after the exploit of Joseph Williams, who reports himself as having killed eighty-four in the summer of 1812.

mestic stock was increasing rapidly, and soon hogs and cattle were marketed in large numbers. Droves were taken east, and store-goods brought back. After the opening of the Ohio canal, the advancement of the county, in wealth as in population, was quite marked. Even the mineral resources of the county began to be regarded as elements of wealth. Coal was shipped to Newark and Columbus. Flour, bacon, and whisky, and even dried fruits,* became very considerable features of commercial transactions. Then fine cattle and sheep began to count largely. The opening of the railroad gave an impulse to the improvement and advancement of the county unequalled by anything else in its history. Butter and eggs and domestic fowls soon had more in them than would pay all the taxes of the people. Shipments of coal in an extensive and systematic way began, and, despite occasional interruptions, steadily grew, bringing into the county large sums to flow into other wealth-bearing channels. Better buildings were erected in both town and country, and fitted with more costly furniture.† Much improvement was made in farm appliances, the growing scarcity of labor, especially during the war, necessitating these. Manufacturing interests were much enlarged; and at length when, in 1875, an examination was made by the proper officers, it was found that the valuation for taxation of the real and personal property was $13,672,770. As the valuation in 1850 was only $5,026,561, it appears that even duly allowing for the fact that the later valuation was affected by the current inflation, the county has in the last twenty-five years more than doubled its wealth; and this, too, in the face of a diminishing population, as elsewhere noted. Of the total valuation about nine and a half millions are in real, and the other four in personal property. The principal items of the latter are as follows: horses,

---

* "Johnny Appleseed," an eccentric but far-seeing man, had frequently journeyed from Wheeling to Mansfield, donating his little sacks of seeds, and planting his little nurseries in out-of-the-way places suited for them.

† In 1850, there were only fourteen pianos in the county; in 1875, one hundred and twelve.

$488,000; cattle, $269,000; sheep, $265,000; hogs, $75,000; bank and other corporation stocks, $569,000 (of which in town of Coshocton, $189,000); moneys, $469,000; book accounts, credits, etc., $1,110,000 (of which $472,000 in town of Coshocton); merchants' stocks, $232,000; carriages, $150,000.

TAXES.

Land subject to taxes was, in the early days, divided into three classes. Of the one hundred and thirty-eight resident land-holders in 1814, only Robert Darling, Isaac Evans, Patrick Miller, James Meskimens, Benjamin Robinson, and Charles Williams had "first class" land. James Meskimens, on one hundred and sixty acres of first class and five hundred and sixty of second class land paid in that year fourteen dollars taxes. Besides the tax on land there were license fees paid into the county treasury for keeping taverns, ferries, and stores. Taxes on personal property were specific, and not according to value. In 1822 horses, mares, mules, and asses were each taxed thirty cents; neat cattle, ten cents per head, and town-lots one-half per cent. on their returned value.

The taxes collected in 1812, amounted to something over $1,000, of which $260 were paid over to the State. The county treasurer for 1816 reported the collections at $1,319. In 1822, the number of resident tax-payers was 1279. In 1825, the collected tax was $2,932.34, and the delinquent list counted up some $700. The tax collected in 1840 was $23,000. The State tax alone in 1875 was $42,417. The paying of the bonds given by the county and townships for the railroad; the great improvements in school line; the construction of half a dozen large and many more small bridges (many of them of iron), and the erection of the new jail and sheriff's house and court-house, have for some years demanded very heavy local taxation. The levy for 1875, for county purposes, was $68,414, and for other local purposes $80,523.

The indebtedness of the county, March 1, 1876, is an inconsiderable sum, and the townships and villages are in debt but a few thousands in the aggregate.

CHAPTER VII.

SOMETHING ABOUT ROADS, FERRIES, BRIDGES, STEAMBOATS, CANALS, AND RAILROADS.

SOME of the earliest settlers of Coshocton county came into it by the route taken by Broadhead's military expedition, and others by that taken by Boquet's expedition—the former from Wheeling, and the latter from Pittsburg to the Tuscarawas valley. The roads were of course Indian trails and bridle-paths. Others of the pioneers used canoes or other water conveyances, floating or poling up or down, as the case might be, the rivers and creeks.

While yet a part of Muskingum county, the road through Coshocton from Marietta to Cleveland had been made.

In 1812, the legislature provided for roads from Cambridge to Coshocton; from the head of White Eyes plains to Cadiz, and from Coshocton westwardly. Congress appropriated three per cent. of moneys derived from the sale of land to the making of roads. For the making of State roads, or the principal ones, commissioners were designated by the legislature. Many roads laid out in early times have in more recent years been somewhat altered, but the chief ones are in alignment wonderfully near the old Indian trails. An immense proportion of the time occupied in the sessions of the county commissioners has been from the beginning, even to this writing, taken up with road matters. With all the alterations and improvements, Coshocton county has even yet little to boast of in the way of roads. There is not prabably at this writing a mile of turnpiked or macadamized road in the county. Fortunately in many parts of the county, especially along the valleys, the natural grade is such and the soil of such composition as to give for most of the year quite fair facilities for traveling.

FERRIES.

Ferries were established very early in the century at Coshocton and near New Comerstown. Later they were numerous on the Tuscarawas and Walhonding rivers and on Will's creek and Killbuck creek. The business was never a very remunerative one to those operating the ferries, and the appliances rather rude. In 1817 the price of license for the ferry at Coshocton was put at sixteen dollars, and for the upper Tuscarawas at seven dollars. The authorized charge for ferriage was: for footman, six and one-quarter cents; horse and rider, twelve and one-half cents; loaded two-horse wagon, seventy-five cents. As might be expected, the attention of the ferryman was not always close. A witness in the court once declared that he "had been entertained (detained) for two hours waiting in the rain for the coming over of the ferryman." At another time the ferryman in charge declining on account of ice to come over, a settler famed for his courage and strength, and fresh from a visit to his girl "up the country," swam over the river, and not stopping to fully dress, "threshed" the ferryman and a dozen bar-room loafers in the tavern near by. At the ferry at the mouth of Will's creek John H. Hutchinson lost a valuable pair of horses, and barely escaped with his own life, the flat having been carried away by the force of the swollen stream, when the horses had not got a complete footing, and were dragged down by the wagon, which was heavily loaded with iron castings being brought from Zanesville for the Coshocton mill. It is said that one of the earlier ferrymen (perhaps an employe of Williams) at Coshocton for a time lived with his family in the trunk of an immense tree, quite after the big kind now attracting so much attention in the Yosemite (California) region.

Sanuel Morrison seems to have been the last licensed ferryman at Coshocton, and James M. Burt's father at the upper Tuscarawas ferry.

BRIDGES.

A toll-bridge was built for the county over Killbuck in 1818 by Adam Johnston, at a cost of $495. Thomas Johnston and others, authorized by the legislature, built one over Will's creek. After many years this was turned over to the county, on condition that it should be repaired and kept up. A bridge was built over the Tuscarawas at Coshocton in 1832 by Elisha Gibbs, Robert Hay, and William K. Johnson, under the supervision of James Renfrew, Samuel Lee, and Benjamin Ricketts, who were designated for the purpose by the county commissioners, and especially represented the citizens, who made donations (amounting to $1,200) for the building of this bridge, in order to have it a free bridge. It was carried away in a freshet about a year after it was finished.*

In 1836 a contract for the present bridge over the Tuscarawas, and also the one over the Walhonding at Roscoe was made with William Renfrew, James Hay, Thomas Johnson, and Robert Hay. The Tuscarawas bridge was finished in 1837, and the other in the following year. The contractors received for both bridges $19,900. That was a large sum for a county expenditure in those days, and there was some difficulty in obtaining it. Sealed proposals for the loan were invited, without response. General Burns was sent by the commissioners to Baltimore to get the money, but failed. Ten thousand dollars of it were at length obtained through the Bowmans of Brownesville, Pa., legal custodians for some parties in Columbiana county, Ohio, and the other $10,000 from the "Ohio Life and Trust Company." For the first ten years the county was to pay only the interest and in the second ten the interest and $2,000 per year of the principal.

The next considerable bridge erected was a wooden one at Walhonding about 1854. It got out of shape, and was regarded by many as insecure, and was rebuilt in 1860.

---

* "Sal's Gut," a bayou near the Tuscarawas bridge troubled the old settlers a good deal, but it was at length filled.

Again giving way, it was superseded by an iron bridge in 1872. Some of the material in the old bridge was used in the masonry of the new. A mistake in dimensions was made, increasing the expense of the masonry, which (almost wholly for labor) cost some $1,200. The masons were Bachman Brothers and N. W. Buxton. The superstructure was furnished by the Coshocton Iron and Steel Works, and cost $7,844. The ice in the winter of 1874 carried away a pier and two spans of this bridge. The latter were replaced by the Cincinnati Bridge Company (of which for a time the Coshocton Iron and Steel Works was a partner) in 1875.

The next bridge built was the Meskimens bridge, on the upper Tuscarawas, about 1854, costing some $10,000. This also was disturbed and somewhat rebuilt. The river having in 1861 cut a new channel, necessitated a new bridge a few hundred yards east of this one, the cost of which was about $9,000.

In 1868-9, the Warsaw and Fry's Ford bridges (wooden) were built. John Shrake, of Newark, was contractor for masonry on both. The superstructure of the former was contracted for by B. & J. Haggerty, and of the latter by John Hesket. The masonry of the Warsaw bridge cost $6,765; of the Fry's Ford, $6,709. The superstructure of the former cost $8,893, and of the latter, $6,100.

The Orange bridge was built in 1870; the masonry—N. W. Buxton, contractor—cost $8,311; the superstructure (iron), J. W. Davenport, contractor, cost $7,258.

An iron bridge was built over the Mohican, a little above Walhonding, in 1871. N. W. Buxton constructed the piers and abutments for $4,465, and the Massillon Iron Bridge Company furnished the superstructure for $5,070.

The Lafayette bridge (iron) was built in 1873; stonework by N. W. Buxton; cost, $6,290; superstructure by Cincinnati Bridge Company (J. W. Shipman & Co., of Cincinnati, and Coshocton Iron and Steel Works); cost, $8,746.

The commissioners are proposing to mark the centennial year by building a bridge near Morris' Ford (two miles below Coshocton), and another at Robinson's Ford (seven miles below Coshocton), over the Muskingum river. The masonry of the upper one has been let to S. H. Moore, of Tuscarawas township, and of the lower one to Perry Collins, of Knox county. The superstructure of both is to be furnished by the Smith Bridge Company, of Toledo. They will be sixteen feet wide (wooden), and cost, together, some $21,000.

STEAMBOATS.

Until the Ohio canal and Muskingum improvements were made, steamboats occasionally came up to Coshocton. The original proprietors of the town designated certain lots on the river bank as "warehouse lots," looking to shipments by river. By act of the legislature, the Muskingum, Walhonding, and Tuscarawas rivers, and Killbuck, Mohican, and Will's creeks, within Coshocton county, have been declared "navigable streams."

They have not, however, on that part within Coshocton county been much disturbed by "prows" for many years.

In 1875, a little steamboat was built at Jacobsport by Mr. Parker, proprietor of the mill, and was running as a pleasure and burden boat for short distances on Will's creek.

CANALS.

That part of the Ohio canal (from Cleveland and Lake Erie to Portsmouth, on the Ohio river) lying in Coshocton county was built in 1827–30. Among the chief contractors were the following citizens of the county, viz.: Thomas Johnston, Wm. Renfrew, Matthew Stewart, Solomon Vail, A. Ferguson, Ephraim Thayer, and A. G. Wood.

A sad incident in the construction of the canal was the death of Judge Brown, a citizen of Coshocton, who had a contract, and was killed while superintending his work by a falling rock. An amusing incident was the exploit of one of the M—e girls, who was employed as cook for a gang of hands. Picking up the rifle of one of the boys who was preparing for a Sunday hunt, she declared she would shoot a man on the other side of the river, who was only an old bachelor, and, therefore, as she alleged, of very little use, and so saying she fired, and actually hit the crown of the man's hat.

The first boat—the "Monticello"—arrived from Cleveland, August 21, 1830. She remained several days at the point of the hill above the aqueduct, attracting wonderstricken visitors in multitudes from this, and even adjoining counties.

The Walhonding canal was commenced in 1836, and finished in 1842. In the engineering corps were William H. Price, Charles J. Ward, John Waddle, Jacob Blickensderfer, Henry Fields, and Sylvester Medbery. Several of the gentlemen named above as contractors on the Ohio canal were also connected with this. In addition to these were John Frew, S. Moffitt, Isaac Means, John Crowley, W. K. Johnson, and others. This canal lies wholly within the county, extending from Roscoe to Rochester, twenty-five miles. It cost $607,268.99, or an average of $24,290.76 per mile.

The first superintendent of the Ohio canal, residing at Roscoe, was S. R. Hosmer, now of Zanesville. Alonzo Ransom, James Hay, John Mirise, James Carnes, and Wm. E. Mead, also held this office. The first collector was Jacob Welch, from Boston, Massachusetts, who (and also John M. Sweeny) had been in the engineering corps under Leander Ransom. At his death E. Bennett was appointed. The following persons have held that position, viz.: John D. Patton (now of Washington City), Houston Hay (of Coshocton), Chauncey Bassett (now in Illinois), Wm. M. Green (ex-postmaster of Dayton), C. H. Johnston (of Coshocton), James Gamble (deceased, of Walhonding), and Foght Burt (now in Illinois).

The superintendents of the Walhonding canal were Langdon Hogle, John Perry, Wm. E. Mead, and Charles H. Johnston.

The first canal-boat launched in the county was called the "Renfrew," in honor of James Renfrew, a merchant of Coshocton. It was built by Thomas Butler Lewis, an old Ohio keel-boatman.

It was intended to have the Walhonding canal extended

to the northwestern part of the State, but there was already (1842) much talk of a speedier mode of conveyance. The work had been very expensive, and the members of the legislature from districts where canals were not regarded as practicable were indisposed to continue the appropriations. In the days of the prosperity of the canals, several gentlemen were required to look after their interests in the capacity of collector, superintendent, and lock-tender, but of late years Samuel Gardiner has held all these offices, and served besides as justice of the peace and county infirmary director.

RAILROADS.

The Steubenville and Indiana Railroad (now merged in the Pittsburg, Cincinnati and St. Louis Railway) was built 1850-54—that part of it in Coshocton county in 1852-53. It was originally planned to go from Coshocton up the Walhonding valley, taking much the same direction as was once proposed for the Walhonding canal, and striking for Northern Indiana and Chicago. But the movements of another company anticipated part of this plan, and the road was built to Newark. A few individual subscriptions of stock were made, but most of the stock, afterward in the possession of individuals, came through the contractors to whom it had been given for work, or was given to the holders of it for right of way, etc. The county, in 1850, took $100,000 of the stock of the company, and the townships along the line of the road (except Oxford) $80,000 more—viz; Lafayette, $20,000; Tuscarawas, $30,000; Franklin, $15,000; Virginia, $15,000; for all of which bonds were issued. Subsequently, in processes of consolidation and extension, nearly one-half of this stock was relinquished, leaving the rest in possession of the county and townships. No dividend has ever been paid on it, and it is all regarded as practically sunken. The road paid into the county treasury, as taxes for 1875, the sum of $5,578.68.

The citizens now readily recalled as having contracts for building the road are Samuel Brown (since removed to Illinois), John Frew, J. W. Rue, John, Ninian, and Geo. Ross. Neither these nor any other citizens specially connected with the building of the road, reaped much benefit from it, but many have gained immensely, and the general advancement of the county, though it has in amount exceeded many times over all that was ever invested in it. Until comparatively recent years, one of the board of directors was taken from Coshocton county. Wm. K. Johnson served in that capacity from the inception of the road until his death, and was succeeded by his brother, Joseph K. Johnson, now of New York city.

In 1872, a railroad was located (as a branch of the Cleveland, Mt. Vernon and Columbus Railroad) through Clark, Bethlehem, Jefferson, Bedford, and Washington townships, and some work was done on it. But "the panic" of 1873 prevented any further progress for some three years. At this writing fresh efforts are being made to complete the work.

The Massilon and Coshocton Railroad, branching from the Cleveland, Tuscarawas Valley and Wheeling Railroad near Massilon (Beach city), and running to Coshocton, was located in 1875, and by the hearty assistance of parties along the line, under the direction of R. B. Dennis, W. L. Holden, and others interested in the C., T. V. & W. R. R., and also in coal-fields near Coshocton, is at this writing being rapidly constructed. A. H. Slayton, J. C. Fisher, E. T. Spangler, and J. C. Pomreue, of Coshocton, have been actively and officially connected with this enterprise. Several other railroads, notably one from Liberty, in Guernsey county, to Coshocton, and thence up the Walhonding valley (a part substantially of T. S. Humrickhouse's projected "Lake Michigan and Tidewater" Railroad); but up to this writing no effective measures have been taken in relation to them.

The first agent of the S. & I. Railroad at Coshocton was John Frew; then J. W. Rue; then E. Denmead; then G. G. Ridgely (1864).

At West Lafayette, J. W. Rue was the first; then S. Ketchum; then Robert Beall.

At Oxford the agent is James Coles. J. Sawyer has been for many years the agent of the Adams Express Company at Coshocton.

CHAPTER VIII.

COUNTY BUILDINGS AND OFFICERS.

FOR a number of years the courts of Coshocton county were held in Colonel Charles Williams' tavern, near the corner of (now) Water and Chestnut streets. Williams was one of the county commissioners at the time the first court was held, and then, and for some years afterward, the only tavern-keeper in the town. He received thirty dollars a year rent for the court-room, and two dollars per term for room occupied by juries. Asher Hart occasionally furnished a jury-room. When Alex. McGowan became clerk to the commissioners (in 1821) they entered into a contract " with Wilson McGowan for a court-room in the building occupied by Wm. Whitten," standing near corner of Second and Main streets (now), the site of part of the present " Central Hotel," and the courts were held there for some four years.

In 1819, the clearing and fencing (with post and rail fence) of the public square was let to Charles Williams and Adam Johnston.

In 1821 the commissioners determined to take some measures for building a court-house, and the auditor was directed to write letters to the townships touching the matter, " as an address to the feelings of the people." Twenty-eight hand-bills, pressing the necessity for such a building, were ordered to be printed and posted up in the several townships. Subscription papers were prepared, soliciting all sorts of building material, and in addition pork, rye, oats, and corn. At the next meeting of the commissioners it was determined to receive only money on subscription. At the April meeting in 1822 a plan was settled upon—a brick building, one story, thirty-two by forty feet, embracing a court-room and two small rooms for juries. Notices inviting proposals were ordered to be printed in the

Zanesville *Messenger* and Tuscarawas *Chronicle;* the bids to be opened July 9, 1822. On that day the letting was postponed until December, and the plan was somewhat changed. At the December meeting of commissioners it was concluded not to build at all unless citizens would aid by subscription, and papers were ordered to be again circulated, it being agreed this time to receive, as at first proposed, produce as well as building materials and money. The letting was fixed for April 18, 1823. At the April session, however, the plan was again changed, and it was resolved to have a house forty by forty feet and two stories high. On the day of the sale (April 18th), Peter Darnes bid $2,185. The commissioners were not willing to award, and adjourned until next day. Then the contract was given to Charles Williams, he being authorized and instructed to associate with him Peter H. Darnes, Abraham Richards, and Andrew Daugherty. It was substantially finished in 1824. The contract price was $1,984. A small allowance was afterward made for extra work, etc. The belfry was completed in 1830 under the supervision of John Elliott. The bell, still in use on the new court-house, was purchased, at the request of the commissioners, by William K. Johnson in 1834.

The structure was sold in April, 1875, and removed by M. Johnston, a grand-son of the original contractor.

It will thus be seen that the building stood for somewhat more than fifty years. Before it was finished a grand ball was given in it, and during all its history it was used for business, political, educational, and religious meetings, and was doubtless beyond anything else the theater of agents and operations affecting and manifesting the character and condition of the people of Coshocton county. Like the men of the day in which it was built, it had a measure of incurable roughness and few trappings, but was thoroughly square and true and strong and abundantly useful.

The matter of building a new court-house having been agitated for several years, was submitted to a vote of the people in the fall of 1872, and decided against by a very large majority. The following winter the legislature passed a special enabling act,* and the matter was proceeded with steadily, according to the requirements of the law and of the case. The contract for the new building was in due time let to S. Harold & Co., of Beaver county, Pa. Work was begun in 1873. The plans had been prepared and the work was superintended by Carpenter & Williams, of Meadville, Pa.

The structure was turned over to the commissioners in July, 1875, the county officers moving in the latter part of that month, and the District Court sitting therein the following month. The contract price was some sixty-five thousand dollars. Additions, extra work, furniture, and appliances vastly added to that sum, and the whole cost may be put down at a round $100,000. On either side of the old court-house there were built, in 1834, county offices (brick), one story, about forty by thirty feet. William C. Blodgett was the contractor, and the contract price was $1,360.

In 1849 an additional story was built on the north building by William McFarland. In 1854 the south building also received an additional story, and W. H. Robinson and William Welch were the contractors. These buildings were sold and removed at the same time with the old court-house. Just on the site of the present court-house stood the first jail, built of logs by Adam Johnston for $1,397; some $900 of this sum being the proceeds of sales of lots in south public square; also the second jail of brick. The latter, with sheriff's house adjoining, was built for $2,200 by Eldridge & McGowan in 1836. The present jail, built of stone, and sheriff's house of brick, were built in 1873. The whole cost of this undertaking was about $30,000. The contractors were M. Johnston and A. Wimmer, the former being a grandson of Charles Williams, the contractor for the first court-house. The plan was fur-

---

*On the urgent solicitation of the citizens of Coshocton, who, by their course in the matter, drew upon themselves the censure of many in the rural districts. A vigorous effort was made by the village of Warsaw to have the new court-house built there.

nished by Carpenter & Williams, of Meadville, Pa., who were consulting superintendents, John Dodd, of Roscoe, being the acting superintendent.

The county infirmary was erected (on the farm of two hundred acres, two miles east of Coshocton, purchased at $15 per acre from W. K. Johnson & Co. in 1848) by E. Davis and others in 1849. It is a two-story brick building, and cost about $3,900. Subsequently an adjoining tract of land was bought from Henry Wheeler for $2,500, making the whole farm nearly four hundred acres.

COUNTY COMMISSIONERS.

The first county commissioners, elected in April, 1811, were Charles Williams, James Meskimens, and Mordecai Chalfant. The following shows the incumbents and time of service in that office:

Charles Williams	1811–13	Isaac Darling	1843–49
Mordecai Chalfant	1811–18	Jas Ravenscraft	1844–47
James Meskimens	1811–21	Samuel Lamberson	1845–48
James Calder	1813–17	Alex. Matthews	1847–50
Squire Humphrey	1817–19	George Wolf	1848–51
Samuel Clark	1818–29	Francis Buxton	1849–52
Samuel Clark	1831–33	Henry Schmueser	1850–56
Robert Darling	1819–25	Thomas Darling	1851–54
Robert Boyd	1821–24	Lewis Swigert	1852–55
John G. Pigman	1824–26	Owen Evans	1854–57
Benjamin Ricketts	1825–28	Abraham Shaffer	1855–58
Gabriel Evans	1826–33	James E. Robinson	1856–59
Richard Moode	1828–31	Wm. Doak	1857–63
John Mitchell	1829–32	Wm. Hanlon	1858–64
John Quigley	1832–34	Jas. M. Smith	1859–65
Andrew Ferguson	1832–38	Thomas Darling	1863–69
Joseph Neff	1833–36	Joseph Keim	1864–70
Daniel Forker	1834–43	Thomas McKee	1865–71
Eli Fox	1836–39	Joseph S. McVey	1869–75
Arnold Medbery	1838–44	John Taylor	1870
Samuel Winklepleck	1839–42	Samuel Moore	1871
J. D. Workman	1842–45	William Forney	1875

COUNTY AUDITORS.

The first clerk (now called auditor) to the commissioners was Thomas L. Rue, but after a few meetings he ceased to attend, and Adam Johnston was appointed to his place, and held the office until 1821. The salary at that time was forty dollars per year. The following persons have held that office since Johnston; the dates following being the dates of their appointment or election:

A. M. McGowan	1821	Wm. Himebaugh	1854
Jos. Burns*	1824	Samuel Forker	1858
J. W. Rue†	1838	C. H. Johnston	1862
H. Cantwell	1848	W. R. Forker	1866
H. Rahauser	1850	Wm. Walker	1871
B. F. Sells	1852	Wm. Wolf	1875

COUNTY CLERKS.

The following is the list of persons who have held the office of clerk, with the date of their appointment or election:

Adam Johnston	1811	A. M. Williams	1854
John Frew	1829	Lemuel Kinsey	1857
A. M. McGowan	1836	Chas. K. Remick	1863
Joseph Burns	1843	G. H. Barger	1869
B. R. Shaw	1851	Israel Dillon	1875

COUNTY TREASURERS.

The first treasurer of the county was Wm. Whitten, holding office from 1811 to 1817. Dr. Samuel Lee succeeded him, and held the office until 1825. The pay of the office for a few years was five per cent., then three per cent. on moneys received, and amounted to from forty to sixty dollars per year prior to 1818. Dr. Lee was succeeded by James Renfrew, who agreed to serve for three per cent., and obligated himself " not to speculate on the county's money." John B. Turner was treasurer for 1827 and 1828. A. M. McGowan for 1829 and 1830. Samuel Rea ‡ became treasurer in 1831.

---

* Resigned.

† Appointed, and afterward elected.

‡ Rea was a son of the well-known Rev. John Rea, of Harrison county. He studied law, and was a man of ability. But he was of too social a turn—fond of " good fellows "—a fine violinist. He was drowned at Fry's Ford, on Walhonding river, in 1834, on his way home from a convivial party which had been keeping late hours. His estate and securities satisfied the county's claim.

In December, 1832, he was removed from office and a suit begun against his securities for a "shortage" of nearly $2,000. Robert Hay was appointed in Rea's stead, and held the office until 1834. Wm. G. Williams was elected in 1834, and held the office until 1846. Benjamin Bonnett succeeded him in 1846. In 1849, he left the county very abruptly, sending in his resignation.* J. W. Rue was appointed to complete the term of office, ending in 1850. Wm. P. Wheeler held the office 1850–52. Lewis Demoss was his successor, and served two terms, going out in 1856. Samuel Ketchum was treasurer from 1856 to 1859; in October of the latter year, owing to the hue and cry about the treasury robbery,† he resigned, and Samuel Lamberson fin-

---

* His cash-box was discovered to be in a very bad shape, and his securities were required by the county to respond. He is understood to have gone to California.

† Ketchum was found by some persons who heard his outcry n seemingly exhausted condition in the treasurer's office, about midnight, January 21. 1859. He alleged that having kept the office open to pay some witnesses from abroad who desired to take a late train, two men came in, and, throwing a shawl over his head, bound and gagged him, and took what moneys were in the safe, reported afterward at about $20,000, the larger part of it State moneys. Subsequently he confessed that the thing was a job, and implicated James M. Brown, from whom he said he had in a strait borrowed some money. They were indicted by the grand jury. A change of venue having been asked by Brown, the case was tried in Licking county, and on law points carried to the Supreme Court at Columbus, but in 1870 Brown was sentenced to pay double the amount abstracted, and spend five years at hard labor in the Ohio penitentiary. Ketchum plead guilty, after Brown was sentenced, and received the same sentence. While in the penitentiary, Ketchum failed rapidly in health, and in this view, having been pardoned, came to his home in West Lafayette, and there died in the summer of 1872, a sad, penitent victim of his own folly, and possibly of the wiles of even more cunning and unscrupulous men. Brown was pardoned by Governor Allen in 1874. A considerable sum was realized by sale on execution of some of the property held in Coshocton by Brown, but finding the legal complications increasing, growing out of claims put forward by his relations, the commissioners compromised on a less amount than originally assessed. The State, however, obtained $10,000, and the county nearly the amount lost. But nearly or quite all that amount was expended in the legal proceedings connected with the case, and the treasury never got back its own.

ished the term, and, being elected and re-elected, served until 1864. His successor was Samuel Burrell, 1864–68. Then Thos. Jones came into office, and held the place for two terms, 1868–72. Richard W. McLain was in the office from 1872–76. John Waggoner succeeded him, and is the present incumbent.

COUNTY RECORDERS.

The first recorder was Adam Johnson, appointed in 1811, and dying in 1829, Jos. Burns was put into his place, and held it until 1836, when Geo. W. Price was appointed. He died in 1840, and Russell C. Bryan took his place 1840–46. The following is the succession, with date of election; G. F. Cassingham, 1846; John F. Williams, 1855 (resigned in 1857, and R. M. Hackinson filled out his time); A. McNeal, 1858; C. W. Stanford, 1861; L. L. Root, 1864; and M. W. Wimmer, 1870.

SHERIFFS.

C. Van Kirk	1811–15	Samuel Morrison	1845–49
Chas. Williams	1815–19	Samuel B. Crowley	1849–53
Chas. Miller	1819–21	Richard Lanning	1853–55
John Smeltzer	1821–23	W. H. H. Price	1855–57
John Crowley	1823–27	David Rodahaver	1857–61
T. Butler Lewis	1827–29	John Hesket	1861–65
John Crowley	1829–33	James Sells*	1865–68
J. H. Hutchinson	1833–37	Thomas Platt	1868–69
Saml. Morrison	1837–41	Joshua H. Carr	1869–73
Jos. C. Maginity	1841–45	John Lennon	1873

PROSECUTING ATTORNEYS.

Wright Warner was appointed, at the September term of court, in 1811, for seven years, but resigned in 1814. Alex. Harper was then appointed, and continued until 1823, when, having been elected judge, he was succeeded by Chas. B. Goddard, who served until 1827. W. Silliman, David Spangler, and Richard Stillwell served for terms of court until 1830 (March term), when Noah H. Swayne was

---

*Sells left the county very abruptly, and his bondsmen had certain claims to satisfy. Platt succeeded him by virtue of being at the time coroner of the county.

appointed for a full term. But in 1833, Josephus Ricketts having been elected, came into office. He resigned in 1834, and G. W. Silliman was appointed and afterward elected in 1835, and his health failing in 1841, the latter part of his term was filled out by T. S. Humrickhouse by appointment. In 1843, and also in 1845, Thomas Campbell was elected. Then the succession was Wm. Sample in 1849; John T. Simmons in 1851 and 1853; John D. Nicholas in 1855; and Charles Hoy in 1857 and 1859. Hoy, in 1860 resigned, and Thomas Campbell finished his term. In 1860, Richard Lanning was elected, but in the second year of his service resigned his office to take that of Major in the army, and Thomas Campbell filled out his term. In 1862, Asa G. Dimmock was elected, and again in 1864 and 1866. His health having failed, and he having resigned and removed in the spring of 1868, R. M. Voorhes was appointed to complete his term, and having been elected in the fall of 1868, and also in 1870, continued in the office until it was taken by the present incumbent, Wm. S. Crowell, who was elected in 1872.

COUNTY SURVEYORS.

The first county surveyor was Wm. Lockard, appointed in 1812. He served until 1817, when James Ravenscraft became surveyor. He resigned in 1819, and Wm. Coulter was appointed until 1824. Wm. G. Williams then came into office, and served till 1830. Jas. Ravenscraft was in the office from 1830 to 1836. Then came John M. Sweney, and then John M. Fulks. Henry Seevers was Fulks' successor, and served until 1852, when Lemuel Kinsey was elected. C. W. McMorris was elected in 1855; R. L. Baker in 1858; T. P. Latham in 1861; he having resigned, Levi Gamble was appointed in 1864, and then elected in 1865 and 1868. John A. Hanlon was elected in 1871, and Geo. Miller in 1874, being in office at this writing.

CORONERS.*

The following persons have held the office of coroner, viz.: David Bookless, Geo. Leighninger, James Ravens-

---

* The list is not complete as to the earlier ones.

craft, Abraham Sells, Benj. Coe, Thomas McAnnally, Addison Syphert, James T. McCleary, Jos. Hitchens, Wm. Jeffries, Thomas Platt, Nicholas Schott, and John Richeson.

INFIRMARY DIRECTORS.

The following have served the county as infirmary directors: Lewis Row, Jas. Jones, Henry Wheeler, Isaac W. Miller, John M. Johnson, Stephen D. Sayer, Thomas Dwyer, D. E. Laughlin, Geo. McCune, J. C. Frederick, Wm. Simons, James McBriar, John Chambers, Nathan Buckalew, John Hawley, Wm. McCoy, C. F. Sangster, Samuel Gardiner, and Thomas Wiggins.

CHAPTER IX.

CONNECTION WITH STATE AND NATIONAL AFFAIRS.

STATE SENATORS.

FOR some years after its organization, Coshocton county was combined with Guernsey and Tuscarawas in a state senatorial district. From 1820 to 1830, the district was made up of Coshocton and Tuscarawas, and after 1824, Holmes, which was in that year organized. Still later, Knox and Coshocton made the district. Since 1850, Coshocton and Tuscarawas have formed the district.

The first citizen of Coshocton elected state senator was Wilson McGowan, serving 1821-22. Samuel Lee was senator, 1826-27; Charles Miller, 1828-29; James, Ravenscraft, 1834-36; James Matthews, 1838-39; John Johnson, 1842-43; F. W. Thornhill, 1845-46; Andrew Ferguson, 1850-51; Wm. Heslip, 1854-55; A. L. Cass, 1858-59; Wm. Stanton, 1864-65; James M. Burt, 1866-67, also 1870-71; John C. Fisher, 1874-75.

REPRESENTATIVES.

The representative was elected, until 1820, by Tuscarawas and Coshocton. Occasionally, at a much later day, to make the proportionate representation, Coshocton would elect a representative, and then Coshocton and Knox or Guernsey together, would have an additional representative.

In 1814, Charles Williams was elected representative by Tuscarawas and Coshocton; in 1816 and also in 1818-20, and 1823, Joseph W. Pigman was chosen; in 1817, Squire Humphrey. In 1820, Coshocton itself became a representative district, and James Robinson was the representative, 1820-21, also 1824; Charles Williams, 1825; John Smeltzer, 1827-28; N. H. Swayne, 1829; James Robinson, 1830; Charles W. Simmons, 1831; James Matthews, 1832; John Crowley,

1833-34-35; Samuel Whitmore, 1836; James Matthews and F. W. Thornhill, 1837; Joseph Burns, 1838-40; Jesse Meredith, 1841-42; Geo. A. McCleary, 1843; Jesse Meredith, 1844; Heslip Williams, 1844-45;* Joseph Williams, 1846-47; James M. Burt, 1848-49; Timothy C. Condit, 1850-52; Geo. McKee, 1852-54; John Pierson, 1854-56; Patrick Thompson, 1856-58; C. F. Sangster, 1858-60; James Gamble and J. N. Fellows, 1860-62; Andrew J. Wilkin, 1862-64; F. W. Thornhill, 1864-70;† John Baker, 1870-72; B. C. Blackburn, 1872-74; John Baker, 1874-76; E. L. Lybarger, 1876.

In 1812, Coshocton county gave Return J. Meigs, candidate for governor, 65 votes; and to Thomas Scott, opposing candidate, 21 votes. In 1814, 248 votes were cast for Thomas Worthington, and one for his opponent. In 1824, Jeremiah Morrow received 634 votes, and Allen Trimble 531 votes, for governor. In 1834, Robert Lucas got 885, and John Findley, 705 votes. In 1844, Mordecai Bartley got 1,749, and David Todd, 2,156 votes. In 1855, William Medill got 2,007, and Salmon P. Chase, 2,064. In 1865, J. D. Cox got 1,979, and G. W. Morgan, 2,374. In 1875, R. B. Hayes got 2,321; and Wm. Allen, 2,913.

In the state constitutional convention of 1851, Coshocton county was represented by John Johnson; and in that of 1874, by Wm. Sample, Esq. The opposing candidates were Captain J. M. Love and E. T. Spangler, Esq.

James M. Burt represented the Coshocton and Tuscarawas district in the state board of equalization in 1860.

James Gamble was chosen a member of the board of public works in October, 1862—entering upon his duties in February, 1863. He died in March, 1864, and James Moore was appointed by the governor to fill the vacancy in April, 1864. He was elected in October, 1866, and held thus the legal term of three years.‡

---

* Dr. Williams is reported as the author of the famous "Liquor Law," passed by that Legislature.

† Speaker of the house, session of 1868-69.

‡ Removed to Indianapolis in 1875.

Connection with State and National Affairs. 71

John C. Fisher was appointed a member of the Fish commission in 1875 by Governor Allen.

CONGRESSMEN.

Coshocton county has furnished four congressmen to represent the district of which it has formed a part, under the decennial apportionments. David Spangler, Esq., was the first of these—elected by Coshocton, Holmes, Knox, and Tuscarawas counties. He was re-elected—thus serving from 1833-37. The next was James Matthews, Esq., also serving two terms, 1841-45. John Johnson was the congressman, 1851-53; and Joseph Burns, 1857-59. Since 1870 the district has been composed of Coshocton, Licking, Muskingum, and Tuscarawas counties.

MISCELLANEOUS.

J. W. Dwyer was for some time (in Delano's administration of internal revenue affairs) supervisor of internal revenue for the northern district of Ohio, with office at Coshocton. He was, at a later date, pension agent, with office at Columbus. W. A. Johnson served, for several years, as deputy United States Internal revenue assessor; and John Frew and James Dryden, and Dr. S. H. Lee as deputy collectors.

U. S. POSTMASTERS AT THE CAPITAL OF THE COUNTY.

Adam Johnson, 1811-29; postoffice on Water street: Wilson McGowan, 1829-30; postoffice on Third street: Wm. K. Johnson, 1830-45; postoffice on Second street: C. H. Johnson; on Water street: R. F. Baker; on Second street: Samuel Rich, 1853-54; on Chestnut street; H. N. Shaw, 1854-61; on Second street: Asa L. Harris, 1861-64; on Second street: A. H. Fritchey, part of 1864; on Second street: W. A. Johnson, 1864-65; on Second street; R. M. Voorhees, 1865-68; on Main street one month, then back on Second st.: T. W. Collier, 1869; Main street, corner of Fourth; between Third and Fourth; between Fifth and Sixth.*

---

*In the "Opera House," erected by J. Heskett, A. Miller, and John Timmons, in 1873-74. Size, 44 by 100; cost said to be $25,000.

CHAPTER X.

THE COURTS AND THE BAR.

THE first term of the Court of Common Pleas for Coshocton county was held on the 1st day of April, 1811. By the legislature the county was placed in the judicial district over which Hon. William Wilson, of Licking county, was president judge. William Mitchell, Peter Casey, and Isaac Evans, three substantial citizens of the county, were also designated as associate judges. The court sat in the parlor of Colonel Charles Williams' hotel, as elsewhere stated. Some choice hickory-wood had been cut for the occasion, and "mine host" was doubtless in his best humor, feeling the importance of the occasion and his own importance as one of the head men of the new county and the host of the court. It is said new hunting-shirts were plenty in town that day. It must, however, have somewhat diminished the glory of the occasion that the president judge did not put in an appearance. The three associates were on hand, and the court "sat" with becoming gravity. Cornelius Van Kirk was sheriff, and the court appointed Adam Johnston clerk for the term. Johnston was also appointed recorder for the term of seven years, and the only other business transacted at that term was the ordering of elections for justices of the peaee for the townships of Tuscarawas, Washington, and New Castle, one each, and for Franklin two. The legislature had provided for three terms of court for that year, as was done for many years thereafter. The second term was held in September. At that Judge Wilson was present, as also the three associates already named. The full-blown dignity of the court was then attained. Thomas L. Rue was appointed clerk *pro tem*. A grand jury was sworn, consisting of the following persons, viz: James Turner, James Craig, Benjamin Fry, Samuel Clark, Samuel Hardesty, John Harrison, Isaac Workman, Charles Miller, Michael Miller, Windle Miller, Henry Miller, Philip Waggoner, Francis McGuire, and John Mills. The jury reported "no business." The docket showed three cases. In two the writs were quashed, and the other case was "continued." At the December term the judges were again all present, and business began to grow more lively. Adam Johnston was appointed clerk for seven years. Elections for two more justices of the peace were ordered for Tuscarawas township and one for Oxford. The most important case tried was that of Charles Williams against Adam Markley; verdict, nine dollars and sixty cents damages for plaintiff. Lewis Cass (afterward so prominent even in National affairs) was Williams' attorney.

The legislature had provided that no term of the court should extend beyond twelve "working days." For the first few years actually from one to five days were occupied. The cases were largely criminal, and especially relating to crimes against the person, assault and battery and slander abounding. The sums involved in civil suits seem insignificant in these days. Pretty large figures were, however, sometimes put upon the records, as, for instance, when a decree was, without resistance, taken requiring Matthias Denman* to execute a certain conveyance on penalty of having to pay $30,000. Among the curiosities as now regarded of the criminal proceedings of the early days is the sentence passed at the December term in 1814 upon one Zeba French, convicted of passing a counterfeit note of the "Miami Exporting Company," viz., that he should be tied to the public whipping-post and receive thirty-nine lashes upon his bare back; also be fined twenty dollars and costs, and be imprisoned thirty days in the county jail. The two "unpardonable sins" with the early settlers of most countries have been passing counterfeit money and stealing horses.

Judge Wilson continued as president judge until 1822, when he was succeeded by Alexander Harper, of Zanes-

---

* He was the grand-father of A. D. and Martin Denman, living in Springfield, N. J., and at that time a very large landholder in Coshocton county.

ville.* He served two terms, and was succeeded in April, 1836, by C. W. Searl, also of Zanesville. Richard Stillwell, of Zanesville, was the next president judge. Owing to ill health he was not able to attend for several terms of court in Coshocton. About the end of his term of office Coshocton county was placed in another district, and James Stewart, of Mansfield, became president judge. He was present at only a few terms of the court before the change was made under the new constitution. The first judge to sit at Coshocton under that instrument was Martin Welker, then of Holmes county, now judge of the United States District Court for the Northern District of Ohio. Having served one term of five years, Judge Welker was succeeded in 1857 by William Sample, of Coshocton. He served for nearly two terms—ten years—(C. F. Downing, of Wayne county, serving two months in consequence of Sample's resignation), and was succeeded in 1867 by William Reed, of Holmes county, the present incumbent.

Under the old constitution three citizens were designated by the legislature to occupy the bench as associate judges. Their terms of office were the same as those of the president judges, viz., seven years. The following citizens served in that capacity: Isaac Evans, William Mitchell, Peter Casey, Lewis Vail, Joseph W. Pigman, Thomas Johnson, Benjamin Robinson, Mordecai Chalfant, John Mitchell, James Robinson, John Crawford, James Le Retilley, Robert Crawford, Benjamin R. Shaw, Samuel Elliott, Josiah Harris, and James M. Burt. Messrs. Casey, Johnson, John Crawford, and Le Retilley were reappointed. John Mitchell served for a brief time, filling a vacancy. Messrs. Harris and Burt served only a few months, having been inducted just before the adoption of the new constitution, by which the office was abolished. B. R. Shaw now resides in Knox county. Messrs. Harris and Burt are still in the county. The others are all dead, and their sepul-

---

* Harper had frequently visited Coshocton as a lawyer, and for several years had acted as prosecuting attorney for Coshocton county. He was exceedingly popular with the bar and also with the citizens. A. H. Spangler and A. H. Fritchey are witnesses—by their names—for this appreciation by both classes.

chers, except that of Peter Casey, who was buried in what is now Holmes county, are with us to this day. For the times and their work, it is claimed that these gentlemen were, almost without exception, well chosen. It has been insisted by some of the ablest lawyers that the associate judge courts oftentimes correctly accomplished an amount of business not always attained under the present system.

There was little claim, by or for these associate judges, of any special knowledge of the law, and the system under which they served came in time to be regarded as a sort of wagon with five wheels—a third estate between the judge proper and the jury, and not demanded in settling either the law or the facts. One of the commonest jokes of their day was that telling of the man who declared that it was terrible to be brought before a court of a thousand men—the president judge being one (1), and the three associates the three ciphers (000).

Under the old Constitution, a term of the Supreme Court of the State was to be holden in each county. In pursuance of this order, the first term of that court was held in Coshocton in 1814, and every year (except one) thereafter until 1851. The judges who were first detailed were W. W. Irwin and Ethan Allen Brown. Afterward came P. Hitchcock, Jacob Burnet, John C. Wright, Charles R. Shernan, Rufus P. Spalding, and others—indeed, most of the judges of the Supreme Court.

Under the Constitution of 1851, a District Court was provided for, and has annually sat in Coshocton. For some years one of the three judges required for this court must be of the Supreme Bench, but under a more recent law the court is made up of the Common Pleas judges of the district.

The Probate Court having special relation to social conditions and primary cognizance of all forms of disposal of property, whether by assignment, testament, or ordinary rule of inheritance, together with concurrent jurisdiction in certain matters of criminal sort, was organized under the Constitution of 1851. It is in daily (week day) session for some kinds of business, while for criminal and some other matters terms are appointed. The first judge of this court was Thomas Campbell, Esq., of Coshocton, who came into office in 1852, and served (the prescribed term) until 1855. C. S. Barnes, of Bedford township, was the next incumbent. Then John T. Simmons, Esq., of Coshocton, served two terms, 1858 to 1864. M. C. McFarland, Esq., of Coshocton, served from 1864 to 1870.

Joseph Burns, of Coshocton, was the next judge, taking the office in 1870. He died in May, 1875, and Governor Allen appointed F. W. Thornhill, of Coshocton, to serve until the fall election, and at that he was elected to fill out Burns' unexpired term. Alex. Hanlon, of Mill Creek township, at the same time was elected for the full term, and is the present incumbent.

THE BAR.

Wright Warner was the first lawyer resident in Coshocton, coming to the place in the spring of 1811. At the September term of the court in that year, he was appointed prosecuting attorney for the county. In a little time he incurred the displeasure of Colonel Williams, and there was a rencounter, followed by several lawsuits for assault and battery, slander, etc., and in 1814 he left the place, removing to New Philadelphia, where, for a number of years, he was in practice, serving also as prosecuting attorney of Tuscarawas county. Nearly cotemporaneous with him was Aaron M. Church—a New Englander and protege of Dr. S. Lee. He died very suddenly with the "cold plague" in 1815. Neither the amount of business done by these gentlemen (Warner received sixty-five dollars for his year's service as prosecuting attorney, and Church left property valued at forty-five dollars), nor their experience was very encouraging to other lawyers to settle in the place. Indeed, for several years the little legal business done seems to have been attended unto by "foreign lawyers," chiefly from Zanesville, such as Lewis Cass, Alexander Harper, Wyllis Silliman, E. B. Munroe, S. W. Culbertson, and Ebenezer Granger.* The next resident lawyer seems to

---

*One lawyer set up in 1819, but the poor fellow was driven, by dull times, to picking up a little in a merchant's store, and soon "lit out." He may have done better in later years, and so his name is withheld.

have been Wm. G. Carhart, in practice about 1821. His practice does not seem to have absorbed his time, and other matters increasingly received his attention. He was of the Carhart family, still well represented in the county. He was born near the mouth of Little Miami river; studied law in Louisville, Kentucky; came to Coshocton county in 1821; was a partner in a store, in a tannery, in the "Union Flouring Mill;" went to California, and is now living in Ottumwa, Iowa.

About 1825, Samuel Rea commenced practice. He was from Harrison county; was elected county treasurer; continued to practice more or less until his death, which occurred (by drowning, as detailed under head of county officers,) in 1834. The next resident lawyer was Noah H. Swayne, coming primarily from Virginia, but directly from Belmont county, in 1827. He was prosecuting attorney for several years; in 1832 removed to Columbus, and is now on the bench of the United States Supreme Court, in Washington, D. C.

James Matthews, born in Columbiana county, read law with Hon. H. H. Leavitt, of Steubenville; came to Coshocton in 1829; was in the Legislature and in Congress; removed to Knoxville, Iowa, in 1855.

Geo. Willys Silliman, native of Muskingum county, educated at Ohio University and at West Point Military Academy; studied law and was admitted at Zanesville; came to Coshocton about 1830. Soon went to Spain as bearer of dispatches from United States government to C. P. Van Ness; returned to Coshocton in 1833; served several years as prosecuting attorney, holding the office till his death. Went to Europe in summer of 1843, and died at sea on the return voyage.*

The lawyer next becoming a resident was David Spangler. He was born in Sharpsburg, Maryland; came to Muskingum county in 1802; studied with Alexander Harper; admitted in 1824; came to Coshocton in 1832; was two terms (1834–38) in Congress; died in 1856.*

---

*See "Biographical Sketches" in this volume.

T. S. Humrickhouse, born in Fayette county, Pennsylvania; graduated at Washington College; studied law with T. M. T. McKennan, of Washington, being admitted in 1832. In November of that year came to Coshocton; abiding a year to acquire citizenship, was admitted at Lancaster in 1833; served a few terms of court as prosecuting attorney for G. W. Silliman; disabled by accident in 1847, and soon gave up practice; now in the nursery and sheep business.

Josephus Ricketts, born in Muskingum county; read with N. H. Swayne; succeeded him as prosecuting attorney; resigned, and soon gave up practice; removed to Millersburg and went into real estate operations; now in Toledo.

Thomas Campbell, born in Jefferson county (Steubenville); came with his father's family to Adams township, Coshocton county, in 1831; studied at Franklin College; came to the town of Coshocton in 1835; taught school and read law with James Matthews; commenced practice in 1841; has been prosecuting attorney and probate judge.

Thomas W. Flagg was born in Rochester, New York; came to Coshocton in 1838; commenced practice in 1840; gave up practice and was chiefly engaged in newspaper work; died May 16, 1863.

J. M. Love, from Virginia, was engaged in engineer's department on the Muskingum improvement; read law in Zanesville; came to Coshocton in 1842; was in military service (Mexican war), 1846–7; removed in fall of 1851 to Iowa; now judge of United States District Court.

Lewis Lewton, practiced from 1842 to 1845; removed to Cadiz, Ohio.

Wm. Sample, born in Crawford county, Pennsylvania; studied law in Steubenville with Oliver C. Gray; admitted March 3, 1843; came to Coshocton November, 1845; was prosecuting attorney one term (two years); elected judge of Court of Common Pleas, 1856, and served two terms (ten years); in 1866 removed to Wooster, and subsequently to Newark, returning to Coshocton in 1873.

A. R. Hilyer, born in Essex county, New Jersey; came to Coshocton in 1837; clerked, taught school, studied law, and was admitted in 1847; was editor of "Coshocton Age" for two years; removed to Iowa; now publishing a paper.

James Irvine, born in Wayne county; studied law with Sapp & Welker, of Millersburg, and admitted there in 1846; went to Mexican war in 1847; came to Coshocton in 1849; taught school and posted up, and in 1850 went into partnership with J. S. Love; was in military service in late war in 1861, and also 1863-65.

John C. Tidball, born in (now) Lawrence county, Pennsylvania; graduated at Jefferson college; labored as a Presbyterian minister some seventeen years at Island creek, Jefferson county, and at Morriston, Belmont county; studied law with C. C. Carroll, of Belmont county, and was admitted in 1843; came to Coshocton in 1848; died in 1863.*

John T. Simmons, a native of Maryland, resided for a time in Belmont county; came to Bedford township, Coshocton county, 1842; taught school and farmed, being the champion tobacco raiser of the county; studied under Wm. Sample, and was admitted in 1850; was prosecuting attorney two terms, also probate judge two; prompted by tastes, and driven by necessities of family, turned to farming for a few years during the war.

B. S. Lee, born in Genessee county, N. Y., September 12, 1812; came to the county (Newcastle township), in 1838; studied with William Sample; admitted September 26, 1850; moved to Coshocton about 1859; died August 2, 1874.

C. C. Leonard, from Knox county; practiced a few years, part of the time in partnership with J. D. Nicholas, about 1855; removed in 1857 to Illinois, and was, a few years later, killed by being run over by a locomotive.

E. T. Spangler, born in Muskingum county; was brought to Coshocton when one year old; graduated at Kenyon College; studied with father (David Spangler), and admitted in 1853; by United States Supreme Court at Washington in 1860.

---

* See "Biographical Sketches."

A. H. Spangler, born in Coshocton county; graduated at Kenyon; studied law with father (David), and admitted in 1853; practiced a few years; gave attention to other matters; now in banking business at Cedar Rapids, Iowa.

John E. Irvine (brother of James), admitted in 1853; went to Mississippi to teach; returned to Coshocton in 1859, and in 1866 removed to Monmouth, Ill., where he continued to practice until his death.

A. M. Williams, born in Culpeper county, Va.; came to Coshocton county November, 1833; was a "forty-niner" in California; studied with Matthews and Stone; admitted in 1853; clerk of court in 1855-58; gave up practice in 1867; since connected with Coshocton Planing Mill Company.

John D. Nicholas, born in Howard county, Md.; read law under direction of William Sample; admitted in 1854; was in military service some time in 1861 and again in 1864-65; was prosecuting attorney one term.

J. C. Pomerene, born in Holmes county; studied under William Reed, of Millersburg, graduating at "Ohio State and Union Law College;" admitted in 1859, and came that year to Coshocton.

R. M. Voorhees, born in Harrison county; studied law with Barcroft and Voorhees, of Millersburg; admitted July 6, 1860; came same month to Coshocton, and went into partnership with Thomas Campbell; was in military service in 1861-65; spent the summer of 1866 at Independence, Mo.; was post-master at Coshocton in 1866-67; prosecuting attorney 1868-1872; admitted to United States District Court at Cleveland in 1875.

Gilbert H. Barger, born in Coshocton county; studied with B. S. Lee; graduated at Cleveland Law School in 1861; commenced practice in 1862; same year went into army; returned to practice in 1868; served as clerk of court from 1870 to 1876.

L. L. Cantwell, native of Coshocton; studied law under Charles Hoy, being admitted by Supreme Court January 9, 1867; has been justice of the peace ever since; served two terms as mayor of Coshocton.

E. W. James, born in Coshocton county; studied with Nicholas and Williams; graduated at Law School of Michigan University; admitted in 1867; spent a few months in practice at Kansas City, Mo.

J. M. Compton, a native of Coshocton county; studied with Lee and Pomerene; admitted in 1869; has been mayor of Coshocton two terms.

A. H. Stillwell, born in Holmes county; studied with C. Follett, of Newark; admitted in 1874; practiced for a time in Muskingum county; came to Coshocton December, 1874.

W. R. Gault, native of Coshocton county; graduated at Wittenberg College; studied profession with Nicholas and Jones; admitted July 20, 1875.

T. H. Ricketts, native of Tuscarawas county; studied with A. Neeley, of New Philadelphia; graduated at Albany (N. Y.) Law School; practiced in Iowa and in Chicago, Ill.; was recognized as an attorney by District Court at Coshocton in July, 1876.

A. E. Creighton, of Coshocton county; studied at Wooster University; read law with William Sample, of Coshocton; was admitted by District Court July, 1876.

A. J. Wilkin, from Washington county, Pa.; was an admitted attorney in 1856, but soon turned to other avocations; was in legislature; now resides in New Comerstown.

Asa G. Dimmock and Richard Laning were about the same time recognized attornies. Each was prosecuting attorney, but not otherwise much concerned with court practice.

Josiah Given, from Holmes county, entered upon practice in Coshocton county in 1857; he gave up practice to enter the army in 1861; removed to Iowa, where his name now floats at the head of a county paper as its candidate for next president.

William Humrickhouse studied with his brother Thomas, and was admitted in 1853, but soon found more congenial employment; now merchandising.

W. N. Cochran, a native of the county; studied his profession at Newark; practiced a few months of 1874-75;

he gave up practice to become a partner (financial and legal man) in an extensive live-stock dealing firm in Pittsburg, Pa., where he now resides.

B. F. Church, having read law with Leonard and Nicholas, practiced at the Coshocton bar, residing in Monroe township from 1857 to 1875; he removed in the latter year to Holmes county.

Charles Hoy, from Ashland county, was admitted to the bar in 1853, and has practiced most of the time since.

W. C. Mayhugh, of Jacobsport, is an admitted attorney, but not in practice.

Robert Beer studied law in his home county (Ashland), and having studied further at Coshocton, was admitted by District Court in 1853; in 1857 he entered upon the study of theology, and is now pastor of the Presbyterian church in Valparaiso, Ind.

I. V. Heslip, M. C. McFarland and L. F. Horton, were also recognized attorneys at the Coshocton bar, but not in practice.

Under the old state constitution a specific tax from two dollars and fifty cents to five dollars per year was assessed on each practicing attorney by the county commissioners.

CHAPTER XI.

AGRICULTURAL NOTES—COUNTY AGRICULTURAL SOCIETY—FAIRS, ETC.

THE agricultural interests of Coshocton county have in all its history vastly exceeded all others in the amount invested and the revenue derived. Manufactures, mines, and commerce never have, even combined, borne any imposing proportion to agriculture. There are in the county something more than three hundred and fifty thousand acres of land, and it is estimated that with the exception of some fifty thousand* all have been productive of crops, of fruit, or pasturage.

The number of cultivators of the soil probably reached its limit about 1850; since which time, there has been little increase in the number of acres tilled. From the outset among the crops raised "corn" has been "king." More acres of it have been planted, and more bushels gathered, than of anything else. In 1857, when the cultivation of this crop reached its maximum, when there was much discouragement in relation to the growing of wheat in consequence of the pests to which it had been for a succession of years subjected, and when the sheep interest had not yet become so great, there were more than a million and a half bushels of corn raised.

The wheat crop has always in Coshocton county ranked next to corn in amount and value. The period of its most successful cultivation may be set down at from 1835 to 1850. The largest crop ever secured was in 1846. The roads to the canal-warehouses and mills were often studded thickly for many rods with wagons waiting their turn to unload. In 1850, there was a larger acreage than in 1846, but the yield was not so great. In 1862, a half a million of bushels was reported as the yield. About 1850, the Hessian fly made its appearance; it was succeeded by the weevil;

---

*Taken up mainly by roads, rivers, canals, etc.

then there was serious trouble about winter freezing, and for twenty years this interest was much depressed. About 1870, farmers began to take good heart again, and in 1874 there was a magnificent crop. The crop of 1875 was very seriously affected by an unusually rainy season just at the harvest time. In earlier and better days the average yield was quite up to eighteen or twenty bushels per acre, but in late years thirteen to fifteen is regarded as good. In the days of high prices, three dollars and twenty-five cents per bushel was paid for good wheat—the lowest price now within the memory of men hereabouts was twenty-five cents.

Rye was more cultivated in earlier days than now, but was never a very big item in Coshocton county. In 1867, the largest acreage for a number of years was put in, viz.: Four thousand seven hundred acres.

In 1862, the barley crop was reported at three thousand bushels, and has never been much above that.

Flax in early days received considerable attention. During the war (1861-5), when cotton goods got so high, renewed interest was manifested in this crop. In 1862, there were sixty acres of it planted.

Broom-corn has never been much cultivated in the county.

Sorghum was a considerable item in war times. Three hundred and eighty-five acres of it were grown in 1862, and more still later.

From 1820 to 1835, maple-sugar and syrup were "big things." Even as late as 1865, there were reported as produced in the county four thousand pounds of the sugar, and three thousand gallons of syrup.

In a good season, forty thousand bushels of Irish potatoes are produced in the county. The Colorado beetle, in 1872-5, affected the yield, but not so largely as they increased the labor in caring for the crop.

In 1868, an average season, thirty thousand tons of hay were produced.

The average amount of butter annually made in the

county for the last twenty years has been about half a million pounds.

There have been several efforts in the cheesery line, but they have not been long persisted in, nor very satisfactory. The most notable cheese factory was one set up, about 1866, in Clark township. The farmers became tired of the constant and regular effort in the matter of furnishing the milk, and competition was heavy, and the factory, after running seven or eight years, was closed.

A considerable amount of tobacco has been raised in Coshocton county. More than forty years ago there was the "tobacco fever." The farmers all went to raising it; the supply exceeded the demand, and there was considerable disgust. In 1858, there were only two and one-half acres raised. During the war, there was a temporary extension of this interest, but not a very wide one.

SHEEP.

The first Merino sheep of thorough blood brought into this county were bought by old Major Robinson and Major Simmons, from old Seth Adams, who, as partner or agent of General Humphries, brought to the Muskingum valley some of General Humphries' importation from Spain, and had them in Muskingum county, near Dresden, as early as 1812. They were not cared for, and no trace is left of them. Fine-wooled sheep, of uncertain and mixed blood, were gradually introduced by farmers from eastern counties, and from the Pan Handle and Western Pennsylvania, between 1830 and 1836 or 1837, when Beaver & Bowman brought out from Washington county, Pennsylvania, about two thousand, and placed them on Bowman's section, adjoining Coshocton. This movement proved a failure, most of the sheep dying the next spring, and the remainder being disposed of and scattered so as to leave no trace.

About 1842, S. T. Thompson and one or two of his neighbors brought from Washington county, Pennsylvania, a few sheep, and founded flocks. These were the first really good Merinos that have left their mark, and still exist.

Wm. Renfrew, Sr., soon after brought out from the same

county flocks a few good black-tops and a few lighter-colored, which he bred separately, and the descendants of which still remain.

In 1846, or thereabouts, Wm. Batchelor and George Wolf brought out a few sheep obtained from General Harmon in the State of New York; they were selected by Mr. Batchelor, and, compared with what were here before, were heavier-wooled and stronger sheep. They did well.

In 1850, Howe & Batchelor brought out from Vermont a French ram, of thorough Merino blood, which had been imported from France by S. W. Jewett, from the government flock at Rambouillet. After trial, they rejected him, and disposed of his increase. They then, in connection with T. S. Humrickhouse, brought out some thirty head of Humphries' Atwood sheep, obtained from Edwin Hammond, of Addison county, Vermont. These are the kind now recognized on all hands as the best, and improving all other fine-wooled sheep. They have been added to from time to time by Mr. Batchelor and others.

In 1834, Isaac Maynard emigrated from England, and settled in this county. He brought with him a small flock of South Downs and a few Lincolnshires. The Lincolnshires were entirely lost, and most of the South Downs. In 1842 or thereabouts, Wm. Henderson, Dr. Edmund Cone, and James Meskimens furnished old Mr. Bache with money to go to England, and bring back with him some sheep. He brought back quite a number of Ellman South Downs and a few Leicestershires, or, as sometimes called, Dishleys or Bakewells, which were divided among the owners. The Leicestershires soon disappeared, but the South Downs are the source of most of the South Downs now in the county. They have been added to by Bluck and others, who purchased rams at different times from various sources. The Cotswolds have been of late tried by various parties—those of Judge Thornhill, Wm. Hanlon, Robert Moore, and J. W. Dwyer having attracted much attention and commendation.

In the times of high prices during the war, one dollar and five cents per pound was paid for a few choice fleeces.

Many were sold at one dollar per pound—one fleece brought twenty-two dollars and fifty cents. When prices fell after the war, and the condition of things was unsatisfactory otherwise as to the profitableness of sheep raising, thousands of the poorest sheep were killed and fed to hogs, the pelts selling for about as much as the live sheep. Thirty years ago there was some talk in certain localities of the county about the sheep having sore feet, but about 1866 there was much complaint of "foot rot." Remedies were devised, and care was taken in the selection of pasturage, and the evil soon passed away.

A Coshocton county Wool-growers' Association was organized about 1864. In February, 1876, the National Merino Sheep Breeders' Association was organized at Coshocton, in a meeting attended by delegates from Pennsylvania, West Virginia, Missouri, and other states.

FINE CATTLE.

In comparatively early times, John Meskimens, Judge Robinson, and Daniel Miller brought some fine cattle into the county. More than thirty years ago, Frank McGuire and Geo. Wolf bought some superior stock in this line from E. P. Prentiss, of Albany, New York, and afterward some from D. D. Campbell, of Schenectady, New York. About 1851, Arnold Medberry and Samuel Brown made purchase of some very fine cattle from Dr. Watts, of Chillicothe. In 1855, Thomas Darling imported a lot from Kentucky, and not long thereafter Samuel Moore, Frank McGuire, and T. S. Humrickhouse became prominently connected with the same line of work. John G. Stewart, a few years ago, exhibited a very superior herd, and has taken much interest in that kind of "stock." J. W. Dwyer has of late also interested himself greatly, especially in the Jerseys and Alderneys.

HOGS.

The hogs of the earlier day in Coshocton county were all that could be made by an abundance of corn and little care; but the original stock not being very good, and little effort being made to improve it, long snouts and blue skins were the rule. The McGuires and the Wolfs were about the first to give attention to improved breeds. Afterward the Lennons, the Burrells, and Matthew Johnson interested themselves in the same line. G. W. Silliman, after his visit to Europe, took an interest in the Berkshires, and brought into the county some of that breed. The Chester Whites became and continued great favorites. The Leicestershires have found many approvers, and are just now with many the favorites.

In early days, one and a half cents per pound was considered a fair price for hogs, live weight. In 1864, Wm. E. Hunt got *fourteen* cents a pound for a few Chester White hogs, but he must have received the usual "Preacher's favors," inasmuch as farmers McGuire and Moore got only eleven and three-fourths cents for their best specimens.

BLOODED HORSES.

"Blooded" horses have from the first received a good deal of attention in Coshocton county. Old Colonel Williams and his compeers had the Virginia notions about these things. The race-course was not then, as now, circular and leveled and rolled, but they had one from the earliest days down. There was one on the Butler place up the Walhonding. The road to Lewisville has been used. But the favorite track for years was on what is now Fifth street in Coshocton, along which two parallel narrow tracks were cleared. "Tests of speed" were there made—not witnessed by elegantly dressed ladies and gentlemen, such as now-a-days throng the county fair-grounds, but by the "homespun" crowd. It is claimed that if the associations of the place were less refined, the honesty was not less than now. They meant square business or simple fun in those days, and were severe on "jockeying." They did not then sell "pools."

Among those actively interested in the horse line, the following may be named: One of the Butlers, in New Castle township, had charge of two horses belonging to Peter Casey, one of the first associate judges of the county, brought in before 1812. They were called "Whistle Jacket" and "Highflyer." Colonel Williams, of Coshocton, bought in from Virginia a horse, long famed in this region, called "Medley." Robert Farwell brought from New England to Keene township "Sir Archie." Joseph W. Rue, about 1830, introduced "John of Jersey," and "Patrick Richards," colts by a horse entered for a race against "Eclipse," the famous trotter on Long Island course, but withdrawn on account of lameness. Matthew Stewart is remembered in connection with "Hickory." Lewis Rice and John Johnson had a horse called "Premium," and A. G. Wood one called "Sir Charles." Sam. Baker's horse was "Snowball."

In 1866, D. L. Triplett and Wm. Bachelor brought from Kentucky "Abdallah," who met the sad fate of being burned to death in a stable consumed in the fall of 1869. The County Horse Fair Association was organized in 1866.

FRUIT CULTURE.

The first orchards planted in Coshocton county were, for the most part, if not entirely, from seedling trees. Top grafting upon these was afterward resorted to in a small degree, but without materially changing the general character of the fruit, except in a few instances. Some of the early settlers coming in from Maryland and Virginia brought with them sprouts from the orchards of their home regions, and these of course contained those varieties. Some of these still have a place in the orchards of the descendants of those who brought them.

In 1832 Joshua B. Hart, of Tiverton township, had a bearing orchard of grafted fruit, consisting of the kinds brought out by the Ohio company when they settled at Marietta. Mr. Hart propagated some by grafting, but could not sell his trees, and quit in a short time.

Joseph F. Munro had a large orchard planted for him by old John Matthews, also of the Marietta sorts. The Robinsons had a few trees of the same.

William Meskimens, on Will's creek, practiced grafting

in a small way, and had bearing apple trees of the kinds common in Western Pennsylvania.

George Henderson had a bearing orchard of apples, and practiced grafting in a small way. His orchard was on White Eyes, and consisted of Western Pennsylvania kinds.

Old Mr. McFetridge had planted an orchard, not then yet in bearing. He brought his trees from Steubenville, and they were of the kinds grown in the Kneisley nurseries.

A nurseryman in Fairfield county, about 1830–31, brought by canal a large lot of grafted apple trees, but found no sale for them for orchard planting, and traded or in some way disposed of them to Nathan Spencer, who planted them in a kind of nursery, and sold them to John Frew. Eighty of them were planted by T. S. Humrickhouse in an orchard on Mill Creek in the fall of 1833.

Old John Elliott planted an orchard of the same kind on his farm in Bethlehem township. Every tree of this lot was true to name, and the whole selection proved most admirable.

Richard Moode, near West Bedford, practiced grafting to a small extent, and had an orchard.

Wishing to plant two or three apple orchards, and not being able to find all the kinds he wanted in any one nursery, T. S. Humrickhouse, about 1835, commenced making a collection and grafting in nursery. He took from all the orchards above mentioned all the varieties they contained, and added from a distance all the kinds he could hear of that gave promise of being valuable, and has continued that sort of work to this day.

When James Matthews was in Congress he procured most of the native and many foreign varieties, and they were thoroughly tried. Most of the foreign and many of the native were discarded. Both Mr. Matthews and Mr. Humrickhouse, about 1840, gave considerable attention to pears, peaches, plums, and grapes, introducing many fine varieties.

About 1838 Robert Seevers started a nursery at West Carlisle, and many of the orchards in the western townships were stocked by him.

Kellis Hord started one near Bakersville. Others in different parts of the county tried the business, but few of them continued long in it.

Traveling grafters, between 1840 and 1850, abounded in the county, but have not left very distinct traces.

For the last twenty years very heavy importations of fruit trees have been made. In one year the sales of tree-peddlers reached nearly $8,000. Those who experimented most largely in the purchase of these trees do not exult much at their success. An immense proportion of the trees died, and many of the varieties which were most highly commended proved really very inferior; and it has been discovered that it is sometimes better to go to a home nursery and get a few good varieties than to get a larger list pressed upon them by some one from without.

Joseph K. Johnson probably planted the largest peach orchard ever set out in the county—some eighty acres—on his place, about a mile east of Coshocton.

Among the most successful fruit-growers of late, as indicated by county fair displays and premiums, have been John Vance and Hugh McFadden, of Tuscarawas township; Simeon Ellis, of Washington; William McCormick, of Keene; and William C. Saunders, of White Eyes.

In this connection it may be stated that in 1855 J. K. Johnson planted quite a considerable vineyard on his place, one mile east of Coshocton, and for a few years soon thereafter a considerable quantity of wine was made under his direction. The most of this was used by sick friends, of whom there proved to be a good many, and for church purposes. From the experiment, as made by him, there was no disposition on the part of himself or neighbors to enlarge this interest.

Some years subsequently, J. B. Elliott and F. Seward established a vineyard in Keene township, but the operation was not accounted a large success.

A Mr. Shitz, in Crawford township, is perhaps the only one now operating in this line in the county. Most excellent grapes of such varieties come into the county as individual tastes approve, are grown in domestic way, and soils and other elements of success are found in many parts, and abound in a half dozen townships.

COUNTY AGRICULTURAL SOCIETY—FAIRS.

As early as 1835, the county commissioners, under provisions of law, directed a call to be issued for a meeting looking to the formation of a county agricultural society. But nothing effective was done under that call, or in any other way, for many years. The association of those chiefly interested in the cultivation of the soil progressed slowly. The matter at length was taken up by such men as Dr. H. Williams, Colonel C. F. Sangster, Dr. E. Cone, Judge Burt, John Davis, and determined and successful efforts accomplished the organization.

The presidents of the society, as obtained from accessible sources,* have been Heslip Williams, E. Cone, James M. Burt, John Meskimens, Wm. Hanlon, J. S. Elliott, and J. C. Campbell.

Secretaries: John Humrickhouse, C. H. Johnston, W. R. Forker, L. L. Cantwell, David Lanning, and Geo. Miller.

Treasurers: Wm. K. Johnson, Matthew Johnston, J. L. Rue, John A. Hanlon.

In the board of managers, besides the gentlemen above named, the following have served: A. D. Denman, T. S. Humrickhouse, Thomas Darling, Francis McGuire, Wm. Renfrew, Samuel Moore, James E. Robinson, D. L. Triplett, Frank Stafford, J. M. Smith, E. L. Robinson, Joseph Dickenson, Francis Wolf, Adam Piffer, John Mulligan, Geo. Factor, Peter Stevenson, J. M. Denman, Wm. McCoy, B. C. Blackburn, Seth Christy, Wm. Hesket, Hugh McFadden, Saul Miller, S. C. Burrell, John Hogle, Philip Moore, Lewis Demoss, G. W. Wolf, Marion Darling, Alex. Dinsmore, Thomas McConnell, Wellington Darling, E. J. Pocock, T. H. Burrell, John M. Adams, John Waggoner, Samuel Gardiner, J. H. Carr, Joseph W. Dwyer, Calvin

---

*The earlier records can not be found, after much inquiry. Plenty of people in this, as in other matters, "can tell *who can tell*" where they are.

Boyd, Joseph Love, Joseph Burrell, M. L. Norris, and John Richardson.

For a number of years the expenses of the society, including the premiums, were defrayed by annual fees paid by the members. Any one may become a member by the payment of one dollar per year; receiving, also, four tickets of entrance to fairs.

The first fair under the auspices of the society was held at Jacobsport, in 1850. The fairs for several years thereafter were held in the public square at Coshocton. From the first there was a choice selection of stock, and a gradual increase in other lines. The Elliotts and John Davis soon had some good displays of agricultural implements. The farmers' wives and daughters warmly seconded their husbands and fathers.

The fair of 1856 was not remarkable for display, but the talks among farmers and stock-breeders had their effect in awakening interest, and then settled these annual gatherings as things to be kept up. That year an arrangement was made for leasing for a term of years the John Burt fair ground (since laid out into lots), extending from Seventh street to the foot of the bluff, and from Main street to the south side of Hiram Beall's property. This tract contained about nine acres. It was properly fenced, and buildings and stalls erected on it, and the fair of 1857 was held there. By 1865, these grounds became insufficient, and in that year the society purchased from Dr. S. H. Lee twenty acres, about four hundred yards east of the Burt tract, and proceeded to fit up more extensive and, as was supposed, more permanent buildings. The amount paid for these grounds was $3,200. To assist the society in purchasing these grounds, the county commissioners agreed to donate $500, and to loan the society $500 more, to be repaid out of their receipts whenever the commissioners should require. It is understood that this was repaid when the grounds were sold by the society, as they were in the winter of 1872–3, having been cut up into lots, the society having in November, 1872, purchased of J. W. Dwyer the grounds now used for fair purposes. These grounds, lying a quarter of a mile south of the Burt fair ground, include a large grove (which was a chief attraction in the purchase), and are more convenient in the matter of access to water, not lying so high above the river level as the Lee ground. The amount of land embraced is thirty-four and fifty-eight one-hundredth acres, and the cost of it $10,488. Of this, from proceeds of sales of old grounds and otherwise, some $4,000 have been paid. For improvements on the new ground nearly $6,000 have been expended. The fair receipts for 1875 were $2,389, and the premiums paid about $1,500.

It is not understood that there are any granges of the Patrons of Husbandry in the county, but there are several "farmers' clubs;" those of Franklin, Linton, and Lafayette townships being seemingly the most vigorous and successful.

The "Centennial Fourth of July celebration" for Coshocton county was held on the grounds of the society, and under its auspices. Messrs. Elliott, De Moss, Dwyer, and Miller were the committee of arrangements. Despite the frequent showers of rain, there was a very large attendance of people from all parts of the county, the number present being in excess of any company of people assembled previously in the county. Music and flags and banners lent interest to the occasion. Thomas Campbell, Esq., was the president of the day. The Declaration of Independence was read by J. M. Compton, Esq. R. M. Voorhees, Esq., read a sketch of the history of Coshocton county, prepared by Rev. William E. Hunt (previously appointed, but detained from the ground by illness). William Sample, Esq., delivered an "Address on the Agricultural Interests of Coshocton County." Appropriate songs were sung by the whole company, led by J. Glover and by the Welsh Quartette, under the leadership of E. Prosser.

CHAPTER XII.

NOTES ON MANUFACTURING, MINING, ETC.

MILLING.

The earliest settlers relied for the most part on hominy or pounded corn. The hominy block was an indispensable article. The finest particles of the crushed grain were made into cakes and the coarser boiled. The hand-mill was the next appliance; then the little neighborhood mills, turned by a run or a horse; then the "one run of burr" mills were set up—one or two in a township. One of the earliest settlers tells how, having grown weary of hominy meal, and having heard that there was a power mill between Dresden and Zanesville, he put some grain in his canoe, and started down the river from near Oxford. The mill was discovered to be quite a patent affair. Two canoes had been fastened just at a ripple in the river, and a small paddle-wheel set between the boats, and this, turned by the rippling waters, furnished the power to turn a large sized hand-mill.

In the "Notices of some of the Earliest Settlers by Township," in a preceding part of this volume, mention has been made of many of the "corn-crackers," as the primitive mills were often designated. Of the earlier mills the more famous were those of Isaac Evans and Michael Miller. Probably the first mill that rose much above the dignity of a "corn-cracker" was that built in Linton township by Thomas Johnson and Jacob Waggoner in 1817, having four run of burrs.

J. F. Monroe & Co. erected the mill near the mouth of Will's creek (now Frew's mill) about 1820.

The mill in Perry township now operated by Adam Gault was built at a very early day.

Soon after the Ohio canal was opened, Medberry, Ransom

& Co. built the "Roscoe mill" (upper), which was burned in 1853.

In 1840 the "Union mill" was built in lower Roscoe by the Union Mill Company (R. M. Lamb, Dr. S. Lee, and John Frew, of Coshocton; Wm. and John Carhart, Jos. Le Retilley and George Bagnall, of Roscoe; and Peter Marquand, of Will's creek). Becoming embarrassed, the company sold this mill to D. N. Barney & Co., of Cleveland, and it was by them sold to Arnold Medberry. It was burned in 1855.

J. S. McVey started his mill at Walhoding about 1844, having enlarged and refitted for the purpose the Gamble distillery.

About 1846, the Linton mill was built by J. V. Heslip, Joseph Heslip, and M. L. Norris. In 1850, Robert Long started the mill at Warsaw; it afterward passed into the hands of N. Rector, subsequently was run by Burrell & Donley, and then by Robert Darling & Son. In 1856, the Empire mill in Roscoe was started by A. Medbery. After his death (in 1862) it was bought by F. E. Barney, Lewis Demoss, S. Lamberson, and D. L. Triplett. These gentlemen, within a few years, have added very largely to the machinery, and extended the buildings, making the establishment one of the largest in the State of Ohio.* In 1874, the Beebe Brothers started their mill in Lower Roscoe. Robert D. Boyd also built one at Wild Turkey Lock. In 183–, a flouring-mill was built, corner of Second and Main streets, by James Renfrew & Co. After a few years it was burned down, and subsequently another, on the same site, was erected by a company, embracing the principal merchants of the town of Coshocton and a few others. It was not very successfully run, and after some years passed into the hands of Love & Hay, distillers, as elsewhere noted. In 1875, C. Balch & Co. started the "City Mill," the large brick mill just east of the freight depot in Coshocton. The following is the list of mills now in operation in addition to those already indicated, viz.: New Princeton, operated

---

*Joab Agnew and N. Schott have been so long with this establishment as to make them seem part of it.

by Beck & Brother; Helmick Mills, Beck and Miller; Clark's Mill, Beck & Co.; West Bedford, Darr; Chili, John Bowman; Avondale (formerly Boyd's) Mill, Thos. Elliott; Emerson's Mill, near Orange.

The manufacture of whisky must be fairly set down as, for many years, one of the leading industries of Coshocton county. Much of the wealth of the county has come through it. A number of substantial citizens have been connected with it. It had the credit of being, for the most part, honestly carried on; and the article made had a good reputation. Even a clergyman of the county advised his remote friends, "if they must have whisky, to be sure and get Coshocton county whisky." Passing by ruder and smaller still-houses, a noticeable one was in operation, nearly forty years ago, near Walhonding, conducted by James Gamble, and a little later, one at that place by Collins, Gamble, and others. Another was on Lower Wills creek, operated by Munroe and others. A few miles below Roscoe was a quite substantial structure, turning out large quantities of corn-juice from 1830 to 1840, owned by John Frew & Co. (the Bowmans, of Brownsville, Pennsylvania). In later times there was a large whisky-mill at Conesville, operated by Cone, and then J. W. Beebe, and then Barney, Corning & Co., during whose administration the establishment was burned. It was rebuilt by Beebe, and a second time burned.

Wm. Renfrew and Robert Hay commenced operations in this line in 1831-2, in Upper Roscoe. The firm afterward became Love & Hay (Samuel Love afterward removed to Champaign county, Illinois, being in first, and afterward his brother Thomas Love). Subsequently, the distillery in Roscoe having burned, they came over to the old flouring-mill at the corner of Main and Second streets in Coshocton, and there continued for many years.* In 1863, T. Love & Co. sold a thousand barrels of their whisky to parties who immediately shipped it to California, and brought back, as the

---

* Fred. Schreid will long be remembered as one of the chief attaches of this concern.

return cargo, thirty thousand barrels of flour. The very heavy capital involved and to some extent imperiled in the seasons of highest prices for corn, and especially the difficulties of competing with less honest distillers, who would run " crooked " whisky, and the ample returns already secured, led to the giving up of the business. There is at this writing no recognized still in the county, and no whisky has been made in the county for some ten years.

Andrew Lybarger was the first man to start a tannery, setting up in that line, about 1808, in Coshocton, on the northwest corner of Second and Walnut streets. This yard afterward passed into the hands of John and Joseph K. Johnson, and, at a still later day, was owned by Andrew Wilkins. It was abandoned some years since. Probably the tannery next started was the one a mile above Roscoe, by the Carharts. Not long after was one at East Plainfield under the control of Thomas Johnston. Among the old establishments of this sort was one near Keene, operated by Geo. Wolf—afterward by Sprague; one at East Union, started by McVey and Bonnett, now run by the Blues; and one near West Bedford, under Wm. Renfrew. At this writing there is a tannery at Plainfield, run by Lewis Carhart; one at Coshocton, by H. N. Shaw & Sons; at Roscoe, by J. & H. Carhart; at New Princeton, by Wm. Wolfe; at East Union, by the Blues; at New Castle, by Jonathan Knight; at West Carlisle, by Lewis Bonnett; and one at Chili, by Gotlieb Feller.

The first iron foundry in the county was started in Coshocton by George Conwell and Morris Burt. It still stands on the lot just south of Dr. Wm. Stanton's residence, corner of second and Locust streets. The Roses, of Roscoe, started the Roscoe foundry. The Coshocton one passed into the hands of J. C. Maginity, and the Roscoe one into Mr. Brown's, and these parties consolidated, making the Roscoe foundry the principal and, after a time, the only one. It is now operated by Henry King, of Coshocton, and James Mirise, of Roscoe.

John Taylor for many years carried on a machine-shop in Coshocton, on the premises used for a tannery by H. N.

Shaw & Sons. His son, Hiram, and Henry King, some eight years ago started a foundry near the Tuscarawas bridge, and operated it (having James Hay also for a partner for a time) until they removed to Roscoe.

A few years ago, a young man, named Edward Kirk, from Pittsburgh, started the foundry on Fifth street in Coshocton. It afterward passed into the hands of T. C. Ricketts, and was operated by Kirk and Robert Hay, then by Ricketts & Evans, and, still later, by Hirt, Palm & Evans.

In May, 1871, a stock company was formed, called the "Coshocton Iron and Steel Company." The company proceeded to erect quite extensive buildings, and put in them the machinery for making springs and axles and iron bridges. The president of the company was Houston Hay; vice-president, F. E. Barney; treasurer, T. C. Ricketts (and they, with Lewis Demoss and John Davis, were directors). The secretary was John A. Barney. James W. Shipman was general manager. He had formerly operated an establishment of the same kind at Fort Plain, N. Y., and the company bought the machinery of his establishment and removed it to Coshocton. This arrangement was made after a committee had visited the works there. Everything needful pertaining to the concern was obtained either from Shipman or other parties. For a time everything went well; but, after running some three years, the company made an assignment. The working capital had all been borrowed at high rates of interest; a boiler had exploded (June 10, 1873), entailing several thousands of dollars of loss; very large sums were paid for salaries and wages, and in some cases not much return in the way of service made; and these and other causes soon swamped the company, and more or less embarrassed the stockholders. The establishment was idle for a number of months, and was then bought on the second offer at sheriff's sale by Houston Hay, who held nearly one-third of the stock of the original company. The price paid was $33,334. Hay soon started the axle department, and not long after, in partnership with J. W. Dwyer, resumed work in the spring department.

This is, at this writing, the largest iron manufacturing establishment in the county, giving employment to nearly one hundred men and boys. George Ayres is the superintendent of the axle department, John Hoban of the spring shop, and Farley Connerty of the foundry.

Some twenty years ago a small foundry was started at Walhonding, and is still operated in a limited way.

There are in the county deposits of iron ore—at least one large deposit of black-band (on the farm of William Hanlon, near Coshocton)—but as yet nothing has been done in either shipping or working these mineral riches.

More than forty years ago certain gentlemen came from Bucks county, Pa., and undertook the erection of a furnace near New Princeton, in Monroe township; but, after cutting immense quantities of cord-wood, and doing some work in building, the enterprise was abandoned. One of the principal operators (B. F. Williams) removed to Richmond, Ind.

A couple of miles northeast of Coshocton is a black-marble quarry. It is claimed to be of the sort used for tiling, etc. A movement was made a few years ago to utilize this, but the project was not well braced, and the capital requisite was not secured. Another effort was made in 1876, with some promise of success.

There was a carding-mill, in very early days, at Plainfield. At a later day, one near Warsaw and another at Bakersville. The first complete mill was started in 1833 in upper Roscoe by Samuel Moffat. After a few years it was burned down, and another built by C. S. Miller and S. Moffat. Miller went to California, and Moffat died, and the property passed into the hands of Thomas Wilson in 1855. With this enterprise, Wilson McClintock, afterward removing to Butler, Missouri, was for some years identified. The building was a frame one, stood a little above the planing-mill, and was burned down in 1867. Wilson proceeded promptly, after the fire, to build the large brick mill now operated by him, upon a site a little west of the old one, drawing water from the Walhonding canal, instead of the Ohio canal.

James Taylor operated a woolen mill in Coshocton for some years about 1840. Within a few years one has been erected by a stock company at Bakersville.

The paper-mill in Coshocton was built in 1863. Thompson Hanna (of Steubenville for many years) was its projector and builder. Messrs. Hay, Johnson, Spangler, Denman, and others countenanced the movement, and aided with the loan of funds. Daniel W. Hanna and Robert Sinclair (son and son-in-law of Thompson Hanna) afterward operated the mill. Want of working capital—made more oppressive by a boiler explosion * and other misfortunes—caused a failure of the proprietors. After some temporary arrangements, the property came into the hands of John W. Cassingham and A. D. Harvey, of Coshocton, and Hugh McElroy, of Pittsburg, Pa., and has been by them successfully operated for some years.

Among the more considerable saw-mills of the earlier days were those of Isaac Evans, on Evans' creek, Thomas Johnson on Will's creek, and Sherry Odell on Mill creek.

At a later day, mills were set up in Upper Roscoe, at Wild Turkey lock, and at Warsaw.

The Coshocton Planing Mill Company commenced operations in 1869. The company was originally composed of Addison M. Williams, Martin Weiser, and W. H. Robinson, Jr. Robinson soon withdrew, and Dr. Wm. Stanton became a partner for a time. For several years the establishment has been owned and operated by Williams & Weiser. The building first used was Jackson Hay's old warehouse, from Canal Lewisville, which the company took down, hauled to Coshocton on wagons, and re-erected. Very considerable additions have been made to this original structure.

A planing-mill was attached to the Roscoe saw-mill by James W. Beebe, about 1871, now owned and operated by Adams & Gleason.

Within a few years, planing-mills have been set up at

---

* By this explosion, John Freeman was killed and John Sherrod seriously hurt. It occurred in 1866.

Jacobsport and Warsaw, the latter now operated by Butler & Leavengood, and the former by Wolf & Williams.

There are still several water saw-mills doing considerable in their way, but a very large part of work in this line has been done for some years by portable steam mills. Among those most largely operating with these have been Messrs. Stafford, Talmadge, Seward, and Joseph Elliott.

The first hatter's shop in the county was probably set up in East Union. Morris Burt was the first in this line in Coshocton. M. Ferguson worked in it for more than a quarter of a century in Roscoe. James H. Donohew, a veteran of the line, now represents the interest in the county at Coshocton.

The first brewery in Coshocton was started in the house opposite the office of Dr. J. Harris, on North Second street, about 1852, by L. Mayer.

Lewis Beiber built the brewery on North Fourth street in 1866. The one in lower Roscoe was started some years later by C. Mayer.

The Coshocton brewery is at this time operated by Chas. Boes.

A small soap-factory was built twenty-five years ago near the bridge in Coshocton by J. Mayer. Some six years ago, the establishment was bought by W. H. Robinson, Jr., and C. Skinner, and torn down, to be replaced with the "Coshocton Soap Works," now owned and operated by D. Adams.

B. F. Sells for a time operated a small soap-factory, at the west end of Main street, about 1858.

J. K. Marsh was the first to manufacture cigars on any noticeable scale—running into the millions. He set up in Coshocton in 1870. A Mr. Horton made a few some years before.

The manufacture of flour and whisky made the coopering business at one time quite an important industry. Among the long-engaged in this line were, of the earlier days, Jonathan Fisk and J. Huff, and of later times, John Mulligan, Robert Crawford, N. Schott, and K. Klossen, of Roscoe, and C. Marks, of Warsaw.

In 1857, E. McDonald and Alex. Manner, from Dresden, set up a carriage manufactory on West Walnut street. After a couple of years, Manner engaged in other business.

In 1869, McDonald erected the extensive shops still occupied by him on South Third street.

The shops on Sixth street, now occupied by Alex. Manner, were erected by G. A. Pieffer & Sons, of Dresden, in 1869. In 1873, Manner bought these premises at assignee's sale, and has since operated there.

Darius Wright for many years carried on wagon-making at Cross Roads, on a scale to become largely known through the county. He is now operating in Warsaw.

Geo. Schleich was the first to do much in this line in Coshocton; subsequently J. Glover undertook the same line of work, and was succeeded by C. W. Frew, who afterward removed to Illinois.

A. Fritz was also engaged for a time in the same line, and was succeeded by Jeffries & Van Allen.

There has been since 1860 a noticeable carriage and wagon-shop, at West Carlisle, in charge mainly of Mr. Welling. There has also been for three years past a considerable amount of work in this line done at New Bedford.

John Shields, at West Bedford, has for many years manufactured threshing-machines and hay-rakes.

John Irwin for a number of years turned out a large number of plows, but he removed, two years since, to Iowa, and this business is now chiefly carried on by King & Mirise, of Roscoe.

The Coshocton gas-works were built in the winter of 1873–4. The contractor was B. Van Steenberg, of New York, who also at the outset was the heaviest stockholder —selling his interest subsequently to Houston Hay. The company was first organized in 1872, F. E. Barney, L. Demoss, John G. Stewart, H. N. Shaw, and W. E. Hunt, directors. H. N. Shaw was succeeded by H. Hay, who, with the others above named, are the present directors.

The local papers of that day say, "The success of the enterprise is to be attributed to F. E. Barney and Wm. E.

Hunt." Isaac McNarry has been superintendent from the start.

H. N. Shaw & Sons (in connection with their more extended tanning operations), in 1875, undertook the manufacture of boots and shoes on a larger scale than had been previously attempted.

The latest manufacturing enterprise is that in charge of J. W. Bebee (United States Yeast Company)—the making of dry yeast. In the winter of 1875–6, he entered upon this work in Lower Roscoe, and is at this writing shipping several hundred pounds a day.

MINING.

Probably the first coal-bank opened in Coshocton county was that of Morris Burt, a mile east of Coshocton, say 1834.

As early as 1836, Matthew Scott mined on his place, in Virginia township, and shipped to Columbus several cargoes of coal.

A few years later, the "Licking and Coshocton Coal Company" commenced quite extensive operations at Coalport, and continued shipping by canal to Newark until about 1860, when the works were taken by others.

In 1856, Foght Burt, from his mine on his farm, about a mile southeast of Coshocton (now in possession of W. K. Johnson's heirs), made a four-feet ten-inch railroad to connect with the S. & I. R. R., making the junction a little south of the freight-depot. At first horses were used to haul the cars; afterward a small locomotive ("Little Giant"), T. H. Burt being the engineer. A considerable amount of money was put in the enterprise, and much effort made by Mr. Burt and his sons, R. W. and T. H., but the project was a costly failure, owing, as is said, to the failure of the S. & I. R. R. Co., "from inability possibly," says R. W. Burt, to meet expectations of assistance in building the coal road, and afterward in furnishing cars.

Not long after the railroad was built Edward Prosser opened a mine about a mile northeast of Coshocton.

The Rock-Run Coal Company commenced operations

about the same time, and the "Shoemaker bank" was next opened.

The coal business received a great impulse about 1868, through the operations of Colonel J. C. Campbell and Albert Christy, who leased large tracts, and organized the "Coshocton Coal Company," enlisting A. H. Spangler very thoroughly. This company bought out Prosser's Beech Hollow bank, and Shoemaker dying, the territory held by him was also embraced in their leases. The Miami Company was formed buying from the Coshocton Company the Shoemaker leases; also the New York Company taking some territory two miles south of the town of Coshocton.

Several companies were also organized to operate in the old Coalport field. These, with some changes in organization, continue. The New York Company's mine passed into the control of the Union Company, now under the management of Colonel Wood. The Miami Company was supplanted by the "Penn Twyn."

In 1870, F. E. and J. A. Barney, D. L. Triplett, S. H. Lee, G. W. Ricketts, E. Prosser, and others formed the "Home Coal Company." Prosser, after a year or so, sold his interest in that company, and opened a mine three and one-half miles southwest of Coshocton, near the canal, shipping by that chiefly to Newark. This bank is still under his control. He also, in connection with J. W. Cassingham and T. Dudley (of Piqua), purchased the Home Company bank. These gentlemen also operate the "Penn Twyn," and are thus the heaviest coal operators in the county at this writing.*

Of the old Coshocton Company, Colonel J. C. Campbell is the president, having the controlling interest in the stock.

Vast amounts of coal of confessedly superior quality have been shipped from these mines, and whatever the result to some of the stockholders and operators, large pecu-

---

*As much as 126,000 bushels (5,000 tons) have been shipped in one month.

niary advantages to the county have been derived from them.

The difficulties connected with the matter of transportation are alleged to be the chief drawbacks to a more successful prosecution of business at any of them.

Besides the merchant mines already mentioned (eight), there are now a number of home supply mines, of which the principal are those of William Hall, J. Lear, William G. Hay, and J. Burt, of Tuscarawas township; and D. Markley and R. Boyd, of Keene township.

Besides the territory embraced in the leases of the companies above referred to, the Morgan Run Coal and Mining Company has several (three) thousand acres covered by its leases, but as yet unworked. It is expected that these lands will be penetrated by the Massilon and Coshocton Railroad, whose projectors are largely interested in them.

The undeveloped coal wealth of the county seems at this time properly to demand the use of large figures for its statement.

COAL OIL STILLS AND OIL WELLS.

From 1857 to 1860 a good deal of money was expended in the making of coal oil in Bedford township, where there are very fine beds of cannel coal. Parties from Boston, New York, and Pittsburg, including such men as Ezra Cornell, of New York; A. E. Kittredge, of Boston; and Robert Forsythe, of Pittsburg, erected stills and opened mines, and made things for a time very lively. But the oil wells in Western Pennsylvania soon set aside the coal oil. Considerable quantities of the coal were afterward shipped to the gas-works at Newark and elsewhere. There was at one time much "oil fever" in Coshocton county.

Messrs. Montgomery and Cowdery came in, and driving about in an elegant conveyance, with silver-mounted harness and whip, made many anxious to get "into oil." They took leases, and gave people to understand that oil abounded in the county. A few of the citizens have reason to remember them, and would rather not hear much about oil stocks.

Certain gentlemen of Coshocton and Roscoe, under the

leadership of F. E. Barney, T. C. Ricketts, and others, formed a "test" company, and sunk a well near the Empire mills in Roscoe, to the depth of some seventeen hundred feet, at a cost of some $6,000, but did not strike oil in paying quantities. Several holes in the ground were also made on Will's creek, and some gentlemen of Coshocton and elsewhere got into companies "on the ground floor."

During the war and soon after, a great many oil leases were taken on ground in New Castle township, and parties, chiefly under the management of Peter Neff, of Cincinnati, sunk some wells. No oil of consequence was found, but there was an immense outflow of gas, and this has recently been turned to account in making lamp-black of very superior quality and in considerable amount.

Soon after the settlement of the county, salt was manufactured on a small scale at Rock Run, three miles south of Coshocton. A few miles further down the river, just over the line of the county (in Muskingum), are, at this writing, quite extensive salt works, with which John H. Klossen, of Coshocton and Roscoe, has for some years been connected. They were operated for years by Retilley & Bagnall, of Roscoe.

Potteries, in the region of New Castle (where excellent materials are found), have been very successfully carried on by the Richs and their successors.

George Bagnall, about 1860, began operations in that line in Lower Roscoe, and afterward sold out to Mr. Rich, who now carries on the business. Bagnall removed to New Comerstown.

The Coshocton Stone Company (Thomas H. Johnson, of Columbus, and John A. Hanlon and L. L. Cantwell, of Coshocton) have for a year past been operating in their quarry (on the Ohio canal and the projected route of the Massillon and Coshocton railway) and in their yard in Roscoe, where they have steam stone-saw apparatus. They are at this writing shipping a contribution of stone for the Ohio building at the Philadelphia Centennial Fair.

CHAPTER XIII.

MERCHANDIZING, BANKING, TAVERN-KEEPING, ETC.

MERCHANDIZING was, of course, for many years on a very limited scale. The "goods" had to be brought from Pittsburg, Steubenville, or Zanesville, either in wagons or by steamboat. For many years, of even later times, it was a common practice to drive stock on east, and in exchange get supplies of goods. Colonel Williams was a "trader."

The first regular "storekeepers" in Coshocton county seem to have been Hedges and Hammond. James Calder was probably the next merchant.

Among the men who achieved a reputation in this line in the earlier days were James Renfrew, Benjamin Ricketts, John Smeltzer, and Robert Hay, of Coshocton; Thos. Johnston, of Plainfield; the Mulvains, of Oxford township; Wm. Brown, of West Carlisle; Chas. E. Marquard, at New Guilford; John H. Pigman, at Clayville; Samuel Holmes, of West Bedford; Welch, of Roscoe; Samuel Ramsey, of Keene; F. W. Thornhill, of West Carlisle, West Bedford, and New Guilford (East Union); G. V. Lawrence and N. Shafer, at New Castle.

The three principal business places in 1820, and for years after, were Coshocton, Caldersburg, and Plainfield.

Of a somewhat later date than above named merchants, we have Wm. Renfrew, W. K. Johnson & Co., John Burns, Bagnall & Le Retilley, John Frew & Co., T. C. Ricketts, R. M. Lamb, Arnold Medbery, H. Meek, Humrickhouse & Co., Samuel Lamberson, John G. Stewart, Jackson Hay, H. N. Shaw, F. X. Fritchey, D. Bretsford, at Jacobsport; R. Cochran, at West Carlisle; H. Beall, at Keene; Seth McLain, in Roscoe; R. Boyd, at Keene; the Denmans and the Shoffners, at Warsaw; Wilson & Thompson, at West Bedford.

There was, of course, a vast enlargement of this interest

after the canals were built, and a very great one along the line of the railway after it was opened.* With this multiplication of establishments has come a division into departments in the larger places, and the same store is now no longer expected, as in the olden times, to have laces and silks and soap and nails. There are, at this writing, in Coshocton and Roscoe *only* forty-six stores, with nearly as many more shops and saloons, etc. The keepers of some of these, as of others in the county, will doubtless be able to secure honorable and extended mention in "Chronicles of 1976."

We append the list for the use of a subsequent historian:

LIST OF PRINCIPAL BUSINESS HOUSES IN COSHOCTON COUNTY IN MAY, 1876.

Coshocton—Dry Goods, etc.—Hay & Wilson, J. Pocock & Sons, J. H. Klossen, Mrs. W. W. Walker, A. F. Maltby.

Drugs, etc.—J. Anderson, Dr. S. H. Lee, J. Wilkin, M. W. McNaughton, J. W. Wright, F. S. Faulkner, L. E. Disney.

Hardware, etc.—Darling & Bonnet Bros., G. W. Ricketts & Co., Forker & McDonald.

China Goods, etc.—B. R. Shaw.

Books and Music—J. Glover.

Periodicals, etc.—F. X. Fritchey.

Boots and Shoes, etc.—H. N. Shaw & Sons, J. G. Magaw, Jos. H. Hay.

Family Groceries—Rue & Son, Humrickhouse & Crowley, A. H. Thomson, L. F. Decker, Williams Bros., Charles Eckert, Lorentz & Long, C. Schweiker, C. Zugschwert, J. Bowen, Bachman Bros.

Furniture—J. Waggoner, D. Rose & Son.

---

* In 1856 the stores in Coshocton were all on Second and Chesnut streets, viz: T. C. Ricketts, dry goods; R. & H. Hay, dry goods; H. Meek, dry goods; A. N. Milner, dry goods; J. W. Dwyer, dry goods; Dryden & Co., drugs and books; Wm. McKee, drugs and books; S. Harbaugh, hardware; F. X. Fritchey, grocery; Mrs. E. Hawley, grocery; H. N. Shaw, boots and shoes; Cassingham & Shaw, leather and findings; G. F. Wilcoxen, boots and shoes; J. Waggoner, furniture; and R. M. Hackinson, drugs.

Wholesale Liquors, etc.—P. McManus, Maro J. Smith.
Grain and Lime, etc.—A. H. Thomson, J. Mulligan.
Restaurants, Bakeries, etc.—B. Stevenson, Mrs. G. A. McDonald, P. Miller & Co.
Marble—Thompson Bros.
Pumps, Gas Fixtures, etc.—J. H. Carman.
Meat Shops—H. Shaw, Burrell & McGill, J. Enoch, Hoselton & Harrison.
Agricultural Warehouse—J. S. Elliott.
Watches and Jewelry—W. W. Bostwick, J. Bostwick, R. B. Black.
Millinery, etc.—Misses Baker, Mrs. N. R. Tidball, Miss Hay.
Saddlery—S. Snyder, Rezin Baker, C. Baker.
Tailoring—P. Hack & Sons, H. Cantwell, D. C. Beach.
Clothing—J. Wertheimer, J. Strouse.
Roscoe—Dry Goods, etc.—Burns & Hack, Crawford & Retilley, Moore & Caton.
Hardware—Harrison & Johnston.
Groceries—L. R. Miller, C. W. Stamford.
Leather—J. & H. Carhart.
Saddlery—A. N. Compton.
Tinware—E. F. Lynde.
Drugs, etc.—John Adams, C. Ferguson.
Canal Lewisville—Burns & Hack.
Keene—Goods—D. G. Whittemore, A. & W. B. Finley.
Saddlery—W. Sprague.
Warsaw—Goods—Jas. Foster, Bard & Carr, Clark, Buckalew Bros., C. Strome.
Drugs—Lawson & Son.
Hardware—G. R. Gamble.
Furniture—Joseph Tiralla.
Saddlery—A. Kaufman.
Hotel—N. Linebaugh.
New Bedford—Renner & Burbacker, A. J. Bowman.
Chili—John Lorentz, Sol. Dewitt, J. J. Lenhart.
Bakersville—Wm. Forney.
Avondale—J. M. Ferrell.
Willow Brook—W. Wright.

Bacon Run—S. Osborne.
Clark's—Pocock & Doak.
Spring Mountain—Baker and Lybarger.
Helmick—O. Miller, Beck Bros.
Mohawk Village—J. W. Given, W. Crago.
New Castle—J. S. McVey, W. Butler.
Walhonding—L. F. McVey.
East Union—Dr. Ralston, J. W. Allen.
West Bedford—Thomas Jones.
West Carlisle—Thomas W. Thompson, Lewis V. Cox, Perry White.
Frew's Mills—D. G. Cooper.
West Lafayette—T. Familton, Leggett & Beall.
Orange—J. B. Peck & Co., J. Richmond & Son.
Jacobsport—T. J. Platt & Bro., Jonathan Wiggins, J. Hugh Johnston.
Saddlery—T. P. Latham, D. Duling.
Linton Mills—T. J. McCartney, Johnston Maple.

BANKING.

The merchants of the earlier day received deposits, and settled any eastern claims in any wise arising against their customers. The first parties who undertook the business in regular way of selling eastern exchange, and doing a full deposit, discount, and exchange banking business, were W. K. Johnson & Co., about 1852. They operated at first in the rear room of those now occupied by J. G. Stewart, and then in the office he occupies. After W. K. Johnson's death, the firm was J. K. Johnson & Co. (the company being John Johnson). After the latter's death, David and John H., sons of Joseph, were received into the firm, and the business was thus conducted until their removal to New York City, about the 1st of January, 1872. Since that time, the establishment is designated "Johnson's Bank"—John G. Stewart, proprietor.

T. C. Ricketts started the second banking-house, about 1855. He also organized the "First National Bank" in January, 1872 (commencing business March, 1872)—T. C. Ricketts, president, and Baxter Ricketts, cashier. In the winter of 1873-4, it was reorganized, Jackson Hay becoming president, Houston Hay vice-president, and H. C. Herbig cashier. Its original capital was $50,000; its present, $90,000.

The Merchants' in 1838, and even later, put out their "scrip," and in 1861 the treasurer of Coshocton county gave out many "pieces of pasteboard" as money; but this was the first bank of issue in the county.

About 1856, the south room in the frame building on Second street, next north of B. Shaw's china and glass store, had over it the sign "Bank," and was the headquarters of one who afterward became quite famous in certain monetary transactions—*i. e.* James M. Brown.

In August, 1868, the "Coshocton Savings and Building Loan Association" was incorporated. Its directors have been F. E. Barney, James M. Burt, Wm. E. Hunt, Hiram Beall, Thomas Campbell, T. C. Ricketts, E. T. Spangler, J. B. Ingraham, J. G. Stewart, D. L. Triplett, H. Hay, J. C. Pomerene, and J. S. Wilson. J. W. Cassingham was secretary through all its history. J. M. Burt, J. G. Stewart, and D. L. Triplett have served as president, and T. C. Ricketts and J. G. Stewart as treasurer. It practically discontinued business in 1875, having at that time, by installments of stock and profits, nearly $100,000 of assets, which were paid out to the stockholders.

TAVERN-KEEPERS.

One of the most prominent features of a country is the public house or tavern, and no proper sketch of a region or people can ignore this feature. For some years Charles Williams was the only man in the county holding himself out in the capacity of landlord, or having business enough to warrant the taking out of a license. In the earlier days travelers expected and received entertainment at almost any house where they pleased to stop. Hospitality was the pride of the whole people, and those agreeing to supply the travelers' wants were not niggardly in doing so. The appliances were sometimes of a rude sort; but the fare was good and the welcome hearty, if the latch-string were out at all.

Illustrative of the primitive way they had in those days of entertaining travelers, the cheapness of the viands, and the anxiety of the early settlers to treat strangers well, we reproduce from Mr. Melishe's journal* his account of a scene between himself and a landlady: "When near Coshocton, I stopped for breakfast at a small roadside tavern. I was anxious to be gone as soon as possible, and urged the landlady to make all the haste she could. She said she would have the breakfast ready in a minute; but the first indication I saw of dispatch was a preparation to twist the necks of two chickens. I told her to stop, and she gave me a look of astonishment. 'Have you any eggs?' said I. 'Yes, plenty,' replied she, still keeping in a sitting posture, with the chicken in her hand. 'Well,' said I, 'just boil an egg, and let me have it, with a little bread and tea, and that will save you and I a deal of trouble.' She seemed quite embarrassed, and said she never could set down a breakfast to me like that. I assured her I would take nothing else. 'Shall I fry some ham for you along with the eggs?' said she. 'No,' said I; 'not a bit.' 'Well, will you take a little stewed pork?' 'No.' 'Shall I make some fritters for you?' 'No.' 'Preserve me, what will you take, then?' 'A little bread and tea, and an egg.' 'Well, you're the most extraordinary man that I ever saw; but I can't sit down to a table that way.' So I allowed her to take her own way, assuring her I would take mine as to eating. She detained me about half an hour, and at last placed upon the table a profusion of ham, eggs, fritters, bread and butter, and some excellent tea. All the time I was at breakfast she kept pressing me to eat; but I kept my own counsel, and touched none of the dishes except the bread, the tea, and an egg. She affected great surprise, and when I paid her the ordinary fare, a quarter of a dollar, she said she didn't want to take anything."

A man once told how he had traveled from Wheeling to

---

* Written in 1816.

Knox county, passing through Coshocton, on a silver shilling. Selecting his house, he would ask for entertainment, and, when about to leave, state that he had only this shilling, producing it, and that it was invariably refused.

An invariable attendant of the early tavern was "the bar," with its decanters and glasses arranged on a shelf behind the counter. The great glory of the tavern was "the ball." A gentleman happened at old Charley Williams' at the time of the usual "court week" dance, and nearly fifty years after gave a graphic, inimitable account of the affair. Becoming at length tired of the revel, he stole away to his bed, but in a little time two of the party came up to him. When on the landing of the stairs, coming down in obedience to their behests, he shrewdly put the candle out, and, slipping past them, got into a nook, where he rested, if not sleeping, until the next morning. The host, as well as the guests, was decidedly festive that night; but the next day he apologized to his stranger guest, and blamed the frolic on "them Zanesville lawyers."

Among the more famous keepers of public houses, besides Williams, were Wilson McGowan, Benjamin Ricketts, B. R. Shaw, Samuel Morrison, J. C. Maginity, in Coshocton; Theophilus Phillips, and Barcus and Mrs. R. Johnston, of Roscoe; B. Magness, of Linton township; Moses Morgan and P. Wolf, of Oxford township; Robert Farwell, in Keene; Joseph Butler, in New Castle; Stryker Morgan, three miles east of Coshocton; Augustine White, of West Carlisle; F. A. Stafford, in Virginia township; Moses L. Neal, Coshocton; Ellis D. Jones, first in Roscoe, then in Coshocton; and Wm. Tidball, who was the first keeper of what is now the City Hotel, and had before taking that won a reputation up in Clark township. W. H. H. Price is now growing gray in the business.

TRANSPORTATION BUSINESS.

Doubtless the citizens of Coshocton county best known in direct connection with the transportation business on the canal were Captain Isaac Evans and Captain Wm. Morrison; both with good reputations; the former dead, the latter still living in the county. Neither this sort of work nor the stage-coach business ever seems to have had a large place among Coshocton county interests. Among "the drivers" there were possibly some whose experiences would be freighted with romantic interest were they set out; but they are, if recorded at all, in some tablet of memory now moss-grown and illegible.

Above the general surface there rises the history of the canal-driver boy, who afterward was governor of Iowa—Wm. Stone—originally from the State of New York, but spending his boyhood and young manhood in Coshocton.

A good many "bare-foot Bills," both in and out of Coshocton county, have gotten well on in the world. For the comfort and encouragement of the present generation let it be recorded.

CHAPTER XIV.

PHYSICIANS—STATISTICS AS TO HEALTHFULNESS OF COUNTY—PIONEER MEDICAL REMEDIES.

THERE is record evidence to show that, in all, not fewer than a hundred and sixty persons have practiced medicine in Coshocton county. With the exception of some twelve or fifteen, these have all been " regulars."

The first resident physician was Dr. Samuel Lee. His biography is given elsewhere in this volume. A ride of twenty miles was in his practice a common occurrence, and for consultation he went to Mansfield, in Richland county. His active practice covered more than forty years.

The next physician who seems to have made his mark distinctly enough to be readily traced was Dr. Hiram Wright. He was a Canadian, coming to Coshocton directly from Western New York. He remained in the county until about 1831, when he removed to Knox county, and not long thereafter died.

In 1831 the physicians of the county were S. Lee, Lewis Colby, Thomas Heslip, William Emerson, Jared Cone, G. R. Morton, Benjamin Hill, and E. G. Lee. Of Dr. S. Lee information is given above and elsewhere.

Dr. Benjamin Hill came to Keene township in 1824 from Cheshire county, N. H. Though very young, he had been in the Revolutionary war in its last year as an assistant to an army surgeon. He was quite eccentric, as people judged; rough in speech, but kind of heart, and especially tender toward the brute creation, horses, dogs, cats, etc. His medical hobby was that all diseases were produced by miasmatic influence. His wife died about 1834, and he returned to New England, and died soon after.

Lewis Colby was a well-educated physician, coming, it is understood, from Vermont to Keene about 1828. In a few years he went to Louisiana, and there died after a brief period of practice.

Thomas Heslip was of the well-known Linton township family by that name, and he practiced for a time near Jacobsport.

William Emerson read medicine with Dr. Lee, and, after attending lectures in Cincinnati, practiced in connection with him, having his residence and office in Roscoe. That was about 1828. He was a promising young man. Died of pneumonia in 1833.

Jared Cone was at West Carlisle about 1828; practiced there some years, and then went to Dresden, whence he removed to Missouri.

Dr. E. G. Lee was at East Union, one of the two towns united under that name having been laid out by him. He came from Knox county, and went back there after some years.

George R. Morton was at Coshocton; came from Norristown, Pa., about 1830; about 1835 he removed to Sandusky city, and there died a few years since.

With the vast throng coming into the county from 1830 to 1845, there was a due proportion of those proposing to practice the healing art. Some of these did not abide very long, and others did not acquire a very extensive practice, and were chiefly occupied with other pursuits. Among these may be mentioned, as pertaining to the earlier day, Henry Miller, afterward so distinguished in business circles in Columbus, who practiced medicine for a short time at Warsaw, as also his brother Jonathan, afterward of Franklin county; or A. T. Walling, now Congressman from the capital district. Or of still later day, Dr. E. Cone, of Washington township, afterward a M. E. preacher, and who recently reported himself as "grower of peaches and apples on sheep lands." Or, in still more recent times, Dr. B. C. Blackburn, who was for a time a merchant, and subsequently a farmer, and has even taken somewhat to politics, representing the county in the legislature. And, by the way, the doctors seem to have been in favor in this matter, the county having sent to the legislature Dr. S. Lee, Dr. Williams, Dr. Stanton, Dr. Cass, Dr. Fellows, and Dr. Blackburn.

Among the physicians who, by long residence and prominence in their profession, are worthy of notice, in addition to those already named, may be mentioned Dr. Willetts, for many years at New Castle; Dr. Delamater, who removed to Indiana, and there died in 1874; Dr. Barger, of New Castle, who was killed by the explosion of a boiler of a steamboat at Louisville, Ky., while on a trip to the west in 1843; Dr. James, who removed from the county about 1846; the Madisons, both dead; Silas Sapp (brother of Enoch), who removed to Indiana, and there died in 1870; R. R. Simmons (brother of John T.), removed to Harrison county about 1860; I. N. Fellows, who died in 1869; L. Howard, who met with his death in Keene at the time of receiving a blow at the hand of his brother-in-law, who was convicted of manslaughter about 1859.

The veteran physician of the county, at this writing, is Dr. Maro Johnston, of Roscoe. He is a native of the county, and studied with Dr. Samuel Lee, of Coshocton; attended lectures at Ohio Medical College of Cincinnati; commenced practice in Roscoe in June, 1833; uninterruptedly in practice.

Heslip Williams, native of Guernsey county, where he studied and practiced for a time, commenced practice at Jacobsport in 1835; was in legislature; otherwise steadily in practice.*

Josiah Harris, from Maryland, graduated in the medical department of the University of Maryland; came to Coshocton county in 1837; practiced in Roscoe until 1840, and then removed to Coshocton.

William Stanton, native of Hartford county, Ct.; studied with Dr. Sears, of Albany, N. Y.; came to Coshocton county in May, 1838; was at West Bedford five years, and then removed to Warsaw. He gave up practicing in 1849, and has since given attention to farming, merchandising, etc. He removed to Coshocton in 1868.

George Day, native of Jefferson county; came in 1839 to Oxford township, where he still resides; attended one

---

* Died August 6, 1876 (while these sketches were passing through the press), of heart disease, aged sixty years.

course of medical lectures at Ohio Medical College, Cincinnati.

A. L. Cass, from Muskingum county, studied with his relative, Dr. John Andrews, of Steubenville; graduated at the University of New York; came to Coshocton county in 1842; and with brief exception, while in the State Senate, practiced uninterruptedly until the summer of 1874. At that time he was prostrated by disease, and has not yet resumed practice. At this writing he is residing at Pittsburg.

W. H. Vickars, of Muskingum county, studied with Dr. Watkins; commenced practice at Otsego about 1840; removed to Coshocton county (Jacobsport) in 1845; and there died in 1873.

J. B. Ingraham, a native of Harrison county, Virginia, studied with Dr. Carpenter, of Athens, Ohio; attended lectures at Starling Medical College in Columbus; came to Linton township in 1848; removed to Coshocton in 1864; uninterruptedly in practice.

David Lawson studied with Dr. Russell, of Mt. Vernon, and commenced practice in 1849; lately in drug-store at Warsaw.

Samuel McElwee, native of New Jersey, studied chiefly with Dr. A. McElwee; holds diploma of Cleveland Medical College; commenced practice in 1849 at New Castle; and has been there ever since.

E. Sapp, native of Knox county, studied with Dr. Houts, of Danville, and came to Coshocton in 1850. For a few years he gave special attention to dentistry.

David McElwee studied with his brother, S. McElwee; established at East Union.

N. Blackman, of Warsaw, studied with Dr. Barnes, of West Bedford.

John Anderson, native of Guernsey county, read with Dr. Kortz; commenced practice in the fall of 1848 at Port Washington, Tuscarawas county; then in Keene, Coshocton county. He came to Coshocton in 1868, and has since been engaged in the drug and book business.

S. H. Lee, native of Coshocton, studied with his father, Dr. S. Lee; commenced practice at Canal Dover, Tuscarawas county; practiced from 1849 to 1856, at Peru, Indiana; then returned to Coshocton; was surgeon in Ohio Volunteer Infantry in 1862, 1863, and 1864. He gave up practice in 1865, and has since been engaged in the drug business.

J. T. Edwards, native of the county, read with Dr. Russell, of Mt. Vernon; graduated at University of New York in 1857; and has since been in practice at West Carlisle.

In addition to those indicated in the foregoing list as still in practice, the following others may be named: J. W. Wright, J. W. Brady, J. C. Brower, W. C. Frew (native of county), at Coshocton; John C. Davis, at Orange; Wm. Bancroft and A. H. Garber, at Jacobsport; W. H. Williams and A. J. Hughes, at West Lafayette; B. W. Chapman and E. P. Stuart, at Bakersville; Peter Lenhart, Chedister, and Volz, at Chili; M. J. Love (native of county), at Keene; S. M. Carr and Beach, at Clarks; John Moore (native of county) and N. Calhoun, at Warsaw; J. W. Winslow, at Spring Mountain; —— ——, at West Bedford; Wm. Smith (native of county), at West Carlisle; A. M. Henderson, at Frew's Mills; J. M. Smith (native of county), at Canal Louisville; T. Ralston, at East Union.

A county Medical Society was formed about 1855, holding meetings at intervals until about 1867, when the organization was practically abandoned. Under the State Constitution prior to 1851, the county authorities assessed a specific tax upon the physicians practicing in the county, running from three to five dollars per year.

Lest some readers might conclude from the number of physicians who have been in Coshocton county, that it was an unusually sickly region of country, it may be well to state that the statistics for many years show an average death-rate of one to every one hundred and thirty-three inhabitants per year. In 1874, when the population of the county was about twenty-four thousand, the deaths reported were one hundred and seventy-seven.

From 1840, on for a number of years, a traveling dentist occasionally visited Coshocton. The poor fellow finished his course about 1858 by hanging himself (while in a depressed condition of mind, produced by discouragement in business and hard drinking) in a stable then standing in rear of the "Central House." The first resident dentist was Dr. E. Sapp. He was succeeded by Disney & Moffitt. Dr. Jacobs next undertook this work. Disney & Moffitt were succeeded by Finlay and Wernett, and Jacobs by Dr. Wait.

Among the more notable practicers of the so-called "irregular" schools of medicine, have been Dr. Alexander McGowan, of the "Thompsonians;" Dr. Martin Roberts, who learned his "arts of healing" from the Indians in Western New York; Drs. Wilson, Walling, Waddell, and Farquhar, of the "Uriscopians;" Drs. Von Ruedegish, Alder, and Burr, of the "Eclectics."

The first Homeopathic physician to settle in the county was Dr. W. W. Smith, who came to Coshocton just after the war of 1861–5. He removed to Pennsylvania in 1874.

At this writing Dr. N. M. Shurick represents that school, having commenced practice in 1875.

The medical remedies in the days of the first settlers, ere the doctors had come around, may have some interest for some young readers. The diseases of children were nearly all ascribed to worms. For the expulsion of these a solution of salt was given, or some scrapings of pewter spoons, or some copperas gathered near coal-bank runs.

A very general remedy for burns, swellings, etc., was a corn-poultice, made of pounded corn. Poultices of scraped potatoes or raw turnips and slippery-elm bark were often used. For the croup (called the bold hives) the juice of roasted onions or garlic was given. For fevers a tea of snake-root. The itch, which was very common, was cured by an application of brimstone and lard. Rheumatism, and swellings generally, were treated with oil of rattle-snakes, bears, geese, coons, ground-hogs, and polecats. White walnut-bark tea was a great favorite. If it was intended for an emetic the bark must be stripped up the tree; if for a purge, down. Some had great faith in charms. The erysipelas, or St. Anthony's fire, could, as some believed, be cured by circumscribing it by the blood of a black cat, etc.

CHAPTER XV.

NEWSPAPERS.

The old citizens tell how they and their cotemporaries used to watch for the arrival of the stage from Zanesville bringing the *Weekly Messenger*. Wm. N. Johnson and other young store-clerks of that day read themselves hoarse for the edification of the customers and loafers, a number of whom were not very good readers, and then, besides, a paper would thus go farther. A President's message, only four days from Washington, was a wonderful thing.

One Dr. Maxwell (who, besides printing the paper, had on sale in the office "Godfrey's cordial," "Bateman's drops," etc.) is credited with having started the first paper in Coshocton county—the *Coshocton Spy*—in the latter part of 1825. It was a sheet twelve inches by eighteen, issued with much irregularity. The concern, after a brief career, was turned over to John Frew, who had furnished supplies from his store for some time. Maxwell went to Mount Vernon, and, in consequence of criminal charges, subsequently fled the country, and the paper was put in charge (as foreman) of one O'Hara, Frew being still the publisher, and steadily paying a little for this honor. O'Hara at length fell a victim to delirium tremens, and Burkit E. Drone became the editor and printer, having also a half interest in the ownership of the paper. After a time, Joseph Medill, afterward famed in Cleveland, and still later and more largely in Chicago, as editor of the *Tribune* and mayor of the city, became associated with the paper. The name of the paper at that time was the *Democratic Whig*. Drone went to Cincinnati, and Medill also removed, and the paper became the property of H. Guild, who at length suspended publication, as some of his predecessors had done. The name at that time was *The Republican*. After some time the office became the property of R. W. Burt (now in the internal revenue service at Peoria, Illinois). How he got it and what he did with it we let him tell:

"In August, 1853, Mr. H. Guild, the editor and proprietor of the old Whig newspaper in Coshocton called on me and desired to sell me his interest in it. He had ceased its publication two or three months previously, having lost hope in its success. I told him I was not a Whig, had been a Democrat, but was now a Freesoiler; that my party in Coshocton county only included about fifty people, and that I saw little or no prospect of establishing a paper in advocacy of my own principles. I also distrusted my ability to do justice to my own cause, never having had any experience as editor, nor even as a printer. I gave him no encouragement, and he went away. But in truth he had awakened a desire in my mind to engage in the work of publicly advocating my principles, which I believed would finally triumph. I thought over the matter, talked with my father and some leading Whigs and independent Democrats, and finally embarked in the enterprise. I was assisted greatly by Hon. James Matthews, and his brother-in-law, Thomas W. Flagg, was taken in as associate editor. I called the paper the *Progressive Age*. The first number was published in September, 1853, and was outspoken on the subject of slavery extension and the fugitive slave law, and strongly advocated the cause of temperance. Wm. A. Johnston was foreman in the printing office. I sent the paper to all the old subscribers of the Whig paper, and also to all the Democrats whose names I could get. I soon found plenty of papers returned ' not taken out of the postoffice.' In two months, however, after my first issue, I had only about two hundred and fifty subscribers, but I did not get discouraged. In a few months, by most persistent efforts, my subscription-list was greatly enlarged, and at the end of a year it had reached seven hundred. The following year the *Age* took part in the formation of the Republican party, and the new party having succeeded in electing nearly all their candidates for county offices, the *Age* came in for a share of the public printing, which gave it a firmer footing. I continued the publication about three years, and the Republican party was in power in the county when I sold the paper to A. R. Hillyer, who published it about a year, and then sold it to J. W. Dwyer. I assisted Dwyer about a year, and then left the county."

J. W. Dwyer succeeded Hillyer, making out of the paper very little direct pecuniary gain. He left it to take office in the treasury department under S. P. Chase.

Asa L. Harris, from Columbus, became the proprietor of the paper in 1861. He changed the name from *Progressive Age* to *Coshocton Age*. About the close of the war, Harris went to Georgia to become postmaster of Augusta (having served in like capacity in Coshocton); and the paper, after being run for a time by J. W. Dwyer and W. A. Johnston, became, in 1866, the property of its present publisher, T. W. Collier, who had resided in Cadiz and New Philadelphia, and had been in service as adjutant of the Eightieth Regiment, O. V. I. The present circulation of the paper is reported at 1,200 copies.

In 1831 John Meredith began the publication of a paper at East Union, Perry township. It was called the *Castle of Liberty*. In 1832 it was removed to Coshocton, and was published until after the presidential election in that year, when it was discontinued. It advocated Democratic principles and the re-election of General Jackson to the presidency. James Matthews assisted in the editorial department for a time.

About 1836 the publication of a Democratic paper, called the *Western Horizon*, was begun at Coshocton. Wm. G. Williams, then county treasurer, was the proprietor, and Russell C. Bryan the editor. For a time John Oliver managed the paper. Subsequently Messrs. Weeks, Wagstaff, T. W. Flagg, and Chauncey Bassett were connected with it. In 1840 its publishers were Flagg & Bassett. It was then about half the size of the *Democrat* of to-day, and bore that name. About 1845 A. W. Avery, who had been a minister of the M. P. Church in Coshocton, was its editor. He removed to Illinois. In the fall of 1850, A. T. Walling, now member of Congress from the Columbus district, was editor and publisher of the paper. In 1853 Rich and Wheaton were publishing it. In the spring of 1856, Asa G. Dimmock, who had edited the Cadiz *Sentinel* and the *Cosmopolite* at Millersburgh, and had just finished his service as warden of the Ohio Penitentiary, became editor and publisher. When nominated for prosecuting attorney in 1862, he disposed of the paper to A. McNeal, a young man from Bethlehem township, who had just served as county recorder. He was drowned while fishing in the Tuscarawas river, a few miles above Coshocton, in August, 1862. Wash. C. Wolfe ran the paper from McNeal's death until after the election, when Dimmock resumed, and soon thereafter (November, 1862) J. McGonagle, formerly of the Cadiz *Sentinel*, became a partner with Dimmock, and continued for some two years. He removed to Shelby, O. In the spring of 1866, the present publisher, John C. Fisher, of Muskingum county, who had been connected with the Newark *Advocate*, became a partner with Dimmock. The health of the latter was at that time seriously broken. He spent the most of the summer in visiting among friends, and died that fall at the home of his brother, in Montrose, Pa., and Fisher became the proprietor and editor of the paper, continuing as such unto this writing, except that during Mr. Fisher's absence in the State Senate it was edited by W. R. Gault and other temporary editors, and that during the summer of 1875, for a few months, W. C. Brownlee (now of Chillicothe) was associated with him. It is understood that in its earlier history the paper frequently required the help of its party friends, and none of its numerous publishers have been able to retire with a large fortune. Its appliances are better now than in any past period of its history. Its circulation is reported at 1,000 copies.

For a couple of years (1849 and '50), a paper, called the *Practical Preacher*, was published some months, at Coshocton, by Rev. Mr. Wirick, then residing at Jacobsport, who was the Methodist preacher on the circuit.* He

---

*Beside sermons, the paper contained communications of literary and miscellaneous sort. Among these were a few sketches of the

had been a printer before becoming a minister. Rev. Mr. Calhoun and other ministers furnished matter for publication. It was printed in the *Age* office—did not thrive—was short-lived.

H. C. Beach and Beach & Elliott, about 1870, and again in 1874, published for brief periods an independent and literary paper.

At least two ladies of Coshocton—Mrs. E. W. James and Mrs. E. T. Spangler—have made some reputation as paper and magazine writers. The latter is also the author of a book, the *Physician's Wife*.

Mrs. Louise Morrison Hankins—a Coshocton-born lady, now of New York City—has achieved considerable fame as a magazine and book writer.

history of Coshocton, partly historical and partly "bar-room stories." The writer of these, in a recent letter, says that the historical matter, then published in the *Preacher*, is found in *Howe's Historical Collections of Ohio*, *Doddridge's Notes*, and other readily accessible publications.

CHAPTER XVI.

SCHOOL MATTERS.

SCHOOL matters did not receive much attention nor attain any noticeable prominence for many years after the organization of the county. The demands of pioneer life were, as is commonly the case, too heavy in other directions to allow of as much time or means for these things as they might in other conditions receive. But there was not much disposition on the part of many to create or improve facilities. There was some study and very earnest efforts on the part of individuals to get something of "book learning," and a very marked individual proficiency in the three great underlying primarily utilitarian attainments of reading, writing, and cyphering; but practically no schools before 1820. About that time, the policy of the State was thoroughly settled and well shaped, and stimulated what of interest there was in localities. The Congress of the United States, in 1803, had granted to the State the one-thirty-sixth of all the lands in the United States Military District for the use of schools in the same, and the Legislature provided for the leasing thereof. But these leases yielded little or no revenue beyond the expense of managing them, and in 1827 they were sold, and the proceeds taken as a loan by the State (now a part of the irreducible debt), with the agreement to pay to schools six per cent. interest on the amount annually. These lands in Coshocton county were appraised by James Robinson and Richard Fowler, and staked out by James Ravenscraft. The sale of them was superintended at first by Samuel Rea. Afterward James Hay was appointed for this work, and he declining, Robert Hay was designated. The sum paid to the county from this fund has been for many years about $800.

In 1821 school districts (school affairs having been hitherto in the hands of township trustees, and almost wholly dependent upon voluntary efforts) were fully arranged for, and the householders in such districts were authorized to select a school committee and a collector and treasurer, and the committee was authorized to receive donations of sites for building, and to assess taxes on their district, as also to receive from the township the rents of the school lands.

In 1825 a school tax was directed to be raised in every county, and yet more complete and practicable arrangements as to districts and directors were made. On certain conditions a tax, not exceeding in amount $300, could be levied for building a school-house. Rate (or tuition) bills could be arranged for and relied on where the tax was insufficient.

Under these provisions, "Dr. S. Lee and his associates," being householders of the district, got from the county commissioners the privilege of erecting a brick school-house (20 by 20) on the southwest quarter of the square, in 1828. Before that, a room in a private house was used. At a few points in the county, family and neighborhood schools of small proportions were carried on for a few of the winter months.

In Coshocton, James Madden, from Virginia, crippled as to one hand, gave instruction in the "elements," especially in writing, in which he was a "proficient."* Then it was, too, that Moses L. Neel,† a "Down-Easter"—a regular genius—handled the ferule, and otherwise, especially by a remarkably fine penmanship, made his mark sufficiently plain to be read to this day. About the same time, David Grimm was teaching in Millcreek, and the father of Dr. M. Johnson in Keene township.

Among the teachers of the earlier day were Wm. B. Hubbard, who subsequently went to Columbus, and became famed as a railroad "magnate;" Noah H. Swayne, now Judge of the United States Supreme Court, and Chas.

---

*He subsequently moved up the Tuscarawas to the Ravenscraft neighborhood, and taught for some time.

†He subsequently kept a tavern in the town of Coshocton.

Elliott, afterward the famous Methodist minister and college president. Out about West Carlisle, Robert McCormic was acquiring fame as a teacher; in Coshocton, Jackson was, after the approved methods of the time, training some of our now well-known citizens, and Thomas O'Neil was giving his youthful vigor to Keene and Lafayette townships. What stories of rude appliances and clumsy tricks of big incorrigible boys and of nice homespun girls the chronicles of that period do tell!

Under the law of 1825, there were to be appointed in each county three school examiners, and in 1826 the Court of Common Pleas appointed for Coshocton county Samuel Rea, Wm. Carhart, and Andrew Grim. A year or two after the law providing for a larger number, N. H. Swayne, Robert Hay, Wm. Wright, Wm. Hazlett, Henry Barnes, Wm. Carhart, and Samuel Rea were appointed. A few years later we find in this position T. S. Humrickhouse, Alex. McGowan, W. K. Johnson, James Matthews, Jos. Burns, and Dr. Geo. R. Morton; and at a yet later day J. W. Rue, Bradley Squires, Richard Moode, Thomas Campbell, Wm. Sample, Dr. Josiah Harris, and Rev. H. Calhoun.

The examiners could individually examine. One of them gives the following as illustrative of the examination then in vogue: A man who had been teaching for some time, came to his office. After hearing the applicant read a few lines, the examiner said: "What is that little mark?" (pointing to a comma.) "Oh! that's one of them there stops that you see in all books." *Examiner.* "Well, what is it for? or what does this particular one indicate?" *Applicant.* "Why, it indicates a stop, of course; they're all stops." Pressed with a few more questions, the applicant insisted on being tried in arithmetic, claiming that he was specially well qualified in that. *Examiner.* "Well, what is arithmetic?" *Applicant.* "Arithmetic! why, it's a book about figgers," etc. The man wrote a really fair hand, and was posted in practical arithmetic, and got a certificate. Grammar was not then required to be taught in the schools.

From 1830 to 1850, the system inaugurated from 1820 to

1830 was not greatly modified by the Legislature, and was being more and more efficiently carried out, and more widely extended. Districts were multiplied with the rapidly incoming population; new school-houses were being built, and teachers were multiplied. The appliances were, even at the best, still rude; methods mechanical. Dr. Harris, the veteran county school examiner, coming into the county about 1838, visited several schools accounted the best, and reports them as exceedingly limited in their range of study—the highest branch being geography—and crude in their methods.

In the latter part of this period, say from 1840 to 1850, there was a growing conviction that thorough and extended scholarship had not been attained under the public school system as then ordered by law, and this fact and a higher sense of the importance of the religious element in education gave rise to a number of private schools and academies. In this work at Coshocton were engaged Rev. E. Buckingham, and especially Rev. Addison Coffey, both of the Presbyterian Church. The latter built quite a good brick house (now occupied by old lady Ricketts), with the view of making room for boarders, and had for his school-house the building now occupied by W. R. Forker—both buildings being on south Fourth street. The Rev. Mr. Sturgis, of the Protestant Episcopal Church, started an academy at Keene. There was a good school at West Carlisle, under Mr. Stevenson; and an academy at West Bedford, which was very successful under W. R. Powers. About the same time, there was an academy at Van Buren (now Spring Mountain), in Monroe township, of which Dr. Haldeman had charge, and afterward Prof. Geo. Conant. This was under the control of a conference of the M. E. Church. The removal from the county of some of the gentlemen, especially Messrs. Buckingham, Coffey, and Sturgis, involved the discontinuance of some of these institutions, and others were less, or not at all, in demand, by reason of improvements in the public school system. The West Bedford Academy, as a combined private and public school, is still in operation.

Taking advantage of the "Akron law" (so called because, as first passed, it had relation to the city of Akron, but it was afterward extended in its application), passed in 1849, the citizens of Coshocton proceeded to establish a graded school. Wm. K. Johnson, Joseph C. Maginity, J. G. Smith, Joseph Guinthur, and Jacob Waggoner, were chosen by the citizens as the board of education. The school examiners first appointed were Thomas Campbell, Wm. Sample, and Rev. H. Calhoun.* Wm. R. Powers, formerly of New York State, then of Utica, Ohio, was employed as superintendent, assisted in the higher department by Miss Sallie Elder (Mrs. Geo. Dewey). There were two primary schools, presided over by Miss Araminta Bodelle (Mrs. H. N. Shaw) and Miss Caroline Stewart (Mrs. Samuel Denman). Soon a secondary school was started, and taught by Miss Elder, her place in the higher school being supplied by Miss Delia Roberts (Mrs. Houston Hay).

The schools at that time held their sessions in a little frame school-house on the north school-house lot, and in the basement of the Methodist Episcopal and Second Presbyterian churches. The little brick school-house on the public square had become dilapidated, and, owing to the location, objection was made to repairing it.† Among the last teachers in it were Messrs. Alexander, Henrigh, James Irvine, and James Dryden.

In 1853, it was determined to erect a suitable schoolhouse. A considerable amount of feeling was manifested in regard to the location of it. Some were anxious to have

---

* The following other gentlemen have served in this capacity : T. S. Humrickhouse, Rev. P. H. Jacob, Dr. J. Harris, A. R. Hillyer, J. C. Tidball, Rev. W. E. Hunt, John E. Irvine, Rev. C. W. Wallace, M. C. McFarland, Rev. S. M. Hickman, J. C. Pomrene, J. R. Johnson, G. W. Cass. The board at present is: Dr. W. C. Frew, W. R. Gault, and W. S. Crowell, Esqs.

† Kindred to this building was one with a tablet over the door, bearing the inscription, "*Know thyself*," about a mile southeast of Coshocton, in the Orangeville district, where the Burts from Orange county, New York, and the Denmans and Condits, from Orange, New Jersey, lived. It was torn down in 1872.

it erected on the quarter block (two original town-lots), at the northeast corner of Fourth and Main streets, fronting the public square. Others insisted upon placing it upon the square in the north end of the town, given by the original proprietors of the town for the purpose. The latter carried the day. The building (a two-story brick, thirty by eighty feet, with belfry, all in Grecian style of architecture) was finished in 1855. A. N. Milner, a merchant and general operator, took the contract at about $4,500. A small allowance was subsequently made, but it was claimed that he was out of pocket very largely, whether by proper cost or through want of management is disputed. The brick work was done by Henry Davis; the carpenter work, etc., by George Hay. The bell was added six or eight years afterward—purchased by the fines paid in that year by violators of the liquor law. When this school-house was built, the board of education was composed of B. R. Shaw, J. C. Tidball, Jacob Waggoner, A. L. Cass, H. Cantwell, and Wm. Sample.

The following names appear in the list of those serving in this capacity subsequently: John Frew, Thomas Campbell, H. N. Shaw, James Dryden, J. G. Stewart, Henry Davis, W. H. Robinson, A. J. Wilkin, J. C. Pomrene, A. H. Spangler, D. F. Denman. The board at this time embraces J. M. Compton, J. S. Wilson, H. N. Shaw, C. H. Johnston, Henry Davis, and W. W. Walker.

To meet the demands by reason of the increased population, the board in 1871 erected a two-story brick on the Denmead and Taylor lots, in John Burt's subdivision. H. Davis and Harrison Waggoner were the builders.

In 1874, a small frame was erected on the north school-house lot, and the accommodations being still insufficent, two primary schools were set up in a private house on Chestnut street just east of the railroad.

In 1876, an imposing three-story front addition was built on the Burt tract. The plans were furnished by Johnson* & Kremler, of Columbus, and the work done by the Cosh-

---

*T. H. Johnson, of this firm, was born and reared in Coshocton.

octon Planing Mill Company—the contract price being $10,885.

W. R. Powers, as superintendent of "Coshocton Union School," was succeeded (removing to West Bedford) in 1854 by W. A. McKee (now of Knoxville, Iowa), and he in 1857 by T. V. Milligan (now pastor of old Presbyterian church in Steubenville), and he in 1859 by John Giles (now of Springfield, Massachusetts), and he in fall of 1864 by C. Forney (now of Pittsburg, Pennsylvania), and he in 1868 by Geo. Conant, the present principal. There are at this time ten assistant teachers.

In 1870, the Presbyterian church of Coshocton made a proposition to give the frame church building for a schoolhouse, and a strip of ground (now occupied by the parsonage) whereon to erect a boarding-house, to a board of trustees appointed by the session, but including representative members of other denominations, to the number of two-thirds of the board, if the community would assist in securing not less than $5,000, wherewith to erect the boarding-house. Over $4,000 dollars were subscribed (all but $300) by members of the Presbyterian church, but the community manifested so little interest in this movement to secure the " Coshocton Female College," that the church, after waiting a year, withdrew the proposition, and proceeded to erect a parsonage with the fund so far as it had been contributed within the church.

A few years later, Rev. Mr. Lee, of the Methodist Episcopal church, the president of an institution called the " One Study University," undertook to establish a branch or feeder of that university, under the name of " Coshocton College," but this effort also was quite abortive—the concern leading a feeble life for a year or so, and then passing away.

Outside of the public schools at this writing the only work in this line being done is at Bloomfield, where Rev. T. D. Duncan, of the Presbyterian church, is conducting a small classical school, and by Rev. Mr. Nunemacher giving lessons in German to quite a large class.*

---

* Rev. Wm. E. Hunt has, during his twenty years' residence in Coshocton, given instruction in the classics to a number of scholars, and

The citizens of Roscoe, at a meeting held at the house of C. W. Simmons, on the 15th of March, 1851, voted, according to law, for a union school, and on the 29th of the same month elected the following board of education, viz: John Carhart, John Dodd, John Burns, James Hill, Maro Johnson, and Arnold Medberry. A month later a site for a school house was purchased for $250, and a contract was made with S. W. Brown, Dennis Chapin, and Samuel Hutchinson for the erection of a brick building, one story, to cost $2,450. When the building was completed some complaint was made as to the workmanship, and the price actually paid was $2,352. The board employed B. W. Lewis, of Ashland county, as principal, and H. Stephens and Charles Hoy were employed as assistant teachers, each to labor half the time. The board of examiners was composed of Dr. M. Johnson, James Hill, and James Le Retilley. Mr. Lewis, after teaching two months, was compelled to resign on account of his health; and, on his recommendation, Charles R. Shreve, of Massilon, was elected principal. He continued in that position until 1858. The principals since have been R. N. Smith, 1859-61; C. S. W. Griffith, 1861-62; M. Travis, 1862-63; S. Cox, 1863-64; A. W. Oder, 1865; R. Hogue, 1866; G. E. Campbell, 1866-69; W. Nicholas, 1869-70; G. E. Campbell, 1870-72; T. Carnahan, 1872 to present time. The assistant teachers, at this time, are Eliza Hutchinson and Juliet Gardiner. The present board of directors are Henry Carhart, J. C. Harrison and Robert Dickerson.

From 1865 to 1876, there has been much improvement in school buildings and appliances throughout the county. Besides the new school-houses in Coshocton, very creditable structures have been erected in a considerable number of localities, and these, and many of the older but still good houses, have been fitted up with the modern and attractive style of desks, etc.

---

fitted for college the majority of those who have gone in that time. Among these last were J. R. Johnson, T. H. Johnson, P. S. Campbell, G. W. Cass, Joseph K. Cass, Miss Jennie Nicholas, Charles Ingraham.

One of the neatest school-houses in the county, outside of Coshocton, is that at West Lafayette—a two-story brick, with belfry. It was built in 1873. T. H. Familton, Velzer Shaw, and Lewis Leighninger, were at the time directors. Wm. Gorseline was at that time, and had been for a period before, in charge of the school. H. W. Harbaugh is, at this writing, in charge of it.

There is also a very nice two-story frame building in Jacobsport, built in 1873. The directors, at the time, were L. Carhart, T. P. Latham, and Alonzo Sibley. The teachers, at present, are S. P. Woodward and Miss Anna Johnson.

In 1871, a good school-house was erected at Warsaw. The directors then were N. Buckalew, Joseph Orr, and John Lenhart. John Crawford is the Centennial year principal of the school. There is a good school-house (two-story frame) at Keene, in which John M. Finley is "the presiding genius." The school-house at East Union is a good two-story frame. New Castle also has a very creditable building.

The school-house at West Carlisle, and the academies at Spring Mountain and West Carlisle, though not new buildings, are all good and well fitted up—each being a frame two-story structure. Canal Lewisville has a neat brick school-house, and the district just east of Coshocton one—both recently built.

The following statistics give a distinct view of the school affairs in the county for the year 1875: Number of school districts, 139; number of persons engaged in teaching during the year, 235; number of pupils enrolled, 7,692; average daily attendance, 3,839; amount paid for sites and buildings, $5,452; contingent expenses, $7,981; for teachers' wages, $39,280; average of teachers' wages per month, $40.00.

The veteran school teachers of the county are M. D. Van Eman, of Bethlehem township, and James Magness, of Linton township.

A complete list of those who have been engaged, in all the years past, in teaching, would embrace the names of very many hundreds of the excellent women and vigorous

School Matters.

men of the county. Of those who, at this writing, may be designated as teachers, not to repeat those already mentioned, the following may be named as most acceptable and successful. Mrs. Conant, Mrs. Carnahan, Misses H. Hogle, Ida Pugh, S. Sample, Isa Campbell, Sallie Anderson, Tip Elliott, Ella Johnston, Pauline Weiser, Cassie Raymer, Rebecca J. Trego, Mary Gorham, Elizabeth Magness, Ellen Horn, Nora Crawford, Linda Lanning, Jennie M. Myser, Lyda Hutchins, Melissa Stonehocker, Kate Elliott, Eliza Hutchinson, Elizabeth L. Barnes, Eliza J. Creighton, Bell Simpson, Nannie Jones, Maggie S. Phillips, Sarah E. Buchanan, Juliet W. Gardner, Lucy Dodd, Charlotte Hogle Kate Boyd, and Emma Massa; and Messrs. John Wagner, S. P. Woodward, H. K. Knaval, J. M. Williams, W. K. Spencer, Jas. D. Phillips, H. S. Mulford, Edgar Carroll, Wm. C. Thomas, Sam'l A. Boyd, S. P. Snyder, J. F. Myser, J. F. Hastings, F. M. Murphy, Lewis V. Cox, Geo. W. McDonald, J. B. Barcroft, Jas. S. Beall, Jas. P. Lawyer, C. C. Emerson, Wm. Gorsline, H. T. Wheeler, Wm. Fulks, Jno. W. Bell, Jacob Brewer, F. M. Ogilvie, O. M. Seward, Geo. D. Hill, W. S. Kilpatrick, D. A. Barcroft, Jonathan Lenhart, Wilber G. Williams, Isaac Loder, and H. B. Barnes.

Under the old law, the school examiners held their office for two years. The number for some time was at least two in each township, and the changes were frequent, so that the list would embrace scores of names. If a man, in those days, was not a school examiner, one of three things might be concluded—either he would not be bothered with the office, or he had not any noticeable literary attainments, or he was not politician enough to secure the appointment.

Under the law (in force since 1851) vesting the appointment in the probate judge, and providing for only three examiners for the county, the following is the list, with term of service: C. R. Shreve, teacher, 1851–59*; John E. Irvine, teacher, 1851–54*; Wm. R. Powers, teacher, 1851–56*; John T. Simmons, Esq., 1854–56; Rev. H. Calhoun, 1856–58*; Wm. A. McKee, teacher, 1854–58;* J. J.

---
* Removed from county.

McSuitt, 1856–60; Dr. Josiah Harris, 1858, still in office; M. C. McFarland, deputy county clerk, 1859–65; Rev. Wm. E. Hunt, 1860-74*; John M. Finley, teacher, 1865–76; W. S. Crowell, Esq., 1874; M. W. Wimmer, 1876, still in office.

With the impulse given, teacher's institutes, under the auspices of the County Teachers' Association, were inaugurated about 1852. By the state law a small amount could be drawn, for this work, from the county treasury, upon the condition that a like amount be contributed by the teachers and friends of education.

Probably the most enthusiastic friends of this undertaking, in its original form, were C. R. Shreve, principal of the Roscoe school, and Rev. H. Calhoun, and Dr. J. Harris, of Coshocton. After a few annual meetings—partly owing to the removal from the county of Mr. Shreve and Mr. Calhoun—the institute work was discontinued. Under the law setting aside, for this purpose, the fees paid by applicants for teachers' certificates, the institute was revived about 1865, and there has since been an annual effort (and for one year, two) in that direction. Dr. J. Harris, Wm. E. Hunt, Prof. Geo. Conant and wife, Prof. T. Carnahan and wife, W. C. Thomas, Wm. Gorsline, W. Nicholas, R. Compton, Geo. Hill, Misses H. Hogle, and Ida Pugh have been officially and prominently connected with this work. The officers for 1876 are as follows: President, J. T. Moore; Executive Committee, Wm. Gorsline, Thomas Carnahan, and Eph. Ellis; Secretary, E. L. Retilley; Treasurer, Ida A. Pugh.

Among the instructors and lecturers engaged in connection with this work have been Professors Tappan, Marsh, Kidd, Henkle, White, Mendenhall, Andrews, Williams, T. W. Harvey, Knisely, and other gentlemen, well known in connection with such matters, residing elsewhere than in Coshocton county. Prof. Conant and Mrs. Conant, Dr. J. Harris and Rev. Wm. E. Hunt, have also been employed in the capacity of instructors and lecturers.

---

* Resigned.

CHAPTER XVII.

MILITARY AFFAIRS.

MILITARY spirit has in all its history been largely manifested in Coshocton county. "Fighting blood" abounded among the early settlers. Nearly every neighborhood had its champion wrestler or fighter. Personal combats were frequent—often accounted a fitting close for every public day, ranking along with horse-racing and rifle-shooting. Pages could be written showing the strength and prowess of some of the old-time heroes, especially as detailed by some of their boon companions. At a term of court held in 1813, twelve indictments were found "for fighting at fisticuffs by agreement," including one against the sheriff of the county. In these appear the even yet well known names, Van Kirk, Markley, Hill, Cantwell, Williams, Cain, Roderick, Newcum, and Clark.

A citizen, coming in some fifteen years later, details how he frequently heard little companies of men quietly talking together and discussing the question as to who was "the best man." And upon the facts coming out it would always appear that this phrase did not denote the man of mind, and heart, and good character, but the man of muscle—the brawniest, bulliest fellow!

The "musters" were the big occasions, brightening the eyes of citizens generally, and affording a fine field for ambition, and producing a large crop of Majors, Colonels, and Generals. Thus came Generals Johnston, Burns, Meredith, Workman, etc.; Colonels Swigert, Ferguson, Ravenscraft, etc.; and Majors Frew, Robinson, etc. Much might be written presenting the tamer or the more ludicrous aspects of the "corn-stalk" musters, and trainings, and drillings of the "citizen soldiery." But these things were in nowise peculiar to Coshocton county, and all the old chroniclers tell of them.

Tom Corwin once pictured* the militia general and the parade as follows:

"We all in fancy now see the gentleman in that most dangerous and glorious event in the life of a militia general on the peace establishment—a parade day! The day for which all other days of his life seem to have been made. We can see the troops in motion—umbrellas, hoe and axe-handles, and other like deadly implements of war overshadowing all the field—when, lo! the leader of the host approaches; 'far off his coming shines.' His plume white, after the fashion of the great Bourbon, is of ample length, and reads its doleful history in the bereaved necks and bosoms of forty neighboring hen-roosts! Like the great Suwaroff, he seems somewhat careless in forms and points of dress; hence his epaulettes may be on his shoulders, back, or sides, but still gleaming, gloriously gleaming in the sun. Mounted he is, too, let it not be forgotten. Need I describe to the colonels and generals of this honorable house the steed which heroes bestride on such occasions? No, I see the memory of other days is with you. You see before you the gentleman from Michigan, mounted on his crop-eared, bushy-tailed mare, the singular obliquities of whose hinder limbs are described in that most expressive phrase, 'sickle hams;' her height just fourteen hands, 'all told.' Yes, sir; there you see his 'steed that laughs at the shaking of the spear;' that is, his 'war-horse whose neck is clothed with thunder.' Mr. Speaker, we have glowing descriptions in history of Alexander the Great and his war-horse, Bucephalus, at the head of the invincible Macedonian phalanx; but, sir, such are the improvements of modern times, that every one must see that our militia general, with his crop-eared mare with bushy tail and sickle ham, would literally frighten off a battlefield a hundred Alexanders. But, sir, to the history of the parade day. The general, thus mounted and equipped, is in the field

---

* In a speech in the House of Representatives, February 14, 1840, in answer to Hon. Isaac E. Crary, of Michigan. Corwin several times spoke at Coshocton—the last time in 1860.

and ready for action. On the eve of some desperate enterprise, such as giving order to shoulder arms, it may be, there occurs a crisis—one of the accidents of war which no sagacity could foresee or prevent. A cloud arises and passes over the sun! Here an occasion occurs for the display of that greatest of all traits in the character of a commander—that tact which enables him to seize upon and turn to good account events unlooked for as they arise. Now for the caution wherewith the Roman Fabius foiled the skill and courage of Hannibal. A retreat is ordered, and troops and general, in a twinkling, are found safely bivouacked in a neighboring grocery! But even here the general still has room for the exhibition of heroic deeds. Hot from the field, and chafed with the untoward events of the day, your general unsheathes his trenchant blade, eighteen inches in length, as you will well remember, and with an energy and remorseless fury he slices the watermelons that lie in heaps around him, and shares them with his surviving friends. Other of the sinews of war are not wanting here. Whisky, Mr. Speaker, that great leveler of modern times, is here also; and the shells of the watermelons are filled to the brim. Here, again, Mr. Speaker, is shown how the extremes of barbarism and civilization meet. As the Scandanavian heroes of old, after the fatigues of war, drank wine from the skulls of their slaughtered enemies, in Odin's halls, so now our militia general and his forces, from the skulls of melons thus vanquished, in copious draughts of whisky assuage the heroic fire of their souls, after the bloody scenes of a parade day. But alas for this short-lived race of ours, all things will have an end; and so even it is with the glorious achievements of our general. Time is on the wing, and will not stay his flight. The sun, as if frightened at the mighty events of the day, rides down the sky; and at the close of the day, when 'the hamlet is still,' the curtain of night drops upon the scene—

> "'And glory, like the phœnix in its fires,
> Exhales its odors, blazes, and expires.'"

WAR OF 1812.

It was proposed originally that this work, as giving special prominence, though far from exclusive attention, to the days of "the fathers," should contain a list of all the soldiers of the war of 1812. But success has not crowned efforts in this direction. The recollection of the few survivors is unreliable and incomplete; the statements made by those supposing themselves informed contradictory. Repeated applications to the War Department were declined, with information that, while answers will be given in relation to individuals, when company, etc., are given, lists will not be furnished or allowed.

There are reports that, at the outset of the war, a considerable number of citizens, chiefly from the south and west parts of the county, joined a company that was being raised by Lewis Cass. This detachment was surrendered by Hull, and sent home on parole.

Under a requisition from the governor, Judge Isaac Evans responded with a full company, marching to Franklinton (across the Scioto from Columbus), where they were mustered into service, and furnished with uniforms and United States muskets. They were in the forces of General Harrison. Their period of service was six months.

There is information of a company in service, under command of Captain Isaac Meredith, raised in the northwestern part of the county.

Captain Tanner is reported to have taken a company from the southern part of the county, and mention is also made of Captain Beard's company.

By the kindness of Matthew Johnston, Esq., the muster-roll of Captain Adam Johnston's company is here given.

MUSTER-ROLL OF CAPTAIN ADAM JOHNSON'S COMPANY OF RIFLEMEN,

Detailed for the protection of "the Mansfield frontier," under command of Colonel Charles Williams, by order of Return J. Meigs, Governor of Ohio:

Adam Johnston, captain; William Morrison, lieutenant;

Abraham Miller, ensign; Thomas Foster, first sergeant; John M. Miller, second sergeant; Frederick Markley, third sergeant; Robert Culbertson, fourth sergeant; John H. Miller, first corporal; Zebedee Baker, second corporal; John M. Bantham, third corporal; John D. Moore, fourth corporal.

Privates—Samuel Morrison, Edward Miller, Isaac M. Miller, Michael Miller, Isaac Hoagland, George Arnold, James Bucklew, John Baker, Matthew Bonar, Joseph Neff, Allen Moore, Benj. Workman, James Winders, John McKean, Windle Miller, John G. Miller, Isaac G. Miller, George McCullough, Daniel Miller, Joseph McFarland, Andrew Lybarger, Henry Carr, Matthew Williams, John Steerman—24.

It will be observed that this force was a volunteer rifle company. The men, as they went out, wore new yellow hunting-shirts, trimmed with white fringe, and each carried his own trusty rifle and tomahawk and scalping-knife. The company was summoned to the field under the impulse given by the account of the massacre of the Copeland family, near Mansfield, by some Indians. It was mustered into service August 25, 1812, and mustered out September 25th of the same year.

Colonel Charles Williams went along with the force in the capacity of scout and general adviser, and in expectation of taking charge of a regiment, if occasion might offer or necessity require.

Thomas L. Rue was with the force as sutler, and Dr. S. Lee was the mustering-in surgeon.

One of the sentinels of the company shot a cow, mistaking it in the dark for an Indian. An Indian, supposed to be a scout, was discovered behind a tree and killed and scalped, the scalp being an adornment of one of the riflemen for years afterward.

In addition to those whose names appear in the foregoing list the following are reported as having rendered service in the war of 1812: Peter Moore, Charles Miller, John G. Pigman, Thomas Johnson, Richard Johnson, Andrew McClain, Samuel Elson, Francis Smith, W. R. Clark, James

Williams, Levi Magness, George Magness, Richard Fowler, Rezin Baker, Richard Hawk, Isaac Shambaugh, James Oglesby, James Wiley, Elijah Newcum, James Butler, Robert Corbit, Thomas Butler, Joseph Soverns, and Isaac Meredith.

Some of the saltpeter used for making powder for the war of 1812 was collected a few miles south of Roscoe. The "caves" formed by projecting rocks had in the decomposed stone on their floors a great deal of nitrate of lime, which, being leached with wood-ashes and exposed to the air and sun, gave nitrate of potash, a high-priced material in those war times, wherewith to make powder.

MEXICAN WAR.

On the first call for troops for the Mexican war, more than a hundred citizens of Coshocton county sprang to arms, although the whole State of Ohio was asked to furnish only some 2,400.

On the 5th of June these embarked on a canal-boat at Roscoe, destined for the "Halls of the Montezumas." Upon reaching Camp Washington, near Cincinnati, a full company was mustered into the service, and became part of the Third Ohio regiment.

A considerable number of the Coshocton boys went into what was commonly spoken of as the Union company, made up of soldiers from Muskingum, Morgan, and Coshocton counties.

The full Coshocton company was officered as follows: Captain, Jesse H. Meredith; First Lieutenant, J. M. Love; Second Lieutenant, S. B. Crowley; Third Lieutenant, Jos. D. Workman. Seven of this company were lost by the casualties of war. This force was under General Taylor, but was not in any considerable battle.

There was also a considerable number of Coshocton county boys in Captain Hart's (afterward Captain Irvine's) company, which became part of the Fourth Ohio regiment. This was raised under the call for troops in 1847. The term of service of the first forces was one year, and they met at Cincinnati the second lot of soldiers.* The latter were in several of the sharpest engagements of the war, being with General Scott.

It is reported that there are now in the county only seven Mexican war survivors, the rest having died or removed. Joseph Sawyer sports the medal of the Veteran Association, a handsome bronze shield, made out of cannon captured in the war.

THE WAR OF 1861-5.

The people of Coshocton county, as those of all other localities, were watching with intensest interest the occurrences of the winter of 1860-61. Whatever the personal sympathies, political attachments, or peaceful proclivities, none were indifferent. When Lincoln, in the latter part of February, passed through the town of Coshocton on his way to the national capital, he was greeted by an immense throng of anxious citizens. The news of the fall of Sumter caused hereabouts as elsewhere a thrill that passed and repassed along the nerves of the people. Many of the settlers had come from south of Mason and Dixon's line, and had tender recollections of their old homes and the people therein. But the war spirit was not wanting, even among these, and as promptly as in any county the masses of the people were up in arms. Under the first call of the president, two companies of men were enlisted for three months' service. One of them was commanded by Captain James Irvine,† and the other by Captain R. W. McLain. They were mustered into the Sixteenth Ohio Regiment, of which Irvine became colonel, John D. Nicholas taking command

---

*Charles McCloskey, of Coshocton (now of Steubenville), at the time of the Mexican war, was a soldier in the regular army, and one of the storming party or "forlorn hope" at the capture of the City of Mexico, when he was terribly wounded, and for a long time near to death. Upon his return to Coshocton, after his recovery, a salute was fired by some of his old comrades, and, by the premature discharge of the cannon, Joseph Sawyer and John Richards lost each an arm, carried away by the rammer.

† R. M. Voorhees, Esq., lays claim to having been the first man to put his name on paper in the recruiting of this company. It is said that N. R. Tidball claims the same distinction.

of the company. The regiment, as will be remembered, was sent to Western Virginia, and smelled a little powder at Philipi. These forces were sworn in for three months' service, and rendered it. Before this time was up, however, it became manifest that the suppression of the rebellion was to be no ninety days' job. Promptly, Josiah Given, Esq., who had seen service in the Mexican War, set about raising another company for three years' service, under the second call of the president, and in a little time another hundred of the youth and strength of Coshocton county were mustered in, and became part of the Twenty-fourth Regiment Ohio Volunteer Infantry. There soon followed another hundred, entering the Thirty-second Regiment Ohio Volunteer Infantry, with Captain Stanley, First Lieutenant C. C. Nichols, and Second Lieutenant Geo. Jack. Then, indeed, were the piping times of war. At every cross-road was a recruiting station. Within a few months, nearly a thousand men were recruited. The most of these were mustered into the Fifty-first and Eightieth Regiments Ohio Volunteer Infantry, which rendezvoused at Camp Meigs, near Canal Dover. In the Fifty-first were Companies D, F, H, and I, commanded respectively by Captains John G. Patton, D. W. Marshall, John D. Nicholas, and James Crooks, and about one-half of Company C, commanded by Captain Hesket, was also made up of Coshocton boys. Of this regiment R. W. McLain was made lieutenant-colonel, and D. W. Marshall, adjutant, both of Coshocton county. In the Eightieth Regiment there were three companies and a considerable part of a fourth. The commissioned officers of the three companies were as follows: Company F, Captain Pren Metham; First Lieutenant James Carnes; Second Lieutenant F. H. Farmer: Company G, Captain Wm. Marshall; First Lieutenant Peter Hack; Second Lieutenant John Kors: Company H, Captain G. W. Pepper; First Lieutenant John Kinney; Second Lieutenant J. W. Doyle. The major of this regiment was Richard Lanning.*

---

* He was killed at the battle of Corinth, Miss., October 4, 1862. He was connected with one of the old families of the county; was a

While the Fifty-first and Eightieth were being collected, J. V. Heslip raised a considerable squad in this county, for the Sixty-ninth Regiment Ohio Volunteer Infantry, and R. W. Burt, formerly a resident of the county, came up from Newark and enlisted a few Coshocton boys for a regiment being raised in Licking county. In the summer and fall of 1862, four companies were raised for the Ninety-seventh and One Hundred and Twenty-second Regiments Ohio Volunteer Infantry. Of one of those in the Ninety-seventh, E. Shaffer was captain, Martin Weiser first lieutenant, and G. W. Smailes second lieutenant. Of the other, C. C. Nichols was captain; N. McLain first lieutenant, and C. H. Matthews second lieutenant.

Of those in the One Hundred and Twenty-second, B. F. Sells and Dr. O. C. Farquhar were captains, Joseph Work and G. H. Barger first lieutenants, and James M. Sells and —— Anderson second lieutenants. About the time these companies were being raised, Colonel James Irvine, commissioned to raise a regiment of cavalry, secured some fifty men in Coshocton county, who were mustered in the Ninth Ohio Volunteer Cavalry. In the summer of 1863, a draft was ordered. The enrollment reported, in August of that year, three thousand and nine persons in the county subject to military duty. Of these some eight hundred were of the second class (between thirty-five and forty-five years of age, and not subject to duty until the first class, from twenty-five to thirty-five, was exhausted). On the day fixed for examination of claims for exemption, there was a pretty good mass-meeting in the public square in Coshocton. Many claims were justly made and allowed. The horrors of the draft were largely diminished as the whole process was better understood. The results of it in securing soldiers in Coshocton county are not readily accessible; but it is believed that they were not widely different from those in the country at large, as follows: On the 19th of October, 1863, the provost-marshal general reported that of every

---

farmer in earlier years; afterward studied law, and was prosecuting attorney of the county when commissioned. He was about fifty years of age. His body was sent home, and lies in the Coshocton Cemetery.

one hundred and fifty men drafted, thirty never reported, being thoroughly disinclined to the service or confident of their legal right to exemption. Of the one hundred and twenty reporting, seventy-two were excused. Of the forty-eight held for service, twenty-four paid the commutation, sixteen furnished substitutes, and the balance, being eight, went to the field. In an effort to arrest drafted men in Crawford township, three men were shot. A few of the citizens of Coshocton county, excited by stories of personal outrage and official mismanagement, gathered their old shot-guns, and repaired to Napoleon, Holmes county, whence fearful accounts of resistance to the draft were soon sent out; but no Coshocton county blood was there spilled.

An incident of the Napoleon excitement was the march of a detachment of bronzed soldiers, in charge of a small gun, which had been sent by the governor to Napoleon, down the Walhonding valley to Coshocton, where they took the cars for Camp Chase.

During the Morgan raid excitement Coshocton became the depository of the treasures of the banks of Cadiz, which were brought hither and put in the vault of Joseph K. Johnson & Co.'s bank. Morgan, on his way to Columbus, after his capture, spent a few minutes in Coshocton.

The men drafted or going as substitutes were allowed the privilege of going into companies and regiments in which their friends and associates were, and the ranks of some of these were thus increased. The generous provision made by the township for the relief of the families of those in the service, and the bounties offered, bore their fruits in the enlistment of many scores of men in the summer and fall of 1863; and, while no new organizations were formed, several hundred men went during that season out of Coshocton county into the military service.

In the fall of 1863, some seven volunteer military companies were, by state authority, organized and drilled under the name of Ohio National Guards. On the 25th of April, 1864, these were ordered by the governor to take the field. They rendezvoused at the fair-ground in Coshocton, and after a few days proceeded to Columbus. After inspection, some five hundred men were selected out of the nearly seven hundred men, and two companies were placed in the One Hundred and Forty-second Regiment, and three in the One Hundred and Forty-third Regiment. The companies in the One Hundred and Forty-second Regiment had the following commissioned officers: Captains L. B. Wolf and Caleb Wheeler; First Lieutenants John Weatherwax and D. L. Lawson; Second Lieutenants B. F. Leighninger and ———— ————. On the staff of the regiment was A. H. Fritchey, quartermaster. Of the One Hundred and Forty-third Regiment, John D. Nicholas was lieutenant-colonel. The commissioned officers of the companies were as follows: Captains N. R. Tidball, Jno. L. Dougherty, and Jas. Ririe; First Lieutenants D. F. Denman, A. J. Stover, and James Crawford; Second Lieutenants John Willis, D. Rose, and Nat. Elliott. They were mustered into the United States service, May 13, 1864, and mustered out September 13th, of the same year,

A few men were secured in Coshocton for the gun-boat service. Dr. S. H. Lee and Dr. A. G. Brown, of Coshocton, and Dr. Edwards, of West Carlisle, represented Coshocton in the medical department, and Rev. G. W. Pepper, of the Methodist Episcopal church at Keene, was chaplain, as well as captain of a company. And there was no arm of the service that did not find some of its strength in the warm hearts and brawny arms of Coshocton county boys.*

It is not in the plan of this work to trace the career of those entering the military service after leaving the county. They were absorbed in the larger bodies of which they became part, and the record of these is in the general history of the war. They were given by the county to this service, and most of them proved worthy representatives of it. It is estimated that in all there entered the service

---

* Major-General William Burns, of the regular United States army, and Lieutenant Poe, of the United States navy, were born and bred in Coshocton county.

nearly twenty-five hundred men, and of these between three and four hundred fell by the casualties of war. There is not a graveyard in Coshocton county but holds the ashes of some of them, and scores of them rest in "the south-land."*

To promote enlistments and serve as counselors in relation to all military matters, the following persons acted, by appointment of the governor, as a military committee for Coshocton county: A. L. Cass, Houston Hay, Seth McLain, J. D. Nicholas, and D. Rodahaver. Soldiers' aid societies were formed in almost every school district, gathering up comforts and delicacies for the camps and hospitals in which were the "boys." Rev. A. McCartney, of Keene township, and Joseph Elliott and Rev. C. W. Wallace, of Coshocton, visited the "Army of the Cumberland" as delegates of the United States Christian Commission.

---

*In the Coshocton Cemetery is buried a young Confederate soldier, who died in the cars when near Coshocton while being transported as a prisoner of war.

CHAPTER XVIII.

BIBLE SOCIETY—S. S. ASSOCIATION—TEMPERANCE MOVEMENTS—SECRET ORDERS.

THE Coshocton County Bible Society was organized in April, 1830. It has distributed by sale and gift some six thousand dollars' worth of Bibles and Testaments in the county, and paid over to the American Bible Society for its benevolent work in the home and foreign field some twelve hundred dollars.

SUNDAY-SCHOOL ASSOCIATION.

Some ten years ago, a county sunday-school association was formed, but after a brief period became extinct. W. H. Robinson was Pres.; Dr. E. Sapp, V. P.; J. Glover, Treas.; J. R. Johnson, Cor. Sec.; W. J. Moffit, Rec. Sec. In the summer of 1876, a new association was organized. Pres., Joseph Frew; Sec., L. Disney; Treas., J. G. Magaw.

TEMPERANCE MOVEMENTS.

The various temperance movements of the country at large have always been to greater or less extent engaged in by the people of Coshocton county. And in few regions has there been either more need for the work or more faithfulness in it. Records which, if given in detail and in such way as to make the account one of personal and local interest, would perpetuate family shame and mortify personal and local pride, tell in general that Coshocton county has contributed its full quota of victims to "the monster evil."

From the days of the Washingtonians, on through Sons of Temperance, Cadets of Temperance, Good Templars, Women's Leagues, there have always been those to "lift up the standard against the enemy." The records of many of these organizations and societies are not now to be had, and it is not deemed best to make herein transfers from them, at best only partial.

The following facts may be noticed:

In early days, every shop, tavern, and trading-place sold whisky. In 1820, there were not less than thirteen such places in Coshocton county, then including the lower half of Holmes county, and having a population of 7,086.

In 1849 there were seven persons licensed, and some thirty indicted for selling without license.

In 1876, with a population of some 23,000, there are in the county forty-five drug-stores, saloons, etc., paying tax to the United States government on sales of liquor.

In 1856, there were two very large distilleries in Coshocton county; in 1876, none.

The first "raising" reported to have been conducted without liquors was that of John Shannon's barn, in Keene township, in 1834.

Lodges of Good Templars are at this date reported in West Bedford, Mohawk Village, and Coshocton; and Women's Leagues in Warsaw, Jacobsport, and Coshocton.

Among the more noticeable movements, we mention two, partly because the record of these was more distinctly made and can now be readily traced.

In the month of March, 1870, in the village of Coshocton, a meeting was called (and held in the Frame Presbyterian Church) to devise, if possible, some more efficient measures looking to the removal of the evils of intemperance from our community. After some discussion, it was resolved to put in the field, at the approaching spring election, a ticket pledged to pass and enforce the "McConnellsville Ordinance," as it was commonly called, or some other of similar sort. Each of the great parties had already presented its ticket. In due time, after a brief but vigorous campaign, the following "Citizens' Ticket" was elected: Mayor, Hiram Beall; Clerk, H. O. Smith; Treasurer, G. F. Cassingham; Marshal, John Taylor; Councilmen, F. E. Barney, W. S. Tidball, Wm. E. Hunt, Geo. Ross, J. S. Williams, and Josiah Glover.* The average

---

* Thomas Campbell was appointed corporation attorney, and Nicholas Tidball street commissioner.

vote for the gentlemen on this ticket was one hundred and forty-three; the total number of votes cast in the corporation that year being three hundred and fifty.

The ordinance having been passed, and vigor displayed as to the enforcement of all temperance laws, four saloons were closed entirely, and the others put under much restraint. But eminent legal ability soon discovered weak places, and the delinquents always got the benefit of them, and of doubts. The tax-payers grew restive under the expenses of trials, etc., and public sentiment, never really as to majority, but only by plurality, on the side of this movement, failed to support the movement, and in due course put into the controlling municipal places those who, while preserving the form of the ordinance, had no sympathy with its spirit.

The recent famous " Crusade," or " Prayer Work," or " Women's Whisky War," as variously termed by the journals of the day, may be said to have been commenced in Coshocton, February 15, 1874.

On the evening of that day (Sabbath) a mass meeting of " the friends of temperance" in the village of Coshocton was held in the Methodist Episcopal Church, to consider the new movement, and the propriety of inaugurating it here. The meeting was presided over by the mayor, and addressed by a number of speakers, the general drift of whose remarks was in favor of " the movement" already sweeping up from the southwestern part of the state, and immensely " written up" in the papers.

On the 21st of February (Saturday), " the visiting band " of women, led by the venerable Mrs. D. Spangler (after frequent conferences among themselves, and direct or indirect conference with those who professed that " the secret of the Lord was with them;" and who, " knew that the Lord was in this movement," and that all the pains and toils would be light when the success was achieved), began their visitation of the saloons. The day was exceedingly stormy; efforts were confined to pleading with those in the business to give it up. After some days, the prayer exercises were entered upon. Usually the ladies were allowed to come into the premises, the proprietor often, however, being out at the time. But at length the exercises were conducted upon the pavement, often in the chill March winds and amid the rain and snow. Meanwhile public meetings were held every evening, at which addresses were made by popular speakers more or less in sympathy with the work, and relations of the experience of reformed drinkers and reports of the women's work were given in. At these great crowds were present, filling the largest rooms available—the Methodist Episcopal Church, Central Hall, the Presbyterian Church, and the Opera House. Morning prayer meetings of large proportions also were held. Pledges were circulated; the newspapers and the lawyers were completely enlisted to put no hindrance in the way, but rather to help "the women," with whom, in their sorrows and general purposes, there was as yet almost universal sympathy, whatever might be thought of some of the methods. Still, no "surrenders" were made, and it was evident, possibly with a view to what followed, that larger sales than ever were being made, especially by a drug store or two, whence flasks were being largely carried out, which probably came into play when the saloons were more closely guarded, or even practically closed.

At length "pickets" were set in each drinking place or as a guard before the door. Two women, often closely blanketed and with warm bricks at the feet, sat hour after hour, until relieved by others sent out by "the officer of the day," by authority of "the League." At length, after days of uneasiness and nights of anxiety and devising, the establishment having the smallest stock and doing the smallest trade surrendered, with the understanding that the liquors should be purchased by the League or its friends, and also the U. S. internal revenue license. And then followed another and another—the liquors were poured into the gutter, the brass band played, the church and courthouse bells rang, the men shouted, the women sang and cried and prayed; the strange enthusiasm was felt in every home to greater or less extent. Then came a lull. Prosecutions, under the temperance ordinance, were now tried. Money was wanted, and came in slowly. Somehow a great deal of liquor was still drunk. Although a few hundred dollars' worth had been captured, it was known that there were thousands of dollars' worth still in the town. With little observable signs of trade—none when the pickets were around—the breath of many still had the odor of beer, or what even seemed more discouraging, whisky; because indicating a readiness to take the stimulant in even more concentrated and damaging form. One man coming out of a meat shop connected with a saloon, with a large basket exhibiting some fine beefsteaks only, he was closely watched, and was detected in distributing flasks to his thirsty old customers assembled in a hay-mow.

Curiously enough, as some thought, the establishments which had females connected with them were the most pertinacious in their rejection of all terms proposed by the League. Still the women held on, evincing the depth of their feeling and the strength of their purpose. At length more surrenders, mainly of empty barrels and old fixtures, were made. These were, in two cases, sold at auction—the proceeds to go to the proprietors.* Glasses brought five dollars a piece, and other things in similar proportion.

But now the actual results of this work, as done elsewhere, were beginning to come out in the papers. Little difficulties began to grow up inside "the League." It was apparent that some were chiefly interested in the movement from its bearing upon personal notoriety, political preferment or supposed party gain, or sexual advancement or denominational popularity. Soon there was talk about bad faith and broken pledges, of divers sorts. An election was approaching, and interest began to center in it. The temperance people were unfortunate in their selection of a ticket, and on the first Monday of April received an unmistakable blow. A few weeks later the temperance ordinance, passed by the temperance council of 1870, was "modified,"

---

* And, *it is said*, ultimately were used to enlarge and refit the establishment subsequently conducted by a relative of the former owner.

and to be brief, in six months after "the movement" was inaugurated, there were more drinking houses in Coshocton than before it was begun.

What occurred at the county seat, with slight mutations, occurred at the villages all through the county. Probably the point of most interest after Coshocton was Warsaw, which, like Coshocton, has always been a little unfortunate in having some of the meanest whisky or whisky-drinkers in the country. To their credit, be it said, that many who "signed the pledge" during this movement, are still keeping it, as some of them had done before for many months, in connection with other movements; and several of those who then relinquished the business have not since engaged in it.

Whatever results followed—whatever extravagances marked its course—no thoughtful one can deny, that in the attention aroused to the monster evils of intemperance in the discussions pertaining to it, in the more thorough instruction of the young, the crusade accomplished much good. The estimate of female influence and essential divinity may be lower. The idea that those who can not prevail with God, and over the passions and appetites of those whom they love and by whom they are loved—their fathers, husbands, brothers, and sons—to the inducing of them to give up the use of drinks, can yet without fail prevail over those, it may be, alien to them in race and religion, to resist their passion for easy living and the love of gain ("the accursed *thirst* for gold," as the poet says), may not be so generally accepted as it once was; but the crusade was no failure, in at least some important aspects. And though, with some, "distance may lend enchantment to the view," its work in Coshocton county was as effective as elsewhere, where it encountered the same conditions.

And what is true of this is also true of the many movements preceding it. People who talk of "no progress" in this great subject, must surely look out only to the narrow circle of their own personal grievances, or have queer ideas of progress. They certainly can not stand with the writer of these sketches, and see the river of fire in its tortuous flow along the years covered by this work. They would at least see indications that the springs of the river were very certainly, if gradually, losing their volume and depth of color. Even in the face of the saddening and disgraceful fact that there are in Coshocton county to-day so many drinking places and so much intemperance, no one who has studied the whole movement will say there has been no progress, unless determined to argue in advance "that the former days were better than these days." From the days that church authorities in Coshocton county must spend hour after hour in cases of discipline arising out of intemperance—from the days that a popular politician could haul a barrel of whisky to the public square, in front of the polls, and, tying a couple of tin-cups to the barrel, after knocking out the head, sing out: "Come on, boys!" there would seem to have been at least some change. From the days when every store kept liquors to the days of back rooms and screens—from the time when the use of liquors was universal to even those in which it is even very general, some progress has been made.

SECRET ORDERS.

Of the Masonic Fraternity, there are four Lodges and one R. A. Chapter in the county, viz:

Coshocton Lodge, No. 96, organized in 1846.
Samaritan R. A. Chapter, No. 50, organized 1852.
Wakatomica Lodge, No. —, West Bedford.
Plainfield Lodge, No. 224, East Plainfield, Oct. 20, 1852.
Warsaw Lodge, No. 255, Warsaw.
Clinton Lodge, No. 42, of Coshocton, suspended 1836. The Thornhill and the Roscoe Lodges also suspended.

Of the I. O. O. F., there are three Lodges and one Encampment, viz:

Coshocton Lodge, No. 44, instituted August 2, 1845;
Coshocton Encampment, No. 191, instituted July 7, 1875;
Sarah Lodge (Daughters of Rebecca), No. 25; all of Coshocton.

Bedford Lodge, No. 446, of New Bedford, instituted June 29, 1870.

There are several other Secret Associations, among which may be named:

OUARGA TRIBE, I. O. Red Men;

CRESCENT CAMP, I. O. of Knights;

COSHOCTON LODGE, Knights of Pythias; all of Coshocton.

In early days there was a famous society called the "Hoo! Hoo! Society," composed of a rollicking set of fellows. Unfortunately for the historian, all their proceedings were conducted by "a dark lantern," but it is said that getting "on the gridiron" or "riding the goat" were tame things compared with their rites and ceremonies.

CHAPTER XIX.

MISCELLANEOUS MATTERS.

1. *The Pre-Historic Race.* 2. *Ancient Burial Grounds.* 3. *Meaning of the names Muskingum, Tuscarawas, and Walhonding.* 4. *Prose Legend of the Walhonding.* 5. *Heckwelder's Famous Ride.* 6. *Temperance Crusade among the Indians.* 7. *Gnadenhutten Massacre.* 8. *Curious Stories Touching Captives Reclaimed by Colonel Boquet.* 9. *Description of Hunting-Shirt.* 10. *The House and Furniture of the Pioneers in Coshocton County.* 11. *Louis Philippe at Coshocton.* 12. *How to Raise a Large Family.* 12. *Indian Stories.* 13. *Backwoods Sports.*

THE PRE-HISTORIC RACE.

DODDRIDGE, in his "Notes on the Settlement of Western Pennsylvania and Virginia," etc., says, touching the earth forts, mounds, grave-yards, stone-hatchets, and other evidences of a race preceding the Indians:

"Most writers represent these as peculiar to America; but the fact is, they are also in Europe and Asia. Large groups of mounds are met with in many places between Moscow and St. Petersburgh, in Russia. When the people of that country are asked if they have any tradition concerning them, they answer in the negative. They suppose they are the graves of men slain in battle, but when or by whom constructed they have no knowledge. Nearly all the mounds which have been opened in Asia and America have been found to contain more or less charcoal and calcined bones. Some have thought that these mounds were used for altars for sacrifice, the offerings being the prisoners taken in battle. The great antiquity of these relics can not be questioned. A curious fact is that they are not found in any great numbers along the shores of the main oceans. This circumstance goes to show that those by whom they were made were not in the practice of navigating the great seas. That they contain nothing with even hieroglyphics is evidence of a high antiquity. Another evidence of the great age of these rude remains of antiquity is that there is not even a regular traditionary account of their origin."

Doddridge gives reasons at length for rejecting the idea that there was any considerable degree of civilization among the people making them. He is inclined to think they were of Asiatic origin, though not holding the idea that they were "the lost tribes of Israel." He is not so wild as some in his estimates of their numbers, wanting something more than one swallow to make a summer, and not familiar with or disposed to accept the processes of the modern anti-biblical "scientists," who made so much out of that tremendous "sell," the Cardiff giant, to disparage the scriptural account of man.

ANCIENT BURIAL GROUNDS.

"In the county of Coshocton, as we pass west on the Pan-Handle railroad, three miles or thereabouts from the county-seat, is seen to the right a large plain in the river bend of several hundred acres, and on the east bank of the river, a few hundred yards distant, a large mound, forty feet high, with trees thereon. In its vicinity, Zeisberger settled Lichtenau, in 1776, and he was attracted to the spot from the numerous evidences of an ancient race having been buried there, more civilized than the Indians of his day. The missionaries have left but meager details of what they there found, but enough to clearly prove that its inhabitants understood the use of the ax, the making of pottery, and division of areas of land in squares, etc. In a large graveyard, which covered many acres, human bones or skeletons were found, less in stature than the average Indian by a foot and a half. They were regularly buried in rows, heads west and feet east, as indicated by the enameled teeth in preservation, so that the disembodied spirits, on coming out of the graves, would first see the rising sun, and make their proper devotional gestures to their great Spirit or God. From approximate measurement this grave-yard contained ten acres, and has long since been plowed up and turned into corn-fields. The race of beings buried there averaged four feet in height, judging from the size of the graves and layers of ashes. Estimating that twenty bodies could be buried in a square rod, this human sepulcher, if full, would have contained over thirty thousand bodies, and the ordinary time required to fill such a grave-yard would not be less than five hundred years in a city the size of Coshocton of the present day, assuming that the generations averaged thirty-three years of life. One skeleton dug up from this grave-yard is said to have measured five and one-half feet, and the skull to have been perforated by a bullet. The body had been dismembered, and iron nails and a decayed piece of oak were found in the grave.

"On the farm of a Mr. Long, about fifteen miles southwest of St. Louis, was found, many years ago, an ancient burying-ground, containing a vast number of small graves, indicating that the country around had once been the seat of a great population of human beings of less than ordinary size, similar in every respect to those found near Coshocton. But, on opening the graves, they found the skeletons deposited in stone coffins, while those at Coshocton bore evidence of having been buried in wooden coffins. After opening many of the graves, all having in them skeletons of a pigmy race, they at length found one, as at Coshocton, denoting a full-developed, large-sized man, except in length, the legs having been cut off at the knees and placed alongside the thigh bones. From this fact many scientific men conjectured that there must have been a custom among the inhabitants of separating the bones of the body before burial, and that accounted for the small size of the graves. The skeletons, however, were reduced to white chalky ashes, and therefore it was impossible to determine whether such a custom existed or not.

"A custom is said to have existed among certain tribes of the western Indians to keep their dead unburied until the flesh separated from the bones; and when the bones became clean and white, they were buried in small coffins. The Nanticoke Indians of Maryland had a custom of exhuming their dead after some months of burial, cutting off from the bones all the flesh and burning it, then drying and wrapping the bones in clean cloths, and reburying them; and, whenever the tribe removed to new hunting-grounds, the bones of their dead were taken along. It is known that this tribe removed to Western Pennsylvania, and portions of them came to the Muskingum valley with the Shawanese. Zeisberger had two Nanticoke converts at Schoenbrunn, and one of whom (named Samuel Nanticoke) affirmed—as tradition goes—that this pigmy grave-yard at Lichtenau was their burying-ground, and contained the bones of their ancestors, carried from one place to another for many generations, and found a final resting place in these valleys, when their posterity became too weak, from the wastage of war, to remove them elsewhere."—*Mitchener's Ohio Annals.*

When the Walhonding canal was being built, a number of skeletons in the sitting posture were unearthed. On the Powelson place, just east of the town of Coshocton, a skeleton was dug up, having upon the head a curious shaped metallic cap or earthen-ware vase. It was forwarded to the Academy of Natural Sciences in Philadelphia, by Rev. Wm. E. Hunt, in 1869.

MEANING OF THE NAMES MUSKINGUM, TUSCARAWAS, AND WALHONDING.

The Tuscarawas river was long embraced with the Muskingum river, as we now call it, under the one designation—the Muskingum extending from Marietta to the headwaters in Summit county. Afterward the Tuscarawas was called the "Little Muskingum." The best accredited meaning of the name Muskingum is "Elk's Eye"—the emblem of placid, quiet beauty.

Tuscarawas, according to Heckewelder (as good authority as any in these things), means "Old Town," the oldest Indian town in South-eastern Ohio being on it near the present Bolivar.

The Walhonding is, with unvarying testimony, said to mean "The White Woman."

PROSE LEGEND OF THE WALHONDING.

Christopher Gist, when looking up lands for George Washington's Virginia Land Company, was at "White Woman's Town," January 14, 1751. He says the town (it stood near the junction of Killbuck and White Woman creeks) was so called from the fact that the ruling spirit in it was a white woman, who had been taken captive in New England, when she was not above ten years of age, by the French Indians, and had subsequently become the wife of "Eagle Feather." She is reported as having been one of the "strong-minded" of her day, and "wore the leggins." She had several children, and was even outstripping the Indian in Indian qualities. Her name was Mary Harris. According to this story, the river was named from the town. Those who prefer this account to the more poetic, and perhaps equally truthful, one given in the chapter of this work entitled "Indian Occupancy," can do so without hurting the feelings of the writer of the book, who has not talent nor time to settle conflicting Indian legends.

HECKEWELDER'S GREAT RIDE.

"There came to Goschachgünk, in the spring of 1778, some disaffected persons from Pittsburg, with Alexander McKee, Matthew Elliot, and Simon Girty—an ignoble trio of go-betweens and desperadoes.

"Soon after the arrival of this party, a second appeared, consisting of a sergeant and twenty privates, deserters from the fort, who joined the British Indians. These men all vied one with another in spreading falsehoods among the Delawares. The Americans, they said, had been totally defeated in the Atlantic States; driven westward, they were now about to wage an indiscriminate war against the Indians. Such reports produced a general excitement in the nation. Captain Pipe, who had been eagerly watching for an opportunity to supplant White Eyes, and overthrow the policy of the council, hastened to the capital, called upon his countrymen to seize the hatchet, and defend their homes. Who would venture to prate of treaties now?

White Eyes barely succeeded in having the declaration of war postponed for ten days, that time might be given to ascertain whether the reports were true or false. But this did not hinder preparations for the conflict. Goschachgünk rang with the war-song; rifles were cleaned and tomahawks sharpened. In order to prevent the rising of this nation and its numerous grandchildren, peace-messages must at once be sent to Goschachgünk. Such messages were prepared, but not a runner could be induced to take them. General Hand's offers of the most liberal rewards were all in vain; the risk was too great.

"In this emergency, Heckewelder and Schebosh volunteered their services. Riding three days and two nights without stopping, except to feed their horses, in constant danger from the war-parties that lurked in the forests, they reached Gnaddenhütten an hour before midnight of the fifth of April. The next day was the ninth of the stipulated term. No contradiction of the reports spread by Girty and his confederates had been received. War was accepted as a necessity even by White Eyes. Of that crisis John Heckewelder was the illustrious hero. Although scarcely able any longer to sit upon his horse, and although it was at the risk of his life, he pressed on after but a brief rest, accompanied by John Martin, a native assistant, and got to Goschachgünk at ten o'clock in the morning. The whole population turned out to meet him, but their faces were dark and sinister. There was no welcome given. Not a single Delaware reciprocated his greetings. He extended his hand to White Eyes, but even White Eyes stepped back.

"Holding aloft the written speeches of which he was the bearer, Heckewelder addressed the Indians from his horse. He told them that they had been deceived; that the Americans, instead of being defeated in the Atlantic States, had gained a great victory, and forced Burgoyne and his whole army to surrender; and that, so far from making war upon the Delawares, they were their friends, and had sent him to establish a new alliance. Such news brought about a sudden change in the aspect of affairs. A council was called; the missives of General Hand were delivered and accepted in due form; the warlike preparations ceased; and, while Captain Pipe and his adherents left the town in great chagrin, the instigators of this whole plot fled to more congenial tribes."—From *De Schweinitz's Life and Times of Zeisberger.*

A TEMPERANCE CRUSADE AMONG THE INDIANS.

"In the year 1773, Rev. David Jones, a Baptist minister, was sent out from Philadelphia city to the Scioto and Muskingum valleys, with the view of establishing a mission. On arriving at Schoenbrunn he found Zeisberger had planted his colonies along the Tuscarawas, and as they gave evidence of success, Jones proceeded on south and spent some time among the Shawanese, but found no encouragement for a mission among them. He, therefore, returned up the Tuscarawas valley to New Comerstown, in the vicinity of the present town of that name. Here the Indians were having a great feast and dance, in which whisky, procured from traders, was the principal performer. Under its influence they refused Jones permission to preach, shut him up in one of their huts, and put a guard around him, and some proposed to kill him; but one of the chiefs, called Gelelemend, or Killbuck, interfered and saved his life.

"After the Indian feast was over they listened to the preacher, and he, having spoken much against the use of whisky, made such an impression on the mind of the chief Killbuck, that he became a convert then, and was ever afterward opposed to its use. While Jones remained at " the New Comerstown," Killbuck destroyed all the liquor on hand, and notified the traders that if they brought any more whisky among the Indians they (the traders) would be scalped. This aroused their enmity against the preacher, and threats being again made by some of the drinking Indians against his life, the chief had him escorted up the river to Gnadenhutten settlement, and from there to Schoenbrunn, from which place the Delawares saw him safe to Fort Pitt, it being midwinter, and the snow, as Jones states in his journal, some four to five feet deep."—*Mitchener's Ohio Annals.*

THE GNADENHUTTEN MASSACRE.

Although this was not an event taking place in Coshocton county, yet as some of the ancestors of the settlers in Coshocton county had to do with it, and the occurrence bore important relations to the Indians whose cherished seat was once in Coshocton county, and to the settlement of the county, a brief account is here given.

In 1781, the Moravian Indians were required to abandon the Tuscarawas valley mission stations and repair to Detroit. Amid the rigors of the winter they were taken to Sandusky and there held for a time. A scarcity of provisions was, however, soon felt in the new location, and in February, 1782, about a hundred and fifty of the Indians returned from the Sandusky region to the Tuscarawas region to get supplies of corn which had been raised the season before, and left in the field unhusked. While they were husking and gathering the corn they took up their residence again in Gnadenhutten and Salem.

Meanwhile the settlers in Western Pennsylvania were experiencing some great outrages at the hands of some redskins. A band had attacked the home of a man named Wallace, murdered his wife and five children, impaling one of the children with its face toward the settlements and its belly toward the Indian country, and had carried off John Carpenter as a prisoner. In the latter part of 1781, the militia of the frontier came to a determination to break up the Moravian villages on the Tuscarawas. For this purpose, a detachment of men, under the command of Colonel Williamson, avowing only the determination to make the Indians move further away or taking them prisoners to Fort Pitt. When they reached Gnadenhutten they found but few Indians, the removal of most of them to Sandusky having already been effected. A few were captured and taken to Fort Pitt and delivered to the commandant there, who, after a short detention, sent them home again. This procedure greatly displeased the settlers, who were demanding a more vigorous policy. Colonel Williamson, hitherto a very popular man, was losing his place of honor among the frontiersmen. At length, in February, 1782, a new expedition under his command set out. This was gathered under the impulse of stories that the Indians released by the commandant at Fort Pitt had, the night after they were liberated, crossed the Ohio and killed a family by the name of Monteur; that an Indian who had been captured after the killing of a family on Buffalo creek had reported that the leader of the band was a Moravian. Williamson's expedition reached the Tuscarawas valley on the 7th of March. Upon pretense of friendly council, and only with the purpose of arranging for the greater peace and prosperity, and especially to take some steps so as to relieve them from their unpleasant situation as between "two fires," of bad Indians and vengeful whites, the corn-gatherers were all called in and actually made prisoners.

The militia now tried to criminate the Indians, charging that despite their peaceful professions they were warriors, and had taken part in the war against the Americans; that they had harbored and fed, in their towns, British Indians on their march to the American frontiers; that their horses were, many of them, stolen; that their houses, in their appliances, and their clothing gave evidence that they had helped to plunder the farms and attack the settlements; that, at any rate, they kept a half-way house for marauding Indians and received stolen goods.

The prisoners appealed to the knowledge of the soldiers themselves as to the general public friendship for the whites; to the efforts they had made successfully for years to keep the nation of which they were part from joining with the British Indians; they explained the necessity which compelled them to entertain British Indians, but showed that they had, at the same time, persuaded many a war-party to turn back; and, further, that when the American general, Brodhead, had come into their country, on his expedition against Goschachgunk, they had furnished his army too with provisions; they admitted often receiving articles of clothing and utensils from other Indians for entertainment; and reminded their captors that they were civilized Indians, dressing like the whites, working their horses like them, and using the same household utensils, mechanical tools, and agricultural implements.

But these explanations were not accepted. A council of war was held. The officers, unwilling to assume the responsibility, agreed to submit the question to the men. They were, accordingly, drawn up in line; Colonel Williamson stepped forward, saying: "Shall the Moravian Indians be taken prisoners to Pittsburgh or put to death? All those in favor of sparing their lives advance one step and form a second rank." Thereupon sixteen (some reports say eighteen) men stepped out of line, leaving an immense majority for the sentence of death.

The mode of execution then created some debate. It was at one time proposed to set fire to the houses in which the captives were and roast them alive; but it was finally determined to kill them and get their scalps as trophies of the campaign. On the 8th of March, the captives (twenty-nine men, twenty-seven women, and thirty-four children) were placed in the "slaughter-houses," as they were designated—the males in one, the females in another—and then butchered with tomahawks, mallets, war-clubs, spears, and scalping-knives. Only a part of the militia were engaged in this dreadful work. Others were gathering up the plunder and making preparations for the march to another town. After the massacre all the houses of the village were burned. The Indians in the second town got timely alarm and fled. Two lads escaped—the one having received a blow that only stunned him, and the other having been scalped. The whole number killed was ninety.

The Rev. Philip Doddridge, a Presbyterian minister, who lived in Western Virginia, where many of Williamson's troops lived, speaking of this massacre, says:

"Should it be asked what sort of people composed the band of murderers of these unfortunate people, I answer that they were not miscreants and vagabonds. Many of them were men of the first standing in the country—many of them men who had recently lost relations by the hands of the savages. Several of the latter class found in the houses of the murderers articles which had been plundered from their own houses, or those of their relations. One man, it is said, found the clothes of his wife and children who had been murdered by the Indians a few days before; yet there was no unequivocal evidence that these people had any direct agency in the war. Whatever of property was found with them had been left by the warriors from the regions beyond in exchange for provisions. When attacked by our people they might have defended themselves, but they did not. They never fired a single shot. They were prisoners, and had been promised protection. Every dictate of justice and humanity required that their lives should be spared. The complaint of their villages being half-way houses, if well founded, was at an end, because the people had been removed to Sandusky the fall before. It was, therefore, an atrocious and unqualified murder. But by whom committed? By a majority of the campaign? For the honor of my country, I hope I may safely answer this question in the negative. It was one of those convulsions of the moral state of society in which the voice of the justice and humanity of the majority is silenced by the clamor and violence of a real minority. Very few of our men imbrued their hands in the blood of the Moravians. Even those who had not voted for saving their lives, retired from the scene of slaughter with horror and disgust. Why then did they not give their votes in their favor? The fear of public indignation restrained them from doing so. They thought well, but had not heroism enough to express their opinion. In justice to the memory of Colonel Williamson, I have to say that, although at that time very young, I was personally acquainted with him, and from my recollection I say that he was a brave man, but not cruel. Had he possessed the authority of a superior officer in the regular army, I do not believe that a single Moravian Indian would have lost his life. But he possessed no such authority. He was only a militia officer, who could advise, but not command. His only fault was a too easy compliance with popular opinion and popular prejudice. On this account his memory has been loaded with unmerited reproach."

In the summer of 1872 (some ninety years after the massacre), ten thousand citizens of the Tuscarawas valley assembled at Gnadenhutten to witness the unveiling of a handsome monument erected through the efforts of the "Gnadenhutten Monument Society" to the memory of the Christian Indians who fell the unresisting victims of the Williamson expedition.

After some excellent music by an immense band of trained singers, accompanied by instrumental music, the Rev. Dr. De Schweinitz, Bishop of the Moravian Church of Bethlehem, Pennsylvania, delivered an oration of rich historic interest and rare beauty of expression.

At the close of the oration, amid music of suitable sort, four Indians of the Delaware tribe, two of them lineal descendants of the massacred Indians, stripped the canvas, and exposed to full view the monument. This is of gray stone, with base and die and shaft, in all about thirty-five feet high. On the die is the inscription: "Here perished ninety Christian Indians in 1782," and on the base the simple legend, "Gnadenhutten."

The assembly having been dismissed for dinner (basket and otherwise), was again summoned to the stand, and the exercises of the afternoon opened by a hymn in the Delaware language, sung by the Indians and their missionary, the Rev. Mr. Riennecke, from Canada.

Brief addresses were made by Mr. Riennecke and each of the Indians, and Rev. Wm. E. Hunt, Presbyterian minister from Coshocton, Ohio, made a few remarks congratulating the Monument Society upon the accomplishment of its work, declaring that the monument belonged to the whole Christian world, and would not only commemorate the Christian virtues of the deceased, but speak to all coming generations of the undying fame of all who do and suffer for the Master.

After a few remarks by Rev. Mr. Harmon, pastor at Gnadenhutten, the benediction was pronounced by Bishop De Schweinitz, and the assembly thus dismissed.

Among those present were many of the dignitaries of the Moravian Church, such as Bishop De Schweinitz and his brothers Francis and Mier, Dr. Riennecke, the Wollfe brothers, and others; but the thousands present witnessed the interest of the whole people of the Tuscarawas valley, and especially those of classic and Christian taste and feeling, in the secluded spot now marked so unmistakably, and even hitherto well known, by all interested in the annals of heroism and the legends of the Christian faith.

CURIOUS STORIES TOUCHING CAPTIVES RECLAIMED BY BOUQUET.

Sherman Day's History of Pennsylvania gives the following curious facts :

"Among the captive children surrendered to Colonel Bouquet, at the 'Forks of the Muskingum,' was one whom no one claimed at the time the people were summoned to the fort for the purpose of identifying and reclaiming their lost ones, and whose after-history is full of romance. In 1756, the wife and child of a Mr. John Gray, living near Carlisle, Pennsylvania, had been taken by the Indians. When Gray died, he willed one-half of his farm to his wife, and the other half to his child, in case they should ever return from captivity. The wife soon got away from the savages, returned home, and, finding her husband's will, proved it, and took possession of the farm. She went to look for her daughter among the Bouquet captives, but, failing to recognize her, was persuaded to claim as the missing daughter the unclaimed little girl above spoken of, and thus secure the whole farm. Taking her home with her, she brought up the strange child as if her own, carefully keeping the secret. The girl grew up as the daughter of John Gray, married a man named Gillespie, and took the Gray estate. This changed hands several times up to the year 1789, when some of the collateral heirs of John Gray obtaining information about the spurious Jane Gray, commenced suits to recover the land, being some four hundred acres of the best land in Mifflin county, Pennsylvania. After legal contests, running through forty-four years, the case was disposed of against the reputed daughter, and the property reverted to the brothers and sisters of the original John Gray.

"At the time of the reclamation, one woman failing to recognize her lost child was lamenting her loss, and telling how she continued still to sing every evening the favorite hymn of the lost child. 'Sing it now,' said the sympathizing officer, and she sang:

> ' Alone, yet not alone am I,
> Though in this solitude so drear ;
> I feel my Savior always nigh,
> He comes my every hour to cheer.'

"She had sung thus far, when the daughter, having her sight quickened by the old sound, rushed forward, and the joy of the restoration was complete."

DESCRIPTION OF THE HUNTING-SHIRT.

Among the earliest settlers of Coshocton county, as elsewhere in the West at the same time, the hunting-shirt was almost universally worn. For the information of our younger readers, we append a description:

"This garment was a kind of loose frock, reaching half way down the thighs, with large sleeves, open before, and so wide as to lap over a foot or more when belted. The cape was large, and sometimes handsomely fringed with a raveled piece of cloth of a different color from that of the hunting-shirt itself. The bosom of this dress served as a wallet to hold a chunk of bread, cakes, jirk, tow for wiping the barrel of the rifle, or any other necessary for the hunter or warrior. The belt, which was always tied behind, answered several purposes, besides that of holding the dress together. In cold weather the mittens, and sometimes the bullet-bag, occupied the front part of it. To the right side was suspended the tomahawk, and to the left the scalping-knife in its leathern sheath. The hunting-shirt was generally made of linsey, sometimes of coarse linen, and a few of dressed deer-skins. These last were very cold and uncomfortable in wet weather."—*Doddridge's Notes.*

THE HOUSES AND FURNITURE OF THE PIONEERS OF COSHOCTON COUNTY.

The house was built of logs laid one upon another, all being notched, so that the end and side logs would hold each to the other. The roof was made out of boards split out of short blocks or pieces of logs, called "clap-boards." The cracks between the logs were stopped with clay. A door was made by sawing or cutting the logs on one side of the house, so as to make an opening about three feet wide. The opening was secured by upright pieces of timber, three inches thick, into which holes were bored into the ends of the logs, for the purpose of pinning them fast, and helping to keep the logs in their place. The door was made of clap-boards, such as were on the roof. At one end was the fire-place, made of a few stones, and the chimney, formed of sticks daubed over with mud. There was a little opening that could be covered by a board for a window, or sometimes an opening covered over with a piece of greased-paper or rag.

As to the furniture, there was a table made by splitting a log and putting some sticks for feet on the rounded side. A few chairs were sometimes made in the same way. Some wooden-pins were driven into the logs, whereon to lay clap-boards for shelves for dishes, etc. A forked-stick was set in the floor, which was either made of split-logs, called "puncheons" or of earth, and into the fork of this one end of a stick was put, the other going into the log in the side of the house. Upon the rest thus made some sticks were placed, the other end of them going in between the logs which formed the wall of the house. Into these wall-logs were driven a few wooden-pins, whereon were hung the gowns of linsey belonging to the women, and the hunting-shirts of the men. Usually two small forks or bucks' horns were fastened up, whereon rested the rifle and shot-pouch, etc. Not a nail nor a piece of glass was anywhere used. A wooden latch for the door was made, and a string of leather or flax ran through a hole in the door to the outside, and when "outsiders" were not wanted this string was pulled in. The "latch-string out" was thus the sign of hospitality. The table-ware consisted of a few earthenware or pewter dishes, and an iron pot or skillet, or both, and some wooden bowls or trenchers, or perhaps a few gourds, made up the kitchen and table furniture. A hand-mill or a mortar and pestle to prepare the grain for cooking was a housekeeping utensil found in some families, but many did not command these, and one served sometimes for several neighbors. The most "fore-handed" men that came into the county had for some years little or nothing better than these things.

LOUIS PHILIPPE AT COSHOCTON.

Among the accepted traditions of Coshocton is one that old Colonel Williams kicked out of his tavern the above-named famous Frenchman, who, having been compelled to flee his own country, was traveling in America about the close of the last century.

Louis was on the throne when G. W. Silliman visited Paris, and he reported upon his return that the king, in an interview, had spoken of his travels in the Western country, and stated that he had been very shabbily treated at a tavern at the forks of a river, whose landlord was described in such way as to satisfy Silliman that it must have been Williams.

The latter, upon being spoken to, said he remembered the circumstance. That Louis had complained of the accommodations as very unbefitting a king, and that he had informed him that all the people in this country were sovereigns, and that, if he did not like what satisfied them, he could get out of the house, and he would help him out, as he then did, with the toe of his boot.

It is said, however, that, as a historical fact, Louis Philippe was on shipboard, on his way back to France, before Williams kept any tavern at the forks.

In later years, there was living in Coshocton a somewhat famous character, who, when in liquor, always fancied himself "Andrew Jackson." It may have been that Williams' French king was a man of the same style.

People who fancy that the importance of either Williams or the town may be increased thereby can still "hold the tradition," and possibly find some way of removing the little anachronism alleged in the case.

HOW TO RAISE A LARGE FAMILY.

One of the "old settlers," who had reared a very large family, though a comparatively very poor man, was asked how in the world he had done it. "No trouble at all," said the old man. "Commenced with a pot of mush, and as each child came, just put in a little more water and gave a few more stirs."

INDIAN STORIES.

"Indian stories," among many of the old settlers, were largely the stock in trade. A man was not much in the old-time bar-rooms, who could not tell some tall stories.

The fact is thoroughly established that after 1795 there were very few Indians within the territory afterward embraced in Coshocton county. In Tuscarawas county, some years later, there were some of the Christian Indians; but such as were found in the region of Coshocton were straggling bands, or sellers of game, or individual strollers.

For thirty years before 1795 the whites had been seeking to occupy the land, and the Indians struggling to maintain their hold; and about that time the whole upper Muskingum valley and the Tuscarawas valley were almost uninhabited, the two races having scourged each other out of them.

Despite all this, stories were told of how frightened the wives and children of the first settlers were, who could hear at night the Indians prowling about the huts and cabins in which they were sleeping.

One of the old fellows, who attached great importance to Indian experiences, was once, when somewhat set up with liquor, relating some wonderful things, when some one, interrupting him, asked him if there were many Indians in the county when he came into it. Eying his questioner sharply, he answered, "Indians plenty! I guess there were. Why, when I came, if a man got off the canal-boat and took a few steps into the woods, he would get shot just full of arrows." This a quarter of a century after the Indians were all removed!

BACKWOODS SPORTS.

In "house raisings," "corn huskings," "fox hunts," and "rifle matches," the early settlers, who had no special interest in horse races or "fisticuffs," found largely their amusements. In some parts of the county, a custom prevailed in relation to observing Christmas and New Year's day that has been thus reported:

The country around was wild, and but little cultivated. A rifle was an indispensable article for house-keeeping, even before the hewed-out log cradle, or the harrow made by taking a forked stick and driving some wooden pins in it. On the days above named, thirty or forty "neighbors" would come together, some of them coming for twenty miles, and, as noiselessly as possible, getting in a circle around a previously selected house, about two or three o'clock in the morning, they would all fire their rifles and simultaneously give a yell. The sequel of the matter was they were all invited into the house and furnished with something hot to eat or drink.

If our readers do not think they would have enjoyed that kind of sport, perhaps they might have enjoyed the following:

Weddings were big things in the pioneer days. The "neighbors" for twenty miles around would commonly be invited. The understanding was that those coming in by certain roads would gather at a designated place on each road, about two miles from where the wedding was to take place. And then for a race!

The mother of the groom was provided in advance with a supply of bottles of whisky, and as the foremost of the horsemen on each road came in he was presented by her with a bottle, and an elegant ruffler was placed upon the horse's neck, ornamented also with gay-colored ribbons. When the horsemen were all in, the hills echoed and re-echoed the shouts of the people, who were braced for this by copious draughts from the bottles.

In the earlier days the amusements may have had more of what is now called "coarseness" than some of the modern ones, but then they were generally more health-promoting, and, according to every testimony, full as "clean" as the latter.

Elements of evil could readily be found in either, and those not less than these had their true character beneath the exterior.

It is certain the social life of the people was not less joysome than now. For a few years, there were not apples enough in the county for "a bee," but they after a time had a place.

In the townships largely peopled by New Englanders and Western Pennsylvanians, the singing-school afforded the diversion as well as often something better.

And then "sparking" was much in vogue—just the thing for a new country—said, indeed, to have originated there. The process was readily learned, generally practiced, and so familiar that old people never stop to inquire about it, but very young do, and for these let it be told how it was done.

The log houses in those days, it will be remembered, had but one room, or, if more, commonly but one with a fireplace. Bed time came, and the children crawled up a ladder into the loft; the old folks went to bed in a quiet way in one corner of the room. The wood fire has been glowing and cracking all through the evening, but has pretty well burned out, and, "for sake of the old people," the fragments are drawn together and slightly covered over with ashes, and thenceforth there is only a dull red glow, with now and then a "spark" springing with a slight snap from the wood. Now was the time for the bashful lover and coy maiden, and then were carried on the love affairs, designated in one locality and set "sparking," and in another "courting," and in another "paying and receiving attentions," but, in one phrase or another, everywhere readily recognized and approved.

CHAPTER XX.

MISCELLANEOUS MATTERS.

1. *The Killing of Cartmill, "the Post-Boy."* 2. *Shocking Murders in Coshocton County.* 3. *Colored People in Coshocton County.* 4. *Fires in Roscoe—An Incident and a Joke.* 5. *A Bundle of First Things.* 6. *Relics and Curiosities in Personal Possession.* 7. *Coshocton Wags in Early Days.* 8. *The Treasury Robbery.* 9. *Humor of the Crusade.*

THE MURDER OF WILLIAM CARTMILL, THE POST-BOY.

The whole Tuscarawas valley was excited in 1825 by the murder of William Cartmill. He was shot from his horse, while carrying the mail, at a point just beyond the line of Coshocton county, in what in those days was called "the Wilderness," near by a station on the Marietta and Cleveland railroad, a few miles south of New Comerstown, now called Post Boy. Cartmill was a resident of Coshocton, a brother of Mrs. Richards, who died January, 1876. John Smeltzer, a trader of Coshocton, who had taken a drove of horses on east, was, at the time, on the road some miles behind the post-boy; and it has always been the idea of many people in Coshocton that the assassin mistook his man, and, when killing the mail-carrier, supposed he was shooting Smeltzer, and would get a considerable part of the price of the drove of horses sold by him. A man named Johnson, out hunting, was the first to discover Cartmell, and declared he was drawn to the spot by hearing the crack of a rifle. The mail-bag was rifled. The neighbors aroused by Johnson arrested him, and he was put into jail in New Philadelphia. The foot-prints on the ground just at the spot where the murder was committed were subsequently measured, and did not tally at all with those made by him. While still in jail, he told the sheriff that he had just caught a glimpse of the murderer as he glided into the woods, and thought he would recognize him if he should see the man again. The entire male population of the locality where the crime was committed were requested to meet at the jail at a time appointed; and they having done so, Johnson carefully scanned each one, and finally selected out of the crowd one John Funston, declaring "that is the man." Funston at once sharply answered him, "You are a liar." He was, however, put into jail, and, after a trial and conviction, confessed the crime.

The murder took place on the 9th of September, 1825, and the execution upon the gallows in New Philadelphia was on the 28th of December in the same year. Of course Johnson was released.

The horse which Cartmill rode belonged to T. L. Rue, and J. W. Rue, of Coshocton, made a business trip on it the same Fall to Cincinnati.

By the way, Cartmill's sister, mentioned in the foregoing, had a very peculiar experience in relation to the violent deaths of no less than three of her near family connections. Her brother's case is given above. Her first husband, John Markley, was killed on election day in 1816, at Coshocton, by a stab from the hands of a man with whom he had an altercation, and who came upon him unawares and escaped. Her son by her second marriage, Joseph K. Richards, had been in a saloon, and some words had passed between him and a man named Ward. Richards had left the place and crossed the street, when an injury was received (either from a stone thrown, or as a consequence of a fall directly after being hit with the stone), that caused his death. This occurred in the fall of 1868.

SHOCKING MURDERS IN COSHOCTON COUNTY.

It is perhaps not best to keep fresh the recollection of those sad manifestations of the weakness and wickedness of human nature which have come out in great crimes. Of course Coshocton county has not been without its share of these things. Some of them committed under the influence of drink, and others growing out of family difficulties based upon jealousy, or unexpectedly arising out of some broil, to the after grief of those having part in them, we may well pass by. And yet they all may be useful to teach a community that extravagant and unregulated passion of any kind is a root full of cost and curse of every kind. One thing is noticeable, and that is this, that although numerous persons have been indicted for murder in the first degree, there has never yet been a case of capital punishment.

George Arnold and John Markley having previously had one or more altercations, the former, on an election day in 1816, in Coshocton, approached stealthily and plunged a knife into the latter, causing his death in a little while. Arnold's reputation as a "rough" was so great, and the confused amazement of the bystanders so great, that he was allowed to escape, never more to be heard of in "these parts." This having been the first shocking murder committed in the county, made an impression not yet effaced nor overshadowed by occurrences of later date.

In the estimate among horrors, perhaps no case has gone beyond that of the Mrs. Wade murder.

At the March (1849) term of the Court of Common Pleas John Gearhart was tried for murder in the killing of one Matilda Wade on the 28th day of September, 1848. Richard Stillwell, president judge, and B. R. Shaw, Sam'l Elliott, and James Le Retilley, associate judges, were on the bench. Thomas Campbell was prosecuting attorney, and William Sample, Esq., assisted in the prosecution. The defendant's attorneys were David Spangler, J. C. Tidball, and James Matthews. The grand jury at the October (1848) term had indicted him for murder in the first degree, James Moore, of Jefferson township, being the foreman. The petit jury were Joel Glover, D. W. Burt, Samuel Winklepleck, John Carnahan, Abraham T. Jones, Thomas Boggs, Daniel Forker, S. C. Crichfield, Joshua Clark, James Whittaker, Stephen Donley, and Andrew Ferguson.

The proof showed that Mrs. Wade, the wife of a druggist in Roscoe, was doing some washing for herself in the basement or cellar of the hotel where she was boarding. In a little time she was missed, and blood was found where she had been at work. Her husband was sent for, and, as there was an unused cistern near where she had been washing, and traces of blood to it, he was let down into it, and found his wife at the bottom. She was drawn up, and it was found that her head had been nearly severed from the body. The defendant had been employed to tend the stables and chop wood, etc., and was seen, a few minutes before the woman was found, whetting his axe. Upon this axe and upon the defendant's clothing blood was found. The plea on the trial was " not guilty "—the line of defense " insanity." The jury convicted of murder in the second degree. Gearhart was sentenced to the penitentiary for life. He died with cholera about three months after being placed in the penitentiary.

The killing of Abraham Wertheimer, and the trial and conviction of Frank Ept therefor, are still fresh in the minds of our citizens.

On the morning of November 21 (Sabbath), 1875, Isaac Wertheimer, a clothing merchant in Coshocton, was called on at his house by a friend, who stated that he had failed to secure some needed articles of wearing apparel the night before, and would like to have him go with him to the store. W. asked him why he himself had not gone to the store, observing that his son Abraham was sleeping there, and could have attended to the matter. The reply was he had been there, but could get no response. Impressed with the idea that something might be amiss, the father speedily accompanied the man, and, upon entering the store, the body of young Wertheimer (twenty years of age), weltering in gore, and evidently dead some hours, was discovered on the couch he was accustomed to sleep on. Alarm was given, and in a little time the excited crowd became firm in the conviction that the murder had been committed by a journeyman tailor named Frank Ept, who was missing. It was learned that a fast train, which usually went east about two o'clock in the morning, had been behind time that morning, not being in Coshocton until eight, and chances of escape by railroad had probably failed the culprit. Patrols were sent out in every direction, and the whole country aroused. Late in the afternoon, word came of the capture of the supposed murderer near Port Washington, in Tuscarawas county, twenty-two miles east of Coshocton, near the line of the railroad; and about dusk, amid the intensest excitement of an immense crowd gathered about the doors of the jail, Ept was lodged in it.

At the February (1876) term of the Court of Common Pleas, a grand jury, composed of the following persons, viz.: John McFarland, New Castle township; Benton Clark, Jackson township; William Biggs, of same township; Daniel McConnell, of Washington; Henry Schmueser, of Franklin; Henry N. Shaw, of Tuscarawas; Oliver Crawford, of Crawford; Thomas Martin, of Franklin; E. C. Haight, of Jackson; John Seitzer, of Oxford; Thomas Smailes, of Virginia; John Mulligan, of Tuscarawas; James B. Heslip, of Linton; L. J. Bonnell, of Tuscarawas; and Waldo Adams, of same township (Henry Schmueser being the foreman), indicted Ept for murder in the first degree, the return being made February 11, 1876. On the 22nd of February, the judge (Wm. Reed) appointed Wm. Sample and R. M. Voorhees, Esquires, to act as attorneys for the accused, who was arraigned on the 26th, and plead not guilty. The case was continued until the May term. A special jury, consisting of Geo. Stringfellow, of Tiverton township; Abraham Weatherwax, of Clark; John Johnson, of Bedford; Daniel Fair, of Clark; R. W. Thompson, of Keene; Laban Headington, of Clark; Highland Wright, of Virginia; Moses Finley, of Virginia; F. W. Powell, of Adams; James Workman, of Tiverton; Willard Nichols, of White Eyes; and Robert Doak, of Crawford, were sworn May 5, 1876. The court-room was crowded during the whole trial, ending with a verdict of guilty of murder in the first degree, on Sabbath morning, May 14, 1876, at nine o'clock. W. S. Crowell, Esq., prosecuting attorney, was assisted by John D. Nicholas, Esq.

The testimony showed Ept (native of Bavaria, born in 1842, having been some three years in this country, having father and mother and other relatives in Columbus, Ohio) to have been working for some time with Isaac Wertheimer; to have gained access to the store on the fatal night by a plea of being sick; to have killed young Wertheimer with a dull hatchet and tailor's goose; to have tried to break open the safe; to have packed up a good supply of fine clothing in a new satchel, along with the bloody tailor's goose; to have taken the watch and revolver, etc., of young Wertheimer; to have left the store and gone up to the railroad about the time the fast train was due, and to have stealthily pursued his way along and near the railroad track until his capture, which was effected by John Bolton, James Reed, and Isaac Mulatt, all of Coshocton. The defence set up was insanity—"homicidal mania."

Sentence was pronounced by Judge Reed, on May 24th, fixing the 29th of September, 1876, as the day for execution by the gallows.

COLORED PEOPLE IN COSHOCTON COUNTY.

Pryor Foster was the first colored man of note in Coshocton county. He was the reputed agent of the "Underground Railroad." About 1839, several "fugitives" stopped with him on their way to Canada. The United States officers were in hot pursuit, but Foster and those in sympathy with him, or so far respecting him individually that they would not involve him in trouble, fixed matters, so that for a time they were safe, lodging the fugitives among some rocks up the Walhonding. They were, however, ultimately recaptured and taken south.

Several of the old families from Virginia were followed to their new homes, in the north-western territory, by some of their servants. The Robinsons had two or three; the Darlings brought one; and "Aunt Letty Thomas" came with the Simmons family. The latter was for many years at service, and afterward kept a boarding-house. She started an eating-house in 1855, for the railroad at Coshocton (then the principal eating station), and made it a favorite place for the hands and passengers. The business proved profitable, and she enlarged and extended the building until it was substantially the "Hackinson House" of to-day. She removed to Oberlin, and later to Washington City. The Waring family came in at an early day from near Richmond, Virginia, settled on Killbuck, and, by their becoming conduct, long enjoyed the esteem of the whole community. One of the young men studied at Wilberforce University at Xenia, and became quite a successful teacher in Ohio and among the freedmen in Tennessee. In 1855, the only colored people in the county were the Warings and Aunt Letty Thomas' family. In 1876, there were about thirty. Old Mr. Darling set up, on a farm in Knox county, the colored man who came in with him, but he did not do well. An effort was made to "abduct" those who had come in with the Robinsons, and place them in bondage in Kentucky. But in some unaccountable way (their captors claimed not by them), they were shot at Chillicothe. This was not long after they had first come to the county. C. Dorsey was the first of his race to do jury duty—served in a corporation case, 1875.

FIRES IN ROSCOE; AN INCIDENT AND A JOKE TOUCHING IT.

Roscoe has had a noticeable experience in the matter of fires. The store of D. L. Triplett, the brick hotel adjoining, the "Union Flouring Mill" in the lower part of the town, the M. E. church, the brick hotel (standing where the Hutchins House now is), and other buildings in the central part, the Roscoe Flouring Mill, two woolen factories, and the distillery in the upper part of the town, are readily recalled as among the chief conflagrations. By the way, it is said that when the distillery burned, one of the most prominent temperance men in all the region was most vigorously at work, with coat off, to stay the ravages of the fire. Some one twitting him afterward about this, he claimed that after all he had been thoroughly consistent, for his main efforts had been directed to saving the *water wheel*!

A BUNDLE OF FIRST THINGS.

The first marriage in Coshocton county was that of John Hershman and Elizabeth Baker, by William Whitten, J. P., in Coshocton, May 1, 1812.

The first white child born on the territory now in Coshocton county, or, at all events, among the white settlers, was Joseph Evans, a son of Isaac Evans, born October 3, 1801. He grew up to manhood, and spent most of his life in the county as a farmer and a canal-boat captain. He removed to Illinois in 1853, and died August 23, 1867. His son, Isaac Evans, lives in Peoria, Ill., having as his wife the great-grand-daughter of an old neighbor of his grandfather, Phebe Wagoner.

The first brick house built in Coshocton was that at the northeast corner of Second and Chestnut streets. The first in Roscoe was built by Theophilus Phillips, and used as a hotel, as was also the one in Coshocton. These houses were both as good in their day as the " Price House," in Coshocton, of to-day, with its three stories and handsome one hundred feet front.*

The first bell in the county was the one now on the courthouse, bought in 1834. When the canal-boat bringing it got within the county the captain commenced to ring it, and continued to do so at intervals until Roscoe was reached, where a vast and pleased crowd greeted it. The bell was bought for the commissioners in Troy, N. Y., by W. K. Johnson, and cost $131.

The first coal-burning cooking-stove used in the county was set up by William Tidball in 1856, when opening what is now the " City Hotel," in Coshocton. By the way, Mr. Tidball himself is almost old enough to find a place among "first things," being now ninety-five years of age. He was born in Alleghany county, Pa., and spent the active years of his life in Holmes county. He had a good deal of enterprise for an old man when he set up that stove.

---

* Erected in 1875 by the Coshocton Planing Mill Company, corner of Sixth and Walnut streets, at a cost of $20,000.

RELICS AND CURIOSITIES IN PERSONAL POSSESSION.

John Burt, of Coshocton, has a watch (tortoise-shell, bound with gold case) belonging to his grand-father (Foght). It was carried by the elder gentleman through the Revolutionary war.

"Aunty" Hay, near Coshocton, has a bible brought from Ireland, more than a hundred years old.

J. W. Rue, of Coshocton, has two books—saved from his father's library when it was burned—one a hundred and fifty and the other two hundred years old.

F. W. Thornhill has a doctor's lance, with which a surgeon in the Revolutionary war used to bleed the patriots and the Hessian prisoners.

M. L. Norris, near Coshocton, has a padlock-key, picked up in Chicago, which *he* avers is the one that locked the door of the stable in which Mrs. O'Leary was milking the cow that kicked over the lamp that started "the great fire."

T. C. Ricketts has the set of books kept in his father's store from 1819 on for some years. John Smeltzer is understood to have been the book-keeper. The penmanship is admirable; the ink was good. The accounts show that somebody used a good deal of whisky in the days of the forefathers. Some of the customers came all the way from near Millersburg, in what now is Holmes county, after a quart, paying only twelve and one-half cents for it. The election and muster days can be readily discerned by the increased sales of "the juice."

James M. Burt, of Lafayette township, has a silver tobacco-box bearing the imprint of a bullet, received while it was in the pocket of his grand-father (Foght) at the battle of Monmouth, in the Revolutionary war.

Joab Agnew, of Roscoe, has a whale-bone cane, with gold head, presented to his father by Commodore Stockton, of the United States navy.

THE TREASURY ROBBERY, AND THE TRIALS.

Brief mention of the robbery of the Coshocton county treasury has been made in another place in this volume, but additional details are here given.

On the night of January 21, 1859, about one o'clock, the attention of Hiram Taylor, who was passing through the public square at the time, was arrested by sounds of some one, as if in distress, coming from the county treasurer's office, that being in the up-stairs room on the north side of the building, just north of the court-house.

He gave the alarm, and soon the sheriff and some other parties were assembled, and proceeded to the office of the treasurer. Bursting open the door, they found Mr. Ketchum, the treasurer, tightly bound, and with a gag in his mouth, displaced enough to allow him to make some outcry.

The court-house bell was rung, and soon a considerable company of citizens was gathered, and the town generally alarmed.

The treasurer told his story—how that having remained in the office to pay, at special request, some witnesses in a case in progress that evening, so that they might take a late train home, two men (one with a big shawl) had come into the office and made inquiries about a little back tax; and that while he was intent upon the books, looking the matter up, the one cast the shawl over his head, and the other seized him, and by their united exertions he was bound and gagged. The keys were taken, and the moneys taken out of the safe, and the robbers withdrew.

Much sympathy was expressed for the treasurer, and at a public meeting of citizens of Coshocton, and some from the county, this sympathy found expression in resolutions which read a little strangely now-a-days. The meeting urged the commissioners to spare no expense or effort in the ferreting out and punishing the bold miscreants who had injured the treasurer and robbed the people. It also advised that Wm. Bachelor, Esq., be employed to go about almost at will in search of the criminal. And there was much hurrying to and fro. But no clue was announced.

At length, two men were put on trial; but the treasurer could only swear that one of them looked like one of the men that came into his office.

After a time, legislative relief was sought, and the treasurer and his sureties freed from the charge of the amount stolen.

Time passed on. Ketchum stepped out of his office by "resignation," but showed no signs of guilt—only seemed worried by his "misfortune."

Among other plans looking to discovery of the robbers, the commissioners of the county requested by special messenger that banks should be on their lookout for such money as was taken—nearly all of it being in bills on the State Bank of Ohio.

In May, after the robbery, notice came from the Bank of Cadiz that a package of stained and musty bank-notes had been presented at their bank for redemption by James M. Brown, of Coshocton. Brown was called upon for an explanation, and his statement was written down and preserved; but as it could not be discovered that he was using more money than he had apparently been using before the robbery, the suspicions against him died out and were forgotten.

Years passed away, and no clue to the robbery could be obtained. Brown, however, was closely watched. While no offense had ever been proven on him, he had established a reputation from boyhood for being eager in the pursuit of money—keen to acquire it, and close to hold it. He had been for some time engaged in "shaving" operations, and had not by some of these helped his reputation, though evidently filling his purse. He was making money rapidly in a year or two after the robbery, and no one could tell just how.

In December, 1864, he was charged with burglary on Ward's drug-store, and at next term of court indicted therefor. About this time he was not to be found in Coshocton, nor thereabouts. An unsuccessful attempt was made to bring him from Canada, where he was after a time discovered operating largely in gold, and with, it was reported, some $58,000 in ready funds.

In 1865, facts enough had come to light to warrant the grand jury in finding an indictment for robbing the treasury, and another for receiving the money stolen. The state proposed a trial in December, but Brown obtained a change of venue to Licking county, and by some informality in proceedings could not then be compelled to go to trial there unless he chose, which he did not.

Meantime, testimony was increasing to show that Brown never got his moneys where he alleged—chiefly from some parties in Kentucky. Just at this stage the attorney-general of the State commenced civil process against Brown for the state's proportion of funds abstracted from the treasury, attaching all his property—his farm, a mile below Coshocton, and many valuable properties he had within a few years purchased in the town. Quarters were now getting close.

At this time, Brown commenced suit in Franklin county against Ketchum for the balance on a note given by him to Brown for $18,000. He alleged it was money loaned to Ketchum in his line of business as a broker. Ketchum said it was " hush " paper given without any consideration ; that in June, 1857, he had discovered a " shortage " in his accounts as treasurer, and had got Brown at that time to lend him that amount ; that he repaid it, and Brown insisted as a matter of comity upon getting occasionally sums from the treasurer ; that, to prevent exposure of his deficits, he borrowed on other occasions, but that ultimately Brown had the advantage, and threatened to have Ketchum prosecuted as a defaulter. On the 22d of January, 1859, the commissioners were to examine the treasury. To cover up the deficiency the sham robbery was planned. On the 21st of January, 1859, Brown came into the office, and suggested the carrying out of the plan, stating that he (the treasurer) must be discovered next day and go to the penitentiary anyhow; that he agreed to the arrangement, provided Brown would give up the $18,000 note, on which he had, as alleged, paid him $14,000 (as the credits on the notes showed), and also give up a $2,000 note, secured by mortgage on Ketchum's house in Lafayette; that Brown promised to do all this, but said he did not have the notes with him, but that after the smoke had blown away he would give up all notes, and give him a good portion of whatever he could get out of the safe that night. The bargain was made; Brown tied the treasurer, put the gag in his mouth, and carried away every dollar, amounting to some $16,000 or $18,000, including the whole sum in the treasurer's private safe.

This was the treasurer's statement, as forced out of him by Brown's suit in Franklin county. And now another indictment was in place.

April 16, 1867, Samuel Ketchum and James M. Brown were indicted for embezzlement, by simulated fraud, from county treasury, and put under bonds of $20,000 each.

Brown got a change of venue to Licking county. The trial began January 14th and closed February 2d, by the jury failing to agree. A subsequent trial, begun March 18, 1869, worked Brown's conviction. This also was held in Newark.

On law points the case was carried to the Supreme Court, but sentence was finally passed, and Brown and Ketchum were fellow prisoners in the Ohio Penitentiary, as elsewhere noticed. The attorneys for the State were A. G. Dimmock, R. M. Voorhees, E. T. Spangler, Wm. Sample, and C. Hoy; and for Brown, Nicholas and James. Campbell and Voorhees were Ketchum's attorneys.

Sheriff John Hesket (who was a bondsman of Ketchum), Colonel James Irvine, C. H. Johnson, and James M. Sells (and Sheriff Rankin, of Licking county), are recognized as having played prominent parts in these famous cases.

COSHOCTON WAGS IN EARLY DAYS.

No greater "wags" ever lived than two Coshocton boys, Bill —— and Sam ——. Old Deacon E——t had raised a nice lot of watermelons, and, just as they were ready for use, found the boys were after them. The two above-named were his apprentices at the time, and finally, as helping the old gentleman to discover what boys had been on hand, proposed to try "the track," when, lo! to the old man's horror, it was discovered that his own shoes just fitted the tracks; the boys, when they went to the patch, taking the precaution to "hook" the old gentleman's shoes as the first step.

A couple of festive youths from the rural districts, on one occasion, came to town, and inquired of one of the above wags if he could direct them to a house of certain (here nameless) sort. He, after a little hesitation, suggested that they might go about dusk to a certain house which had just been left vacant, and matters would be all right. He then notified his cronies, and while the aforesaid young men were seeing the lions in the groceries, etc., they hastily gathered into the old house a few articles of furniture and utensils, giving the place an inhabited appearance. At the appointed time, one of the town "b'hoys," arrayed in female apparel, received "the guests" at the door, and they were just beginning to feel at home, when in rushed a party of young men, who made things so lively for the rustic gentlemen that they were glad to escape with their lives!

HUMORS OF THE CRUSADE.

Among the humors of "the Crusade" was the case of one "Christ" S——h. He had been put on trial for violating the beer ordinance. The case being about over, there was some little talk between the justice and the lawyers about the penalty, and especially about going to jail. At this juncture, "Christ" broke out with—"Jail! oh me can no go to shail. Vy, vot would become of mine shop and mine bakery? Now, dare is Christ E——t; he got nuthing to do, vy can't he go to shail, and leve me alone?" The point made was a double one, especially in view of the fact that the "substitute" proposed having been out of employment for some time, had been acting as a sort of Deputy Marshal, especially in Crusade cases.

CHAPTER XXI.

THE CHURCHES—GENERAL STATEMENTS—DETAILED ACCOUNTS OF THE BAPTIST, CHRISTIAN, CATHOLIC, AND LUTHERAN CHURCHES.

THERE are in Coshocton county, at this time, some eighty congregations, representing the various religious bodies. These congregations own church buildings costing about $225,000. Ten of the congregations are reported as owning parsonages, which cost some $15,000 in all, ranging from $500 to $5,000 apiece.

Many of the earlier settlers of the county did not have much appreciation of the clergy, and were not more inclined to the church than to the school, and none of the denominations made much headway for nearly a score of years after the county was organized. Some of the settlers, however, invited the ministers of their old homes to come and preach to them in the wilderness, and these responded. Ministers passing to and fro stopped and conducted religious services. Of course, at that day, there was no need to carry rifles to the meeting-places to protect from the Indians, as in the days of the fathers in Western Pennsylvania. " Grove-meetings " were often held. Some log churches were built, but even these were arranged for fire, and were not in this like the first sanctuaries in New England, and they had puncheon floors, and at least split-log seats; and while there were " backwoods " appliances, there was little to now recall in amazement. Now and then there were at the services " some fellows of the baser sort," and it is said that on more than one occasion the preacher had occasion to display his muscle as well as mind and heart.

Some of the doings would call to mind the story of the preacher, who, upon sending his hat around for a collection, exclaimed as he surveyed its contents: " Thank God, I got my hat back from this crowd." One of the earliest preachers was reported to have been "a great fighter" in his old Maryland home, and, it was said, lost a piece of his nose, it having been bitten by his antagonist in a fight before he came into the church. People came from a long distance to church, all usually on horseback. Poverty and ignorance and their glazed-eyed daughter indifference were in the way to the success of the churches; but, after all, most of the trials were mutual to people and ministers, and had in them very little of romantic interest or striking character. What weariness and pain came to individuals —what struggles were required by godly women and noble men—in the building of the church even to its present height, in this county, would take more than a volume to tell. And yet these were of such sort as that they must appear in individual history, or necessarily lead to invidious discrimination, and even then to tiresome repetition.

BAPTIST CHURCHES.*

Previous to 1825, we have no solid history of this denomination of Christian workers, more than that there were a few pioneer Baptist preachers, who traveled and preached the gospel in dwellings, school-houses, etc., wherever and whenever opportunity and circumstances made it their duty. As among the most prominent of these self-sacrificing ministers, we mention the names of Elders Stephen Norris, Wm. Spencer, and Amos Mix. But there were other ministers and devoted laymen, who aided much in planting the gospel in this county at that time.

The first Baptist church organized in Coshocton county was the White Eyes Plains. This church was organized at the house of Isaac Evans, on said plains, November 5, 1825, by Elders S. Norris and Wm. Spencer, with fourteen members. Elder Norris was the first pastor, and labored for them three years, when he was succeeded by Elder Wm. Spencer, who continued with them until about the

---

* By Elder A. W. Oder.

year 1831, at which time the church numbered about twenty-four members.

Their places of worship were dwellings, school-houses, etc., in Oxford and Lafayette townships. In the later part of 1847, they completed a house of worship in the village of West Lafayette, having previously been at times nearly prostrate in power and influence.

At the time of the formation of the Coshocton Baptist Association, August 25, 1845, this church had a membership of thirty-four, as nearly as can be ascertained from their records, which at times were badly kept.

In the year 1850, the church built another house of worship, near the center of Oxford township, to accommodate the eastern portion of the church, making it also a regular place of worship.

In 1870, the church having increased largely in numbers, efficiency, and territory, divided into two separate and independent bodies. That portion which remained with the eastern part retained the name ot the *White Eyes Baptist Church*, and the other portion took the name of the *West Lafayette Baptist Church*. Since the separation, both have been doing good work for the Master, and are having regular service, and also keeping up good Sabbath-schools. The White Eyes church has a membership of about fifty, and Elder E. B. Senter is their successful pastor. The West Lafayette church has about sixty-five members, under the well-received ministry of Elder J. F. Churchill. The order of the pastors that have labored with the White Eyes Plain church is as follows: Stephen Norris, William Spencer, ———Pritchard, S. Price, L. Gilbert, H. Sayer, L. L. Root, H. Broom, A. W. Odor, J. G. Whitaker, L. Rhineheart, and E. B. Senter, who was serving them at the time they separated, and who continues with the White Eyes church. The ministers that have labored with the West Lafayette church since it became an independent body are E. B. Senter, G. W. Churchill, and J. F. Churchill, who is yet with them.

Jefferson Regular Baptist Church, located in Jefferson

township, was organized in May, 1840, by Elder B. White, with six members. It grew rapidly, and, in 1846, its membership was nearly one hundred, and in 1850, one hundred and thirty. Subsequently, it began to decrease in numbers, caused mostly by removals West and elsewhere. Not more than ten years elapsed until it was but a weak church, and since 1860 it has not been able to sustain preaching, and in fact is no longer to be properly called a church. The ministers that have labored for this church are as follows: B. White, William Mears, L. Gilbert, J. M. Winn, R. R. Whitaker, S. W. Frederick, A. W. Odor, under missionary employ, and A. W. Arnold. The old frame house of worship is almost a wreck. There are probably eighteen members.

Tomika Regular Baptist Church, situated in Washington township, was organized January 5, 1828, with but three members, by Elder Amos Mix, who was its first pastor. For several years they had no house of worship, and the first one they built was a log one. In 1845, their membership had increased to about seventy-five. They have had their misfortunes and successes alternately, and at present have a frame-house of worship, capable of seating from three hundred to four hundred persons, and a membership of nearly sixty, with a good working Sabbath-school. Their pastor, Elder S. C. Tussing, closed his services with them a short time ago. The order of the pastors who have labored for them since their organization is as follows: A. Mix, J. Frey, Sr., William Mears, L. L. Root, L. Gilbert, H. Sampson, J. Frey, Jr., S. West, R. R. Whitaker, B. Alen, E. B. Smith, J. W. Reed, A. W. Odor, E. Frey, J. C. Skinner, and S. C. Tussing.

Clark Township Regular Baptist Church was organized June 19th, 1833, by T. G. Jones and E. Otis, with eleven members. Shortly after the organization, the church licensed one of her members, B. White, to preach, and in June, 1834, he was ordained as an elder and called regularly to the pastorate, in which relation he continued about nine years. This church did not grow rapidly, and at no time could it boast a large membership, yet it has lived, and continues to this day to hold forth the word of life through the labors of S. W. Frederick, who is their present pastor. After Elder White closed his labors as pastor of the church they went into strife and contention, until finally they divided into three separate bodies, but were afterward united as before, Elder White again becoming the pastor of the church. At this time the church has a membership of about thirty-five. They have a new frame house of worship, capable of seating three or four hundred persons. The order of pastors is as follows, viz : B. White, ——— Ammerman, H. Sampson, J. W. Dunn, and S. W. Frederick.

Mill Fork Regular Baptist Church, located in Virginia township, about eight miles southwest of Coshocton, was organized May 1st, 1840, by Elders William Mears and L. Gilbert, with fifty-two members. After the organization, the church grew rapidly, and in a few years had over one hundred members. Having reached a membership of one hundred and forty, the number decreased, and at present it is about eighty-five. Since 1850, this church has sent four of its members into the ministry, viz.: J. W. Reed, E. B. Senter, F. C. Wright, and A. W. Odor. The present pastor is Elder S. C. Tussing. The ministers that have served this church as pastors are as follows : Wm. Mears, L. Gilbert, T. W. Grier, L. L. Root, J. G. Whitaker, R. R. Whitaker, T. Evans, E. Smith, A. W. Odor, J. C. Skinner, and S. C. Tussing. They have a commodious frame house of worship, built in 1870.

Mohawk Regular Baptist Church, located in Perry township, was organized about the year 1841 or 1842. In 1846 the membership was forty-nine, and in a few years was about one hundred; but since that time has been gradually decreasing until 1870, when it was thirty-five. The present membership is about fifty. They have no minister at the present time. They have a small frame house of worship, in tolerably good repair. The ministers that have labored as pastors are as follows; S. Wickham, J. Frey, jr., R. R. Whitaker, A. W. Arnold, E. B. Senter, and S. W. Frederick.

Tiverton Regular Baptist Church, located in Tiverton township, was organized in 1841. In 1854 there were about fifty members, and in 1860 over one hundred. Since that time the number has decreased, and although the membership is about seventy it can not be properly called an active church. They have a strong and capacious frame house of worship, but it is not in proper repair. The ministers that have labored with this church as pastors are as follows: L. Gilbert, R. R. Whitaker, R. W. Lockhart, B. M. Morrison, A. W. Arnold, and S. W. Frederick. The Sunday school still manifests some life.

White Eyes Regular Baptist Church, located in White Eyes township, was organized in 1839, with fourteen members. For a time after the organization the church prospered, and in 1854 had a membership of sixty. From that time the number has decreased, and more than a year ago they met and disbanded, having at that time about fifteen members. Their house of worship is a small frame one, quite old. The ministers who have served this church as pastors are as follows: H. Sayer, B. White, R. R. Whitaker, A. W. Odor, J. W. and H. Broom.

Monroe Regular Baptist Church, located in Monroe township, was organized in 1847, under the name of the Wolf Creek Church, and was subsequently changed to Monroe. When first organized she went forward, with seeming zeal for success, and in a few years had a membership of over sixty. In 1867 she changed her location, at that time having a membership of only twenty-seven. At present they report fifty-five members, but have no house of worship, using a school-house for that purpose. The ministers that have served as pastors to the Monroe church are as follows: J. M. Winn and L. L. Root, the latter having served the church for over twenty years and still continues.

Pleasant Hill Regular Baptist Church, located about five miles west of Roscoe, in Jackson township, on the graded road, was first organized in 1845, with about forty members. They advanced steadily for a few years, but in about fifteen years became virtually extinct. In 1862 they were reorganized, being named the Rock Hill Church. They made some progress, and in 1869 built a comfortable house of worship on its present site, being renamed Pleasant Hill. The ministers who have served as pastors of this church, from its first organization, are as follows: L. L. Root, H. Sampson, J. G. Whitaker, R. R. Whitaker, W. S. Barnes, A. W. Odor, S. W. Frederick, and E. B. Senter, who is their present pastor.

Evan's Creek Regular Baptist Church, located in Adams township, was organized in 1845, with about twenty members. In ten years the membership was about fifty. From that time the number began to decrease, and in 1866 they ceased to be a church. They once had a log house of worship, but it has ceased to be serviceable. The ministers that furnished pastoral service to this church are as follows: R. R. Whitaker, J. G. Whitaker, A. W. Odor, and J. W. Moreland.

Perry Regular Baptist Church, located in the western part of Perry township, and formerly a branch of the Tomaka Church, was organized in 1860 as an independent body, with twenty-seven members. They have been slowly but steadily advancing, their number now being about forty. They have a small but neat frame house of worship, in tolerably good repair. The ministers that have labored with them as pastors are as follows: S. West, R. R. Whitaker, E. B. Senter, A. W. Odor, E. Frey, and A. W. Arnold.

Darling's Run Regular Baptist Church, located in Jefferson township, was organized in 1866, with ten members. They advanced for some years, but have now come to a stand-still condition, with a membership of a little over twenty. They have no house of worship, using a school-house for that purpose. They have had as pastors Elder W. S. Barnes and Rev. H. Clark. They have no pastor at present.

Harmony Regular Baptist Church, located in Monroe township, was organized in 1866, with about twenty members. Since that time it has steadily advanced, having at the present time over sixty members. They have no house of worship, using a school-house instead. They contemplate building soon. They have had as pastors A. W. Arnold and J. K. Linebaugh. The latter is still with them.

Canal Lewisville Regular Baptist Church was organized in 1866, with twenty members. Since that time the number has increased to about forty. They have a small frame house of worship not very well adapted to the purpose. As pastors, they have had Elders L. L. Root, W. S. Barnes, and S. W. Frederick.

Chestnut Ridge Regular Baptist Church, located in Tiverton township, was organized in 1873, with about twenty members. It has been striving for three years to do work for the Master, and the membership has increased to twenty-seven. They have built a comfortable frame house of worship, and paid off all the incumbrances. They meet regularly, and have a good Sunday school. Elder J. K. Linebaugh preached for them before their organization, and has continued to do so up to the present time.

Chestnut Hill Regular Baptist Church, located one and a half miles east of Coshocton, was organized in 1875, with twenty members. They have no house of worship, but use the district school-house. They have a good Sabbath school kept up throughout the year, and at the present time have a membership of twenty-four. They have been visited occasionally by different ministers, and for some time were regularly supplied with preaching by Rev. H. Clark. At present they are under the oversight of Elder J. F. Churchill, of West Lafayette.

A Regular Baptist Church was constituted at Coshocton on the 23d of August, 1834—the services being held at the house of Wilson McGowan (who was a leading member, and for many years clerk of the congregation), and conducted by Elders John Pritchard, Geo. C. Sedgewick, Wm. Spencer, and Wm. Purdy. Elder Sedgewick Rice was the minister until May 5, 1838, when he was at his own request released. He died sometime thereafter, leaving a pleasant recollection of him in the community as a godly man and an able and earnest advocate of his church. After his services ceased, the church was supplied by several brethren for several years, until it seemed to have become practically dissolved about 1848. The McGowan, Bryant, Welch, Burt, Coe, Carhart, Farwell, Loder, Miller, Estinghausen, Whittemore, Babcock, Sprague, Elliott, Wright, and Oder families seem to have been connected with this movement. At one time there were some thirty-seven members. The services were held in the court-house. Benjamin Coe was the last clerk of the congregation.

Keene Regular Baptist Church was organized in 1850, with about twenty members, several of whom had been members of the church which had been organized and kept up for several years in the town of Coshocton, but at the above date had ceased to exist. The Keene Church built a good frame house of worship, but never made a successful advance, and in 1866 failed to report to the association, having ceased to be a church proper. The house has since been burnt, and naught remains. The ministers who labored with this church were J. M. Winn, B. White, M. J. Barnes, and T. Evans.

There were at different times four other organizations of Baptist Churches in Coshocton county beside the ones already noticed, but they were not of sufficient importance to merit a sketch.

The probable number of Regular Baptists in Coshocton county is not far from 950.

CHRISTIAN CHURCHES.

There is a *Christian* church, having at present one hundred and fifteen members, in Virginia township. It was organized by Elder J. W. Marvin, of Knox county, Ohio, in 1832, starting with five members, of whom two are yet living. For some twelve years the congregation met in the woods, or a barn, or a school-house. In 1844, a frame meeting-house (twenty-eight by thirty-two feet) was erected, which, in 1873, was replaced by a better and a larger house of worship. The pastors of the church have been J. W. Marvin, James Hays, Wm. Bagley, Jacob Harger, A. E. Harger, A. Bradfield, B. Rabb, Wm. Overturf, M. M. Lohr, E. Peters, and John W. Wright, at present in charge.

The whole number of members enrolled in connection with this church during its history is two hundred and thirteen. Formerly there were three other active churches of this communion—the West Bedford, the Antioch, and the Severns—each with a good house of worship for the day and locality; but they are now almost extinct.

It is understood that there is at least one congregation of German Baptists known as "Dunkards," gathered in the Saul Miller neighborhood, quite small, having no house of worship, and without much ministerial service.

No organized society of "The Disciples" has been reported as at this time in existence, although there is a considerable number of adherents of that church in the county.

CATHOLIC CHURCHES.

There are four of these in the county. The oldest—*St. Mary's*, of Linton township—was organized about 1840. A small log building was used by the congregation until about 1873, when this was replaced with a neat frame. This church and the few scattered Catholics elsewhere in the county were for years ministered unto by priests from Zanesville, who would make three or four trips a year, traveling on horseback. About 1855, the Rev. T. Bender, of Cincinnati, was appointed pastor of the Newark church, having also the charge of the Coshocton county Catholics.

He went vigorously to work, and by 1857 had succeeded in gathering and establishing the church of *St. Nicholas* in Franklin township, and the church of *St. Elizabeth* in Monroe township. Each of these erected small log-houses of worship, built by the labor of the members, who also furnished the ground and materials. These congregations have both been greatly depleted by emigration to the Far West, and they have made little or no progress since their organization. They have been mainly supplied by weekday services by the resident pastor of Coshocton.

In 1858, the Rev. Serge De Stchaulepinkoff (a Russian priest, who, on becoming Catholic, had been compelled to leave his country) was sent to Coshocton, and was the first resident pastor. Under his direction, *St. George's* church, of Coshocton, was built. He continued in charge for some three years, and was succeeded at short intervals by Fathers Andres, Ranch, and Nordmeyer—all sent by Rev. J. B. Purcell, archbishop of Cincinnati.

In January, 1869, Rev. John M. Jacquet was appointed pastor of Coshocton by the Right Rev. J. H. Rosecrans, who, the year before, had been made first bishop of Columbus. In the membership of the *St. George's* church, there has been no great change for some years. Through the instrumentality of Father Jacquet, both the church building and the pastoral residence have been much improved, and all debts against the charge paid off. The country churches have also been repaired and much improved.

The total membership in the county is about seven hundred, of which some four hundred are communicants.

LUTHERAN CHURCHES.

There are three evangelical (English) Lutheran churches in the county. The oldest of these is *Zion Church*, in Crawford township. It seems to have been gathered and organized through the labors of Rev. E. Greenwald (long settled in New Philadelphia), about 1832. Rev. J. B. Reck succeeded him in 1835; but, after a few years, the care of the church again devolved (in 1838) on Mr. Greenwald. In 1840 Rev. E. C. Yunge took charge of the church, and in 1846 Rev. E. Melsheimer, who died in 1849. In 1850 Rev. A. U. Bartholomew became pastor, and in 1859 Rev. M. M. Bartholomew. Rev. S. S. Samson took charge in 1862, and Rev. David Sparks in 1864. The present pastor, Rev. J. W. Myers, has been in charge some ten years. The elders have been Andrew Eichmier, Jacob Myser, Henry Grimm, John Smith, A. Winklepleck, William Stall, and Frederick Everhart. The Mysers, and Winkleplecks, and Frocks, and Doaks, and Everharts, and Michael Grill, John Smith, James Christy, Frederick Barrick, and Nicholas Storm have been among the more prominent members, who have varied in number from thirty to eighty. The congregation has a good house of worship in Chili.

About 1840 an effort was made for a church in Franklin township, and an organization was effected and building secured, but, after some years, the enterprise was abandoned. About 1856 Rev. S. Kammerer began preaching in that (the Wertz) neighborhood, and a church building about thirty by forty feet was erected, and a congregation called *St. Paul's* organized. Rev. A. N. Bartholomew became pastor, and continued for twelve years. He was succeeded by Rev. J. S. Sleutz in 1870, and he in 1872 by the present pastor, Rev. John Weber. This church and the church at Adamsville, in Muskingum county, have always been joined as a pastoral charge. Daniel Gaumer gave the land for the church and burial-ground. The church building is of frame, and cost about $1,500. The elders have been John Wertz and Zachariah Glaze. The number of members at the organization was thirty; at this time it is about ninety.

The third church is at West Carlisle—a neat frame building. But few services have been held for several years; and the congregation, especially since the removal of Mr. Billman from the township, is very feeble.

There is a church near New Bedford, a little way over the line in Holmes county, with which a considerable number of residents of Coshocton county are connected.

St. John's Evangelical Lutheran (German) Church, at New Bedford, was organized by Rev. G. Doepken in 1854, and ministered unto by him for twenty years, at the end of which time he removed to Marietta. The minister at present is Rev. O. Primer. The house of worship, a large frame, was built in 1855. At its organization there were connected with the congregation some twenty-five families; in 1876 there are about sixty-five families. Among the more prominent have been the Schaumeeker, Schmelz, Schmidt, Schlegle, Baad, Steel, and Holt families. The church is in connection with the Joint Synod of Ohio.

CHAPTER XXII.

THE CHURCHES—DETAILED ACCOUNTS OF THE METHODIST EPISCOPAL, METHODIST (PROTESTANT), PRESBYTERIAN, UNITED PRESBYTERIAN, PROTESTANT EPISCOPAL, CHRISTIAN UNION, ETC.

METHODIST EPISCOPAL CHURCHES.

In relation to the Methodist Episcopal churches south of the rivers, the following has been furnished by Rev. B. F. Beazelle, the pastor of the one in Coshocton :

The first preacher who occupied this territory was the Rev. John Mitchell. That was in 1812. He was most likely the first Methodist preacher of Coshocton county. He organized three classes that year — one near where Plainfield now is, one at Maysville (Marquands), and one in the Robinson neighborhood, now called Bethany church. Religious services have been maintained in these places ever since, and after the lapse of nearly two generations, the fruit of this "handful of corn" is seen in a comfortable and tasteful house of worship at each place, and larger and more vigorous societies than perhaps ever before.

They were at first connected with the Tuscarawas circuit, Muskingum district, Western conference. Subsequently, it is said, they formed a part of Norwich circuit. Not later than 1820, they were included in Muskingum circuit. From 1813-23, the district was called Muskingum also, then for a time Lancaster.

That old Tuscarawas circuit included within its boundaries the following circuits and stations: Zanesville, now of the Ohio conference, Norwich, Sonora, Adamsville, Cambridge, Liberty, Washington, Milnersville, Plainfield, and Coshocton, of the Pittsburg conference, and parts of what are now Dresden and Roscoe circuits in the North Ohio conference, and doubtless other territory which can not be designated.

Bishop Morris, writing in 1839, says: "The Muskingum

circuit, when the Rev. Charles Elliott was my colleague, in 1818-19, included what is now called Zanesville station, Putnam circuit, Cambridge circuit, and parts of others; and the following year, when Samuel Brockunier and James Gilruth were my colleagues, we so enlarged it as to include Washington, Coshocton, and other intermediate settlements. Those familiar with the country can see the extent of our plan by running a supposed line from Zanesville on through the settlements of Jonathan's creek to Wolf creek, below McConnelsville; thence up the river to Putnam; then by a zigzag route on to the bend of Wills creek, and all the neighborhoods down to Cambridge; thence to Washington, Sugar creek, Wagoner's plains, Coshocton, and Johnson's plains; and finally, by numerous angles, right, acute, and obtuse, back to the place of beginning. This, when I went to it, was a four weeks' circuit; but when I left, it required a tour of six weeks, with little rest for man or horse. Our first year's work resulted in a small decrease, chiefly on account of strictly enforcing the rules of the discipline, and laying aside many delinquent members; but the second year we received about two hundred new members, which, after deducting all losses, gave us a considerable increase."

About the year 1833, as nearly as I can tell, " the radical split," as it was commonly called, occurred. This rupture was produced originally by the question of " lay delegation," and led to the formation of the Methodist Protestant Church, in 1828. This event was very disastrous in its consequences to the appointments of which we have been speaking. The Plainfield society, then perhaps sixty in number, was reduced to eight. This little band, headed by Judge Thomas Johnson, continued faithful to the old church and its principles, and continued to meet on a week day, for preaching, in the school-house. From this fact, I infer that the seceding party, by odds the largest, retained the original house of worship.*

---

*A house of worship was erected, chiefly by Judge Johnson, in 1835. Subsequently, the congregation erected a building (frame) in Jacobsport. For the erection of this, M. L. Norris (afterward so extensively

The Marquand appointment was for a number of years seriously enfeebled, but through unflagging faith and labor, under the leadership of the earnest men, Marquand and Ballentine, quiet and order were again restored.

At Robinson's, the society shared a similar fate. At times, prosperity would seem to return, when, by deaths, removals, or other untoward events, it would seem to be left in the same or worse condition. But the little company of earnest men and women, chief of whom, I believe, was Judge Robinson, stood firm, and the result is the substantial success of to-day. Judge Johnson died in 1840, having, however, lived to see prosperity restored to the church of his love. Judge Robinson fell at his post in 1856. Peter Marquand passed from earth about eight years ago; and Hugh Ballentine removed to the West some years since, where he still lives.

For about five years prior to the organization of the Coshocton circuit, those appointments were connected with the old Roscoe circuit, which, during that period, was served by the following-named preachers: Blanipied, Lynch, McDowell, Cooley, Goof, Lowell (who died of small-pox in Dresden, and was succeeded by Perkins), Camp, Brown, and Kalog. During that time, David Young and W. B. Christie served as presiding elders. I am not certain that this list is correct, nor can I give the date of appointment or length of service of any one. As we approach our own time, however, our information is more abundant and accurate.

Rev. I. N. Baird, D.D., now of Allegheny City, Pa., in a letter to the writer, says: " I was sent to Coshocton in the summer of 1840. Found the territory I was to organize into a circuit to be bounded by the Muskingum river from Coshocton down to the mouth of Wills creek; up the same to the neighborhood of Linton; then north to the plains near Evansburgh; thence down to the place of beginning. There were societies at East Plainfield, Mar-

engaged in building operations in Coshocton) had the contract. This building was somewhat enlarged and greatly improved in the summer of 1875.

quand's, and Robinson's. There was no society in Coshocton—indeed, but one member was found there, Sister Spangler, still with you. Thomas C. Ricketts had, a little before that, united with the church in Roscoe—was yet on probation, and afterward came to us when we organized. There was a brother Conwell, also, who had been a member of the church somewhere, and joined us when we organized. But Mrs. David Spangler was the only member of the church at the time of my arrival, and to her as much as to any preacher, perhaps, our struggling enterprize there is indebted for its success. Her noble husband, though not a member, was always helpful in every way."

In 1841, Dr. Baird organized a class near the present Mount Zion appointment, the planting from which sprang the church of that name. In 1854, the following appointments were attached to the charge: Liberty, Hopewell, Peoble's, and Early's. The arrangement not proving mutually agreeable, at the end of one year they were detached.

In 1855, the church at Lafayette was founded, which in recent years has attained considerable strength. Until 1859, the circuit retained substantially its original shape, but in that year a division was made. Coshocton, Robinson's, and Lafayette formed one pastoral charge, retaining the old name. Maysville, Mount Zion, and Plainfield formed another, under the latter name. Lafayette, by request, was next year placed in the Plainfield circuit. For nine years, Robinsons and Coshocton constituted one pastoral charge; but in 1868 the former was again included in the Plainfield circuit, since when the latter has been a station.

The first quarterly conference of the original Coshocton circuit was held at Bethany church, October 17, 1840. It will be of interest to know the names of the men constituting that body, which have been furnished me from the original record by one of the members: Rev. Edward Taylor was the Elder; Rev. I. N. Baird the Preacher; James Robinson, Robert Johnson, David Richason, Hugh Ballentine, T. C. Ricketts, and John M. Johnson, the Stewards. Exhorters: E. Davis and Charles Grimes. Leaders: Adam

Wallace, John Chamberlain, Charles Wilcox, and Thomas Elliott. This, I believe, is the entire list.

We have seen that, at the organization of the circuit in 1840, no society of the Methodist Episcopal Church existed in Coshocton; but for some years previous the Methodist Protestant Church had maintained one. Different men had, however, preached in the town from time to time as occasion offered, for a number of years—such as Thomas A. Morris (afterward bishop), David Young, Jacob Young, Robert O. Spencer, Wm. B. Christie, John Dillon, and others, no doubt, of whom I have no certain knowledge.

As to the founding of the church in Coshocton, Dr. Baird further says: "I preached in the court-house, and organized the first class of twelve members in the old jury-box. It was during my second year that some steps were taken toward building a church. I can not now recall the stage of the work when I left in 1842. I left a considerable society—near seventy members, I think—and was succeeded by Rev. John J. Swayze, at that time the most popular man in the pulpit, in the conference." The twelve members of that first class were: Elizabeth Spangler, Thomas C. Ricketts, George E. Conwell, Felix Landis, David Frew, Benjamin R. Shaw, Henrietta Shaw, Nancy Decker, Martha Wallace, Mary Wallace, Abraham Sells, and Lucy Thomas.

Fortunately, from the original record-book, I am enabled to transcribe the following: "At a meeting held in the town of Coshocton, May 9, 1842, by the friends and members of the M. E. Church, for the purpose of consultation as to the propriety of erecting a house for public worship—Wm. McFarland having been called to the chair, and B. R. Shaw made secretary—on motion of David Spangler, it was unanimously resolved that we take immediate measures to secure a site and erect a suitable building." Accordingly a committee of five persons was appointed to secure a location and solicit subscriptions. Thomas C. Ricketts, James Robinson, David Frew, and Wm. McFarland composed the committee. An additional committee, consisting of James LeRetilley, Theophilus Phillips, and Samuel Hutchinson, was appointed to secure subscriptions in Roscoe. At a subsequent meeting, David Frew, B. R. Shaw, and George E. Conwell were elected a building committee.

After some good-natured difference of opinion, the present location was agreed upon for the church, the ground then being owned by Joseph Rue. Whether their friends of to-day regard their selection as a fortunate one, I can not say.

A vote of thanks for the liberal subscriptions of the community is recorded, and then, among other things, the following: "*Resolved*, That we accept the proposal of Mr. John Elliott to erect said building for the sum of $2,500, as per contract"—paying him at the same time $1,099, the amount of subscriptions then obtained.

A complete list of the contributors, with the amounts of their contributions, is also preserved. The men of that time—for we are to remember that all this took place a generation ago—believed in the pay-as-you-go plan. Numerous records of minor subscriptions were made during the four years the church was building; but when it was finally ready for use, little or nothing remained to be paid.

The church was dedicated in the early summer of 1846, during the pastorate of Rev. E. P. Jacob, by Rev. Wesley Kenny, D.D., then of Wheeling, more recently of the Philadelphia Conference, lately deceased. Since that time it has been repaired and improved at different times at an aggregate expense of not less than double its original cost. In 1862, the parsonage property was secured. In the spring of 1863, the Pittsburg Conference held its annual session in it.

The Sunday school was organized August 8, 1845, with George E. Conwell superintendent, Russell C. Bryant secretary, and W. Wells librarian.

THE PREACHERS.

1812–13, John Mitchell; 1813–14, John Clingan; 1814–15, William Dixon; 1815–16, Joseph Kinkead; 1816–17, William Knox; 1817–18, John Waterman and Thos. Carr; 1818–19, John Tivis and Samuel Glaze; 1819–20, Thos. A.

Morris, S. R. Brockunier, and Jas. Gilruth; 1821–22, Jas. Hooper and Archibald McIlroy; 1822–23, Leroy Swormstedt and M. M. Henkle; 1823–24, Burnis Westlake and David Young; 1824–25, Wm. Cunningham; 1825–26, Edward Taylor and Ezra Brown; 1826-27, Zarah H. Coston, M. Ellis (sup.); 1827–28, Cornelius Springer and James Callahan; 1828–29, Joseph Carper and C. Springer; 1829–30, Joseph Carper and Wm. B. Christie; 1830–31, Alfred M. Lorrain and Gilbert Blue; 1831–32, Jacob Delay and Wm. Young; 1832–33, John W. Gilbert and Levi P. Miller; 1833–34, J. W. Gilbert and Charles C. Leybrand; 1834–35, James McMahon, Cyrus Brooks, and Samuel Harvey (until 1840, names given above); 1840–42, Isaac N. Baird; 1842–43, John J. Swayze; 1843–44, John D. Rich; 1844–45, Thomas McLeary; 1845–46, E. Jacob; 1846–47, James Henderson; 1847–49, D. P. Mitchell; 1849–50, C. Wyrick; 1850–51, D. Trueman; 1851–52, C. A. Holmes; 1852–54, J. E. McGaw; 1854–55, H. Sinsabaugh and R. S. Hogue; 1858–59, T. Davidson and H. M. Close; 1859–60, T. Davidson and J. J. Neigh.

PREACHERS OF PLAINFIELD CIRCUIT SINCE 1860.

1860–62, George McKee; 1862–64, Joseph Shaw; 1864–65, John Crisman; 1865–66, same (left, his place filled by W. L. Dixon); 1866–67, T. H. S. White; 1867–68, J. E. Storkey; 1868–69, same, and M. C. Harris; 1869–70, J. W. Weaver and T. W. Anderson; 1870–71, J. W. Weaver and J. W. Toland; 1871–72, same, and H. W. Rader; 1872–73, A. V. Galbraith and T. S. Luccock (sup.); 1873–75, A. V. Galbraith; 1875–76, H. H. Pershing.

PREACHERS OF COSHOCTON SINCE 1860.

1860–62, S. M. Hickman; 1862–63, W. R. Fouts; 1863–65, W. D. Stevens; 1865–67, E. W. Brady (who, retiring before the expiration of his term, was succeeded by J. W. Bushong, who served during the remainder of the term); 1867–68, E. Birket; 1868–71, S. Crouse; 1871–73, J. D. Vail; 1873–76, B. F. Beazell.

Of statistics prior to the foundation of the Coshocton circuit, we know nothing. The contribution—or, at all events, the allowance—of the entire circuit the first year (1840) for the support of the gospel, was $100 for the preacher and $10 for the presiding elder.

Benevolent collections were of course not thought of, and Sunday schools were yet in the future. The entire membership of that year was about 60. The membership of these two charges, as shown by the conference minutes of 1875, is 640. The amount paid for ministerial support the same year, $2,120, and for benevolent purposes, $640. There are also six Sunday schools, with an aggregate attendance of 600 scholars.

Of the churches to the west and north of Coshocton (in North Ohio Conference) we have these notes:

The first (*Chalfant's*) meeting-house in Washington township was built in 1811, and the church there is regarded by many as the oldest in the county. There is a good church at Moscow, in that township. In the northwest part of the county the Methodist church was planted at several points in New Castle and Perry townships, concentrating at East Union, at a very early date, largely through the zealous efforts of Joseph W. Pigman, a famous class leader and local preacher, settled in that locality, of whom mention is elsewhere made in this volume.

Churches were subsequently established at West Bedford and West Carlisle, which, with varying numbers, have always been accounted (especially the former) as among the more important ones in the county.

The *West Bedford* church antedates the other several years, and is one of the oldest churches in the county. It was organized about 1819.

Roscoe.—From 1820 to 1826, there had occasionally been a sermon preached in Roscoe (then Caldersburg), in the dining-room of a tavern kept by one William Barcus; but in 1826 two Methodist ministers were appointed by the Annual Conference to the Circuit in which Roscoe was embraced, and in the spring of that year the first class was formed by those ministers (their names were Abner Gough and H. O. Sheldon). The persons forming the class were Theophilus Phillips, Mrs. Samuel Brown, James Le Retilley and wife, Mrs. William Barcus, Rachel Le Retilley, and Joseph Shoemaker and wife. Meetings continued to be held in the same tavern until about 1828, about which time Samuel Brown joined, and the meetings were after that held at his house until 1831, in which year they built them a nice little brick church, twenty-four by forty feet. A little incident in regard to Samuel Brown. He was, by his own account, a very wicked man then. There was to be a love feast held on Sunday morning, and he went along with his wife to carry the child, not intending to stay in, but when they got there it was about time to close the door, as it was the custom in those days. So, when he stepped in to hand the child to his wife they closed the door and drew a bench against it, so that he could not get out, and was compelled very reluctantly to remain, and during the exercises he became powerfully convicted, and then and there joined the church.

In 1853, the old church being too small, they concluded to build a larger one. The old one was torn down, and one erected forty by sixty feet; and in March, 1874, it was burned and rebuilt the same year at a cost of $8,000, exclusive of materials out of old building. It is a handsome brick, same size as old one, with brick tower and fine bell. The windows are of stained-glass, and the pulpit and pews are very neat; manufactured at Richmond, Indiana. It was dedicated December 27, 1875.

The *Branch* church, some six miles west of Roscoe, has long been associated with that church in a circuit, and takes rank as one of the older and stronger country churches.

Warner Chapel, on Bowman's section, three miles south of Roscoe, is a neat brick building, the erection of which was accomplished some six years ago, largely through the efforts of the Austins, Biggs, and others formerly connected with Roscoe. It is a point in the Roscoe circuit.

Three miles further south is the *Conesville* church. Frank Wolf was largely instrumental in securing this church. The building is a good brick one of moderate dimensions.

The *Warsaw Methodist Society* was organized in 1843, by Rev. Mr. Thatcher, the presiding elder at the time being the Rev. Mr. Yocum. For five or six years meetings were held in the old school-house, still standing on the hill. The first members were Langdon Hogle, Andrew Weatherwax and wife, Joseph Meggs and wife, John Hook and wife, William Pancake and wife. The church was built about five years after the society was organized—a frame building worth something over a thousand dollars. Rev. Mr. Thatcher was followed by Rev. Finley Leonard, during whose ministry a great revival occurred, the result being an addition of some forty to the church. The number of communicants at this time is fifty, and the church is in more prosperous condition than for several years.

The *Mohawk Village* Methodist church was organized in the fall of 1840. In the preceding year a company from Ireland had settled in the Mohawk valley, until that time a comparative wilderness. They were followed the next year by other families of the same connection. The first company embraced James Moore, deceased (father of Robert Moore), James Moore, Sr., John Moore, and William Moore. Those coming the next year were William and James Given, William and James Thompson, and William Moore, all now living. And these families, with Thomas Treadaway and wife, composed the society at its organization. In 1841, there was an addition to the settlement, including, besides others, John Moore and family, and the well-known James and Robert of the present day. For about a year from the organization, the meetings were held in the Whittaker school-house; then a school-house was built in the settlement, and meetings held in that. In 1849, the church was built—worth some $1,500. Within a few years it has been repaired and very much improved as to its interior. It stands near a refreshing spring of water, and is convenient and attractive in all its appointments and arrangements. The minister first in charge was Rev. Mr. Camp. Rev. Leonard Parker succeeded him, and Rev. Henry Whittemore (still preaching in Northern Ohio Conference) succeeded Parker. Under his ministry quite a noticeable number were added to the society. Rev. Homer J. Clark followed Whittemore. Then came Austin Coleman, during whose ministry the church building was erected. Just prior to building the Methodist Episcopal church, he held a protracted meeting in the Baptist church, which had been built the year before. During this revival there were a great many valuable accessions. The history of the society has been marked by great prosperity. The number of members at this time is eighty-seven.

In relation to the church at *Keene*, two respectful applications, at some months interval, were made to the minister in charge for information. Both were unanswered. An intelligent gentleman was then commissioned to make direct personal application. His answer is in these words: "Nothing can be learned of the early history of the M. E. Church here that can be made available for your purposes. There seem to be no 'records' to refer to, and there is no member to consult who was living here at the time the church was organized. I can get no information from the Rev. Mr. Disney, and succeed no better with his laymen. I can only abandon the fruitless search."* The society is an old one, and the building a good frame.

At *Canal Lewisville* a very neat frame church was built in 1872, chiefly through the efforts of David Markley. The appointment is one in connection with Keene, and the congregation has had a pleasant history and enjoyed great prosperity.

In 1874, mainly by the efforts of John Richmond and J. B. Peck, a tasty and convenient Methodist church was

---

* Was not this the church in which Rev. Charles Elliott, D.D., and other worthies of Methodism were trained?

built at *Orange*, and a congregation formed, supplied for the present from New Comerstown.

The church at *Bakersville* was organized about 1848, and is now enjoying its second house of worship (dedicated February 7, 1875), the old one having become unadapted to the size and character of the congregation. Making part of this charge are several appointments in the county round about, chief of which is White Eyes. The number of members at Bakersville at this time is about seventy, and in the whole charge some two hundred and twenty.

The church at *Bloomfield* was built during the summer of 1871. It was dedicated January 14, 1872. Its cost was about $2,500. The congregation was organized with a membership of twenty. Thirty-three were soon thereafter added under the labors of Rev. A. E. Thomas, the minister at that time in charge. The present membership is about seventy-five. The Sunday-school has always been a most interesting department of this church. It was organized in March, 1872, with E. J. Pocock as superintendent.

The whole number of members of the M. E. Church in the county is reported at sixteen hundred.

METHODIST (PROTESTANT) CHURCHES.

The Methodist (Protestant) Church dates its organization in Coshocton county in 1830. The first movement seems to have been at Jacobsport, where to this day probably the strongest organization is found. The building is a commodious frame.

On the plains above Lafayette a church (the appointment was called "Phillips'") was organized at an early day in the history of the denomination, which has always since manifested much vigor. It occupies a substantial brick building.

At Coshocton, some thirty years ago, the M. P. Church was a comparatively strong one, with the best house of worship (the brick on Locust street between Second and Third) and largest congregation of the place. It soon thereafter began to decline, and for a number of years has not attempted to hold any service. The building has of late years been occupied by the German Lutherans.

The interest of the M. P. Church about Coshocton has of late years been concentrated at Moore's school-house, two miles below Coshocton, where there is at this time quite a fair congregation.

Besides the points thus far noticed as occupied by this denomination, there are appointments at Littick's, in Franklin township; at Union Church, in Oxford township; at Wolfe's; at Bird's Run, in Linton.

The pioneer organizer among the early Methodist Protestants was Theophilus Richison.

Among the more prominent ministerial laborers in the advancement of the interests of this denomination have been Cornelius Springer,* N. Sneethen, J. Dolby, William Munhall, Israel Thrapp, Joseph Hamilton, John Baker, D. Truman.

Among those connected with the various organizations in the earlier days were: In Coshocton, David Waggoner† and wife, and Zebedee Baker and wife; in Franklin township, Isaac Shambaugh and wife, the Litticks, Browning, Bancroft, and Maston; at Moore's school-house, the Moores, the Porteus', and McBanes; at Jacobsport, John Davis, S. V. Powelson, the Bakers, Chapples, and Magness; in Lafayette township, the Loozes and Phillips, etc.

It is said that there are some fifteen localities (all south of rivers) at which services under the direction of this denomination are held; and the number of members in the county is estimated at some five hundred.

PRESBYTERIAN CHURCHES.

Coshocton Church.—The largest Presbyterian church in the county is that of Coshocton. It can hardly be called

---

* Recently died in Zanesville at a very advanced age, and greatly beloved.

† Residing just out of Coshocton, in the southeast. He is a son of Phillip Waggoner, elsewhere mentioned as one of the first settlers in Oxford township; now in his seventy-sixth year.

the oldest, it being in fact a twin church with that at Keene. Ministers traveling to, or living in the counties west and south, occasionally preached in the town from 1812 until 1818. In the latter year, Rev. James Cunningham, then living in Utica, Licking county, supplied what was denominated "the congregation of Coshocton and Mill creek," in which were fifteen communicants. The separation of the congregation seems to have occurred about 1833, about which time Rev. Geo. Warner was preaching to the church. Rev. Nathaniel Conklin followed him. The first elder at Coshocton was James Renfrew, and a little later John Elliott was elected. The former had served as an elder in the united church of Coshocton and Mill creek, and the latter had served at Keene before removing to Coshocton. The services were held at first in private houses, and then in the court-house. In 1824, James Renfrew started a Sunday-school. It was held in the currying-shop of the tannery on the northwest corner of Second and Walnut streets. In April, 1834, the county commissioners gave Samuel Lee, William K. Johnson, John Porter, and their associates, a lease of a site for a church on the southwest quarter of the public square, and the congregation, by a great and protracted effort, put up a substantial frame building, thirty by forty-two feet. It stands at this writing on the northeast corner of Fourth and Main streets —used for stores. Rev. Joseph S. Wylie, the first pastor of the church, began his labors in 1835, and remained pastor about six years, passing to Apple creek in Wayne county, and afterward to Florence, Pennsylvania, where he died. Eight members made up the original organization of the Coshocton church. There was a steady increase until 1838. In that year fourteen members withdrew, and were organized into a second Presbyterian church. Rev. Addison Coffey, coming from Lebanon, Ohio, began preaching to the old church as stated supply, August 8, 1841, and was installed pastor in 1843. Shortly before Mr. Coffey came, Jacob Elliott and Jonathan Fiske* had been ordained elders,

---

* Father of Rev. Ezra Fiske, D.D., of Greencastle, Indiana.

and in his pastorate (ending September 2, 1847), David Noble, Samuel Wheeler, Rolla Banks, J. F. Traxler, and Wm. Loder. From 1847, when Mr. Coffey removed to Peoria, Illinois, to the fall of 1851, the church was supplied by Rev. H. K. Hennigh and Rev. R. Robe, now in Oregon. Rev. Prosper H. Jacob (now of Knoxville, Iowa) was pastor from 1851 to 1854. In his pastorate, Wm. Sample, Wm. Laughead, and Jos. K. Johnson were installed elders. Rev. T. J. Taylor (who died in Illinois, 1867) supplied the church for a few months in 1855-6.

Wm. E. Hunt (licensed by Steubenville Presbytery), the present pastor of the church, became such May 14, 1857, having supplied the churches of Coshocton and Keene from the July preceding. At that time there were fifty-six members of the church. At the time of Mr. Hunt's installation the Johnson Brothers (John, Joseph K., and Wm. K.) proposed to give lot 314 (on Main street) and the house then on it for a parsonage, provided the rest of the congregation would build an addition, all of which was done. In 1866, the brick church (forty-three by seventy feet, two towers, steeple one hundred feet, slate roof, frescoed walls, stained glass windows, etc.), corner of Fourth and Chestnut streets, was begun and finished in spring of 1868, at a cost of $15,500.* The synod of Ohio met in it that fall. In May, 1867, T. S. Humrickhouse, T. C. Ricketts, and James R. Johnson were installed elders.

The second church was organized January 12, 1839, and in the following spring Rev. E. Buckingham, from Newark,† became the pastor. Samuel Lee and A. R. Hillyer were the first elders. Mr. Buckingham remained until April 22, 1846. During his ministry, eighty-four were added to the fourteen original members of the church, and a frame house of worship was erected on Fourth street between Main and Chestnut streets, now "Equity Building."

---

* The carpenter work was done by W. H. Robinson; the brick work by C. Daugherty, of Newark, Ohio.

† Afterward at Canton, Ohio; died March, 1876.

Phineas Tuttle and James Hill were elected elders March 27, 1843.

Rev. H. Calhoun (now of Ironton, Ohio), was stated supply of the church for eleven years from April, 1846, and was followed for brief periods by Reverends Mussey, John Henderson, and Wm. Bridgeman. From November, 1861, to November, 1865, Rev. C. W. Wallace (recently of Monroeville, Ohio), supplied the church.

A. D. Denman and Josiah Glover were elected elders September 23, 1860; Chester Wells, September 13, 1862; and W. H. Robinson and Dr. S. H. Lee, March 11, 1863.

A temporary arrangement was entered into July 1, 1867, by which the first and second churches were to worship together under the ministry of Rev. Wm. E. Hunt, pastor of the first church, each church retaining its organization. This arrangement continued until the formal union was accomplished in virtue of the action of the General Assemblies, under which the churches had respectively been. This was consummated September 11, 1870. The united church took as the corporate name "The Presbyterian Church of Coshocton," and engaged Rev. Wm. E. Hunt as pastor. At the time of union, there were on the roll of the first church one hundred and twelve names, and on that of the second church seventy-four. In 1871, the brick parsonage next the church was built at a cost of about $5,000. The old parsonage was sold for $2,500, and the second Presbyterian church building was sold in 1873 for $3,000.

The elders at this time are William Sample, A. D. Denman, T. S. Humrickhouse, S. H. Lee, T. C. Ricketts, W. H. Robinson, Josiah Glover, and James R. Johnson. The number of members in April, 1875, was one hundred and seventy. A large proportion of the funds for the new brick church was raised through the instrumentality of the "Ladies' Society"—they having in the outset purchased the lot, costing $1,000.

Keene (Township) Church.—As stated in the preceding sketch, Rev. James Cunningham, living in Utica, Licking county, as early as in 1818, occasionally preached to what was denominated the Congregation of Coshocton and Mill Creek. The prominent members of the congregation (in which were fifteen communicants) were James Renfrew and Samuel Lee, of Coshocton, and Timothy and Jacob Emerson, in the neighborhood of Keene. Services were held in pleasant weather under the trees of the forest, standing on the site of the present church of Keene. The church probably became the church of Keene distinctively in 1833. The oldest sessional record now accessible is dated July 14, 1827. On that day the Rev. Thomas Barr preached, and fifteen members were received into the church. The elders were Timothy Emerson and James Renfrew. The church was supplied during 1828 and 1829, Rev. James Culbertson and Rev. J. B. Morrow, among others, preaching. Rev. George Warner then "supplied" for two years. In 1832, Rev. Wm. Cox preached, and the session received ten members. Rev. N. Conklin was stated supply for two years ending June 1836. Rev. J. S. Wylie followed Mr. Conklin, and served for three years. Both Mr. Conklin and Mr. Wylie also served at the same time the Coshocton church, and these churches have frequently been associated in ministerial charge. Rev. B. I. Lowe followed Mr. Wylie, remaining as stated supply for two years. From 1841 until 1843, the church was supplied by Presbytery. Rev. John D. Whitham was installed pastor July 7, 1843. In 1844, a division occurred, and a New School church was organized. After a little time this was reorganized as a "Free Presbyterian" church, which, after a feeble life, protracted through a dozen years, became extinct.

Of the old church Rev. J. W. Knott became pastor, June 28, 1845, remaining in charge until October, 1847. Rev. Samuel Hanna (son of Rev. A. Hanna, of Wayne county) became pastor, November 11, 1848, and continued his labors until his death, in 1850. His memory is still among the people as "ointment poured forth." Rev. John Trubit, Rev. William Edgar, and Rev. C. C. Bomberger supplied the church from 1850 until July, 1856. At that time Rev. William E. Hunt began to preach, and continued until the next year, when, being invited to spend the whole time at Coshocton, the Keene church called Rev. R. W. Marquis, then preaching in the Linton and Evans creek churches. He was installed November 14, 1857, and continued as pastor until his death, in May, 1875, and is now gratefully recalled as "the faithful *pastor*." Since his death, the church has been supplied by Rev. A. Cone. In 1832, John Elliott and Nathan Shannon were added to the session. John Elliott was afterward dismissed to Coshocton. Timothy Emerson died in 1874. The present elders are Nathan Shannon, Joel Glover, Robert McClure, Liverton Beall, James Leggett, and W. H. Crawford. Rev. I. N. Shannon, pastor of the church of Terre Haute, Indiana, and also of Mt. Vernon, Ohio, was a child of this church, his father, Nathan Shannon, having long been an honored elder in it, and his own body rests in its grave-yard.

The church building, standing on a gentle acclivity, embracing several acres, dotted with young forest trees, is a large frame structure, most substantially built. It was erected in 1834 by Charles Farwell. The number of communicants in 1875 was one hundred and twenty-eight.

West Carlisle Church.—This church was organized on the first day of November, 1828. Rev. James Cunningham (originally from Washington county, Penn., first settled near Marietta, afterward at Utica), had been preaching occasionally in the neighborhood, for some time, and continued to preach for the church until 1834. Rev. Jacob Wolf then served the church for about a year, and after he left Mr. Cunningham again preached for the congregation a couple of years. In 1838 and 1839 the church was supplied by Rev. Enoch Bouton and Rev. Nathaniel Conklin. Rev. J. Matthews seems to have been the first pastor—installed November 11, 1840. Until 1846 he gave it half his time, and then the whole time until 1853. During his time the church building still in use was erected. In 1853, C. C. Bomberger was ordained and installed pastor, giving to this church half his time. During the war the congregation was greatly distracted, and finally divided, Mr. Bomberger and a considerable portion of the congregation putting themselves in connection with the Presbytery of Louisville (Declaration and Testimony), and the new church coming afterward under the care of the Presbytery of Central Ohio in connection with the Synod of Kentucky. After several years of embarrassment, with only occasional supplies, John Foy was ordained and installed in 1870. During his pastorate the church rallied to a considerable extent, and the house of worship was repaired and improved at a cost almost equal to its original cost. Mr. Foy removed, in 1874, to Martinsburgh, Knox county, and the church since has been supplied chiefly by Rev. S. Mehaffey. At its organization the number of members was twenty-four. In 1860 there were eighty-six; in 1874, one hundred. The first elders were Thomas McKee, James Crawford, and Adam Gault. Subsequently the following have served: A. H. Lyons, Christopher Crothers, John Lyons, Jas. McKee, Robert Crouch, Wm. Harvey, *Geo. McKee, D. D. Johnson, Lewis Bonnett,* and *Thomas McKee.* Those in italics compose the session at this time.

Jefferson Church.—This is situated in Jefferson township, about one mile south of Warsaw. Among those chiefly interested in the organization of the church were the Elder family, and the building was located on a site given for the purpose on the farm of old John Elder. The church was organized August 19, 1837. A colony was sent out for the purpose from the West Carlisle Church, with which it has nearly always been associated in making a pastoral charge.*
The principal ministerial labor has been rendered by Reverends Matthews, Bomberger, John Moore, and Foy. It had, at the outset, twenty-four members—had, in 1875, about seventy. The elders first elected were Thomas Lowery, Isaac Skillman—subsequently Wm. McCullough, James Anderson, James Douglass, Matthew Elder, Wm. Crouch, J. V. Stevenson, *John McCluggage, Cyrus Elder, D. E. Laughlin.* Those in italics constitute the session at this time.

---

* See sketch of that church.

Clark Church.—The Clark (township) church was organized March 22, 1834. Rev. N. Conklin and others had occasionally preached in the region, a number of Presbyterian families having therein settled. John P. Kerr and Thomas Guthrie were the first elders. There were twelve members.

The services, for three years, were held in the house or barn of Wm. Craig. The first church building was erected in 1837, by Geo. Weatherwax. Cost, about $200. The site of the building originally donated was deeded to trustees May 19, 1846, by Wm. Craig and wife, in consideration of one dollar. In 1867, a new edifice was erected—a good-sized and neatly-built frame structure.

The ministers of the church have been: N. Conklin, 1834–38; Messrs. Washburn, Turbit, and Gordon were supplies from 1838 to 1845; S. M. Templeton, 1845–47; Samuel Hanna, 1847–51; John M. Boggs, 1851–56; R. W. Marquis, 1857–72; A. S. Milholland, 1871–75; T. D. Duncan, April 11, 1875.

The elders: John P. Kerr, Thomas Guthrie, Robert Huston, George Weatherwax, *Thomas Shannon, Wm. Weatherwax, Geo. R. Altman, James Endsley, Jr.,* and *John T. Crawford.* Those in italics composing the session at this time.

The original membership was almost wholly from Western Pennsylvania. There were twelve members at the organization; in 1876, one hundred and fifteen.

Linton (township) Church.—Was organized August 15, 1833. Ten persons presented certificates from other churches (most of them from the church on Island creek, Jefferson county), and five persons asked to be received into the church on examination, among them John Glenn, afterward an elder. The church was supplied by Revs. N. Conklin, N. Cobb, J. Matthews, D. Washburn, S. Hanna, Wm. Lumsden, and Robert Robe, for nearly nineteen years. Rev. R. W. Marquis was the first pastor; settled April 10, 1852, and remained in charge until the fall of 1857. The church was then supplied for a time by Rev. J. B. Akey.

In 1860, Rev. John Moore, D.D., became pastor, and continued as such for some two years. Rev. G. W. Fisher was the next pastor, 1864–68. After being supplied for two years, the church called to the pastorate Rev. J. B. Stevenson, and he was in the place more than a year. Rev. W. B. Scarborough, the present pastor, took charge in 1872.

At the organization of the church, there were fifteen members; now there are ninety-three.

The first elders were Alex. Matthews, Sr., and Alex. Matthews, Jr. Being unacceptable to the congregation, they were soon removed. Eldredge Foster, J. Fort, John Glenn, and Wm. Love were in the office. All dead.

The present session is composed of A. Shaffer, A. Sibley, John Glenn (second), and Robert Daugherty.

The congregation is using its second house of worship. The first was an old wagon-maker's shop, repaired and refitted. The present is a very neat frame building, erected in 1868.

Mr. John Gunby, residing at Snow Hill, Maryland, but owning land in the vicinity of this church, left it a legacy of $1,000 in 1874.

Evans' Creek Church.—The first house of worship stood on a hill, about a mile out of Bakersville, overlooking the creek. It was a log one. The present is a neat frame structure, in Bakersville, built in 1861. The church was organized April 29, 1833.

During almost its entire history, it has been associated with the Linton church, having the same pastors, except in the case of Rev. John Moore, D.D.

The elders have been: James Jones, David Walters, Wm. Shannon, Robert Lyons, *John Buck*, *David G. Miller*, and *John Miller*. Those in italics are the present session.

The number of members at this time is seventy-three.

Roscoe Church.—The Roscoe church was organized April 25, 1847. Rev. H. Calhoun supplied it for eleven years, and it received a part of the time of Revs. Henderson, Wallace, and other pastors of the Second church of Coshocton. At the organization there were fifteen members. Under the care of Mr. Calhoun, and also at a later day under the labors of Rev. C. W. Wallace, Rev. S. P. Hildreth, and Rev. H. C. McBride, considerable accessions were received to the church; but it has, at this writing, hardly as many as when first organized. The elders have been James Hill, George Bagnall, T. Carnahan, S. Sayre.

Chiefly through the spirited exertions of Mrs. P. W. Medbery, a good frame building was erected about 1849.

In 1847 a church was organized at "the Valley," on the road from Coshocton to Newark, six miles west of Coshocton, and a squared-log church built. Rev. P. H. Jacobs, of Coshocton, and Rev. C. C. Bomberger supplied it from 1847 to 1860.

The neighborhood had at first a few Presbyterian families, but death and removal to the west soon effaced these, and as the territory was occupied from the start by other denominations, this retired from the field.

In 1863, the old organization having become extinct, a second effort was made, but with no better success than the first. To this second congregation, Rev. John Moore, D.D., while settled in Jefferson church, ministered. In the first organization, William Crooks was an elder; in the second, John McCluggage. The church never numbered a score of members.

At East Union, in early days, an unsuccessful effort to establish a Presbyterian church was made; also at Wakatonita Cross-Roads.

After "the split" of 1838, attempts were made to start "New School" churches at Linton and Keene, but there was no success at either place.

The whole number of Presbyterian communicants in the county at this time is about eight hundred and fifty.

UNITED PRESBYTERIAN.

An "Associate Reformed Presbyterian" Church was planted in Adams township nearly forty years ago. Its chief friends were the Campbells, Daughertys, McFaddens, Funks, Smiths, and Warrens. The principal ministerial service was rendered by Rev. D. F. Reed, the congregation being associated with Millcreek. A house of worship was built about 1840, but it was many years ago burned, and the church became, after a time, extinct.

In relation to the other United Presbyterian churches, a member of the Amity church communicates the following:

The United Presbyterian Congregation of *Amity*, Keene township, is composed of the Associate Reformed Congregation of Millcreek and the Associate Congregation of Keene, which occupied substantially the same territory.

The first members of the A. R. Church came to Keene township during the summer and fall of 1817, of whom Robert Boyd was the first, who came May 4, 1817. He was an educated man, and was considered by some of his friends as at one time the best scholar west of the mountains. His wife was a sister of Rev. Gilbert McMaster, D.D., of the Covenanter Church, father of Rev. E. D. McMaster, of the O. S. Presbyterian Church. He came from Ireland when quite a young man. His father, William Boyd, was an elder in Rev. Kerr's Church, Cookstown, Tyrone county, Ireland, father of Revs. Joseph and Moses Kerr, of Pittsburg, Pa. The first preaching they had was in the summer of 1818, by Rev. George Buchanan, of Steubenville. He preached occasionally afterward; and Robert Boyd and George Ford, formerly elders in his congregation at Steubenville, acted as a session here. George Ford said there was no other organization between this and Steubenville. After 1822, Revs. David Proudfit, David Norwood, and Moses Kerr supplied occasionally.

The first communion was held in the fall of 1828, by Rev. Samuel Findley, D.D. The members at that time were Robert Boyd and wife, George Ford and wife, John Williams and wife, Thomas Hamilton and wife, Joseph Marshall and wife, Robert Boyd (Jr.) and wife, Mrs. Nancy Foster, Mrs. Sarah Ford, et al.

In 1834 George Marshall, Samuel Hamilton, and John Irvine were elected elders.

Robert Boyd died November 25, 1826. George Marshall died September 30, 1834. He was a solid farmer, and the father of Colonel William Marshall.

George Ford lived until some ten years ago, dying at a very advanced age. He was a man of strong will and ardent piety.

John Irvine removed a few years since to Iowa.

The brick church was erected in 1834. The present frame church was erected in 1856.

Rev. D. F. Reid settled as first pastor in 1841, in connection with Millersburg and White Eyes, and labored with a good degree of success for about sixteen years.

William Richie and Richard Richie were ordained elders November 10, 1857.

The Associate Congregation of Keene was organized August 26, 1838. Robert Boyd and Robert Karr were ordained elders. Rev. Samuel Irvine officiated. Members: Robert Boyd and Elizabeth, his wife, Robert Karr and wife, William Boyd, John Karr and wife, Sarah Boyd, John Boyd, John Elliott and Martha, his wife, Robert Tidrick and wife, John Williamson and wife, James Johnson, Samuel Boyd and Nancy, his wife, and John Loder.

Revs. S. Irvine, Joseph McKee, Samuel Hindman McCleans, and others, supplied occasionally. In April, 1845, Rev. James M. Henderson was settled as pastor, one-fourth of his time in connection with Northfield and Claysville. He labored thus one year and nine months with a good degree of success, when he was released from this part of his charge. He was a strong advocate of temperance and opponent of slavery. The most striking instance of his labors here was a sermon that he preached from the text "Thou shalt not surely die." A Universalist preacher, by the name of Eaton, was making quite an excitement, and drawing a number of influential and enthusiastic followers after him. Mr. Henderson gave four weeks' notice that he would preach on the subject in the Keene O. S. Presbyterian Church. There was a large audience to hear him, and he handled the subject in such a manner that Universalism has had a quietus on it in these parts ever since. August 26, 1853, James T. Boyd and James Boyd were ordained and installed elders.

In November, 1854, Rev. John P. Scott was settled one-third his time in connection with Millersburg and labored one year and nine months with success, when he was released from this branch of his charge.

June 16, 1855, John Williamson and James McKenzie were ordained and installed elders.

September 4, 1858, the A. R. Congregation of Millcreek and the Associate Congregation of Keene formally went into the United Presbyterian Church.

July 1, 1859, Rev. William A. McConnell was settled as pastor of the congregations of Millcreek, White Eyes, and Keene.

Pursuant to a notice given on the last Sabbath in April, the congregations of Millcreek and Keene voted unanimously to consolidate into one congregation and session, under the name of Amity. This " action was ratified " by Presbytery, October 15, 1861.

The session was Rev. W. A. McConnell, George Ford, John Irvine, William Richie, Richard Richie, James T. Boyd, John Williamson, and James Boyd.

Mr. McConnell labored with ability and success until some difficulties arose. He resigned his charge at the meeting of Presbytery, June, 1864, on the ground that he had not got the encouragement and support to harmonize the charge he was led to expect. He left on the 13th of September, 1864. At that time Amity had one hundred and thirty members. Amity has had no settled pastor since. The membership at present is forty-seven.

The Rev. J. C. Boyd, of Utica, Ohio, and the Rev. Joshua W. Wait, of Lincoln county, Tennessee, were reared in this congregation.

The congregation of *Avondale* was organized autumn of 1873, Rev. Andrew McCartney officiating. Elders Robert C. Warren, Claudius Hamilton, James T. Boyd, and John

Doherty. Membership, about forty-five. They have a very neat frame building.

PROTESTANT EPISCOPAL.

Bishop McIlvaine preached in Coshocton in the old Presbyterian church, standing on the square while it was not yet quite completed, 1835. Several unsuccessful movements have been made looking to the organization of a congregation of the P. E. church in Coshocton. For more than a year, preaching by a minister of that church was kept up in Roscoe. Rev. C. Sturgiss lived for some time, about 1844, in Keene, conducting an academy and preaching to a little flock at "the Knob," in Millcreek township, where, through the influence of John Mitchell and others, a church was organized about forty years ago. There is, at that place, a neat little stone church, but only a few members, and there has been no service for nearly two years.

A movement was made for a church of this order at Newcastle, and services were conducted for some time by the professors at Gambier, but little headway was made.

Rev. J. D. Nunemacher is preaching to a congregation (without organization) composed mainly of Lutherans, in Coshocton, following in a line of work carried on for twenty years. There is also a congregation of similar sort at Helmick, in Clark township.

At "Ramur Meeting-house," in Keene township, there is gathered a "Christian Union" church—a denomination growing out of the late war, proclaiming as one of its cardinal doctrines, "no politics in the church."

Another organization of same kind was organized in East Union, in 1866, and numbered over a hundred members. Still another church of this order is on Severns' Ridge in New Castle township.

UNITED BRETHREN.

Twenty-five years ago there was a considerable church of the "United Brethren" worshiping in the Ramur Meeting-house in Keene township, but during the late civil war it was so divided and distracted as to become practically extinct, and was supplanted by the "Christian Union" church, now worshiping in same building.

It is understood that there are two respectable congregations of United Brethren in the east part of the county, one in White-eyes and one in Crawford township, but no detailed accounts of them have been obtained.

CHAPTER XXIII.

BRIEF BIOGRAPHICAL SKETCHES.

Charles Williams, the first white settler in Coshocton county, was unquestionably one of the most remarkable of its citizens. He was born near Hagerstown, Maryland, in 1764. In his boyhood, the family removed to Western Virginia, near Wheeling. He married there Susannah Carpenter, and moved to the neighborhood of the salt works on the Muskingum, ten miles below Coshocton, and subsequently to "the forks of the Muskingum." Of hardy stock, he grew up in the severest discipline of pioneer life. He was a successful trapper, hunter, Indian scout, and trader, and held every office (being almost all the time in some) in the county possible for a man of his education, from road supervisor and tax-collector to member of the legislature. He was famous as a tavern-keeper, and in that and other capacities became very popular. Clever, genial, naturally shrewd, indomitable in purpose, not averse to the popular vices of his day, and even making a virtue of profanity, he was for forty years *a* controlling spirit of the county, and for twenty-five, *the* controlling spirit. He died in 1840 (in his seventy-sixth year), leaving a considerable number of relatives, many of whom are still in the county. Two of his children were burned to death by the destruction by fire of the cabin built by him when he first settled at Coshocton. It is said that one of his daughters (the mother of C. H., Matthew, and Wm. A. Johnston), when twelve years old, was in the habit of doing the milling for the family, taking the grain on horseback to Zanesville, and bringing back the flour. The family was emphatically of the Pioneer sort.

Thomas L. Rue, appointed as clerk of the court in 1811, and candidate for the legislature in 1814, was the oldest son of Rev. Joseph Rue, of Pennington, New Jersey—a well-known Presbyterian minister. He came to Coshocton county in 1811; a little later, went to New Orleans, coming back the overland route. He married Miss Fulton, and for some years gave himself to the management of a large tract of land (since known as the Rickett's lands) near Coshocton, acquired by that alliance. Afterward he was engaged in trade with C. Van Kirk. He died in Roscoe, February 17, 1871 (aged eighty-eight years), at the house of Dr. M. Johnson, who had married his only child. He was a brother of Joseph W. Rue.

James Renfrew, one of the earliest merchants in Coshocton county, and for a few years county treasurer, and otherwise connected with public affairs, was born at Lisburn, county Antrim, Ireland, in 1767. He brought to America a healthy body, a strong mind, and a little of this world's goods, which were steadily increased until his death. He commenced keeping store in Coshocton about 1815. In 1820, while in Pittsburg, whither he was in the habit of going for goods, he married Mrs. Johnson, a widowed sister of old Dr. Kerr, of the A. R. Presbyterian church in that city. The children of this woman found in Mr. Renfrew a most worthy step-father. He was an admirable counselor and helper while living, and a generous friend when dying. Both himself and his wife were most zealous Presbyterians, and sought to have all connected with them honor the Lord. Beside the Johnsons (John, Jos. K., and Wm.), Robert Hay was an object of Mr. Renfrew's interest and business training, and always spoke in highest terms of him. Wm. Renfrew (quite prominent as a merchant and otherwise) and James Renfrew, Jr., were children of Mr. Renfrew by a connection formed prior to his coming to Coshocton. He had no children by the widow Johnson. Mr. Renfrew died in 1832, being in his sixty-fifth year.

Abraham Sells was for more than half a century a resident of Coshocton county. His father's family located very early in the century near New Comerstown. Abraham learned his trade of cabinet-making at Marietta, and set up in Coshocton in 1814. He was for some time a justice of the peace, and also coroner of the county. He died September 22, 1869, in his seventy-sixth year. His widow, now about his age at death, resides in Coshocton with her son B. F. Sells.

Dr. Samuel Lee was for more than sixty years a resident of Coshocton. He was born, and spent his boyhood, on a farm near Pultney, Vt. Having studied medicine at Castleton, Vt., he came to Ohio in 1809 on invitation of, and along with, Rev. Timothy Harris, of Granville, Licking county, who was then minister of the church of Granville, and had gone to visit his friends in the east, and act as a sort of emigration agent. The trip to Ohio was made on horseback. The Doctor was always specially interested in horses, and once remarked that the first thing he ever owned was a horse, and he guessed it would be the last thing he would give up. After he had been in Granville about two years (in which time he married Miss Sabra Case, who was an help-meet indeed, and who preceded him to the grave some three years), he came to Coshocton on the hunt of an estrayed or stolen horse. The town was then a mere hamlet, and wanted a physician, and he removed at once. Practice was then no play. A ride of forty miles in visiting a patient was of common occurrence. The perils and exposures of the new country gave the Doctor plenty of work, and his originally vigorous constitution and active habits were heavily taxed, and drafts made upon them bearing heavily upon his later years. For years before his death he was much crippled and very hard of hearing. He died at the house of his son, Dr. S. H. Lee, on the 19th of March, 1874, having completed within four days his eighty-ninth year.

Dr. Lee had undoubted adaptations for his time and place. The roughness and freedom and economy of pioneer life did not misfit him. He was very genial; could tell a good story, and crack a joke with the jolliest of the men and women of his day. He used to tell with zest how he had taken aback some old ladies who had been summoned to attend a young unmarried woman who had been "unfortunate," and was then in straits, by proposing very gravely "a corn poultice," a favorite application of that day, and pretending that he did not understand the case, being misled by the fact that the woman was an unmarried one.

His patriotism and philanthropy are pleasant things in the remembrance of his friends. Although holding public office but twice—that of county treasurer, in very early days, and that of State senator in 1826-27—he was always interested in public affairs. While an intense hater of the system of slavery, he was anything but bitter to those who were entangled, by their birth and surroundings, in that system. There are abundant evidences of his friendly disposition in his readiness to go on their official bonds, and otherwise stand for his neighbors. His conscientiousness and diligence in his profession none have questioned. He had a quick-wittedness and strong common sense that often stood in lieu of profundity of attainment. Among those with whom he had to do, he could, with a lancet and a little calomel, and jalap and a corn poultice, effect all that many now-a-days can do with the nicer instrumental appliances and amply furnished apothecary shops. He was not what might be called a scholarly man, but always the friend of intelligence. The first school-house built in Coshocton was on a site granted to Dr. Lee and his associates. By industry and economy he always lived comfortably, and at his death left a considerable portion.

He really reared two sets of children—his own and those of his daughter who married Robert M. Lamb—beside having some care over the children of another daughter, Mrs. Jamieson.

The Doctor, at an early day, owned almost the entire square bounded by Fourth, Fifth, Main, and Walnut streets. He had a farm just east of town; but his residence was for the most of his life in the brick house at corner of Fourth and Main streets.

His shrewdness and strict honesty in business transactions were prominent features in his character. His creditors were generally few, and debtors many.

Before leaving his New England home, Dr. Lee openly committed himself to the service of God, and espoused the religion that stood him in stead unto the last.

For adherence to his convictions of duty in a religious way, he was well known; and in exhibiting gave and bore much. For thirty-five years he was an elder in the Presbyterian church.

Feeble in body and failing in mind, for some time in latest years, he never forgot the Bible and his family worship, and wanted to be reckoned a child of God.

James Robinson came with his father's family into the locality now known as Franklin township, Coshocton county, then the Northwestern territory, in 1801. He was born in Clarksburg, Harrison county, Virginia, in 1787. He served one term as associate judge, and two terms in the legislature; but he seems to have taken most interest in his broad acres, and to have been chiefly famed as a large land-holder and enterprising farmer. He was also very actively interested in the Methodist Episcopal church, being chiefly instrumental in the planting of the Bethany church, where his descendants still worship. He died May 7, 1856.

Thomas Darling was born in Hardy county, Virginia, November 7, 1799. His father brought the family to the Walhonding valley (near Warsaw) in 1806. The journey was made on horseback, the mother having an infant on the horse before her, and the little boy, Thomas, holding on to her, as he rode behind.

His life was mainly given to farming. He was, however, a public-spirited citizen, and for a number of years served the county as a commissioner, the record of which service appears in another part of this volume. In later years, he was much interested in blooded cattle, and introduced some valuable stock into the valley in which he lived. He died December 27, 1874, being seventy-five years and about one month old.

He married Miss Demie Butler, and reared a considerable family; and his family connections enter largely into the social fabric of the Walhonding valley, as well as extending into other localities.

Benjamin Ricketts was born near Cumberland, Maryland. Learning his trade as a hatter in that town, he afterward opened a shop at Marietta; still later, had one in Zanesville. Giving up his shop, he set up a store in West Zanesville. He commenced selling goods in Coshocton in 1818, and in the spring of 1820, brought the family to the town. His successful prosecution of business was most clearly apparent in the accumulations attending it. He became a large land-holder and well-known citizen.

He served one term as county commissioner. He and the opposing candidate were "tied" on the vote, and by lot the office devolved upon Mr. Ricketts. He was never much enamored of public office, and, it is understood, never held any except this one.

His church connection was with the Methodist Episcopalians.

Like many, indeed nearly or quite all, of the successful and prominent men of Coshocton county, Mr. Ricketts was greatly aided in all his life's work by his wife, who, at the good old age of nearly eighty-five years, is still living in Coshocton. She was from Hampshire county, Virginia; was married when about sixteen years of age, in 1807.

Mr. Ricketts died July 1, 1857. His descendants and connections are many, and few families have been better known "in the gates" than his.

John Carhart stood for more than half a century before the people of Coshocton county as a steadfast worker and zealous Christian man.

He was born near Dresden; learned the tanner's trade in Zanesville; came to near Roscoe (one mile north) about 1821, and set up a tannery. He was also in mercantile line for a time—was one of the partners in "Union Mill;" latterly, gave whole attention to leather business.

Early in life, identified himself with Baptist church, and was steadfast in the faith. Was an enthusiastic Sunday-school man; and, as none of his own views were in the place, co-operated zealously with the Methodist Episcopal and Presbyterian schools.

He died December 6, 1873, being a little more than seventy-three years old.

James Le Retilley was born in the Isle of Guernsey, in 1788. He came to this country in 1806, settling in Guernsey county, where was a settlement of people from the island of the same name. Removing to Muskingum county, at a point about ten miles below Coshocton, he engaged in the manufacture of salt, along with George Bagnall. They made about six bushels a day at three dollars a bushel, or exchanged a bushel for twelve bushels of wheat. Their salt was carried to remote points, some of it by canoes and pirogues up the Killbuck almost to Wooster. In 1825, the Kanawha and lower Muskingum salt coming into market, largely rendered the business of Retilley & Bagnall unprofitable, and they removed to Caldersburg (Roscoe). Retilley and William Wood set up a dry-goods store (in a log-cabin), the first in the place. After a few years Wood retired, and the firm became Bagnall & Retilley, and for years was very prominent in trade circles, doing a very large business.

Mr. Retilley was one of the associate judges of the county, and an active adherent of the Methodist church in Roscoe. He died in December, 1850, aged sixty-two years. He was twice married. His second wife (the daughter of T. Emerson of Keene), now resides in Granville. His descendants are still well known in the land.

Thomas Johnson, by the documentary history of the county, and the concurrent testimony of survivors, was one of the most prominent and spirited citizens. He was born in the parish of Glentubert, Monaghan county, Ireland, on the 16th of March, 1783. Early in youth he manifested a great desire to go to America, and urged his father to emigrate. He, being a very quiet, unobtrusive man, with quite a family of young children, could not think of bringing them to the wilds of America. Thomas remained with his father until he was twenty-four years of age, and had brothers grown up. He then told his father he was determined to go to the new world, and urged his suit with so much ardor that his parents could no longer withhold their consent. He left Ireland in 1806, and landed in New York with but one sovereign in his pocket. He there met with Joseph T. Baldwin, of Newark, New Jersey, who offered to employ him. He remained with Mr. Baldwin for three years. In 1808, he married Sarah Parker. About this time his parents and three brothers, Richard, William, and Robert, and his only sister, Margaret, joined him in Newark. Thomas then determined that Newark was not the place for his father's family to settle, and in 1808 he and his father's family came to Coshocton county, where they bought a quarter section of land from Esaias Baker, on which now stand the old homestead and also the village of East Plainfield and cemetery, in which his first son, William, was the first to be buried. In 1812, he and his brother, Richard, were in the army under General Harrison. He held the office of justice of the peace, and was long an associate judge of the Court of Common Pleas. He and Jacob Waggoner built the first mill of any note on Will's creek, of four run of burrs, that tapped a radius of twenty miles. From 1820 to 1830, he ran several flat-boats to New Orleans and other points south. He nearly lost his life the first cholera season. In running the dam at Zanesville one time he and two of his oarsmen were thrown out of the boat by the oars striking the pier of the bridge. Mr. Rankin, being a good swimmer, got out, William Smith was drowned, and he was rescued from the water by the exertions of sheriff Daniel Brush. Once, finding yellow-fever prevailing in New Orleans, and markets dull, he concluded to coast out his load of provisions, and poled his boat up the Tennessee as far as Florence, where muscle shoals prevented his further passage. He had large contracts on the Ohio canal. Owing to the high banks and mud bottoms, there was a difficulty in fording Will's creek at his mills, and the commissioners being unable or unwilling to assist in bridging said stream, he petitioned the legislature, in 1834, to authorize him to build a bridge and collect toll. This was the first bridge spanning Will's creek in Coshocton county, and remained a toll-bridge about twenty years, when his son made a free-will offering of the bridge to the county commissioners, they agreeing to repair and keep it up. He was connected with the building of the bridges that span the Tuscarawas and Walhonding rivers between Coshocton and Roscoe. From 1838 to 1840 he had heavy contracts on the Walhonding canal. In 1812, the pioneer Methodist preacher founded this settlement, and the Johnson family were the first to unite in church fellowship. Thomas was appointed leader of the class, and also steward, which office he held to the day of his death. His house was always the preacher's home. About 1835, he built the largest meeting-house in the vicinity, on his land and principally at his own expense, giving it by will to the trustees of Coshocton circuit, and their successors in office. After a protracted sickness, which first made itself manifest while attending court in Coshocton, he died, August 20, 1840, in full resignation and in great peace. His widow survived him almost twenty-two years, dying at the old homestead, March 29, 1862. His father also survived him eighteen days, dying September 7, 1840, in the eighty-first year of his age. Robert Johnson, his youngest brother, moved from near Plainfield, twenty years ago, and settled in Colwell county, Missouri, being in his seventy-eighth year, and the only survivor of the old stock.

Joseph Burns.—His father, Samuel Burns, removed from Waynesburg, Augusta county, Virginia (where Joseph was born), to Ohio, in 1815. The family were about a year in New Philadelphia, and then came down the river in a pirogue, or large canoe, to Coshocton, making their location in this county in 1816. Joseph was at that time about sixteen years old, having been born March 11, 1800. Favored by nature with a good appearance and great affability of manner, and being skilled in the art of penmanship, he was soon a young man of note in the neighborhood. His first appearance in public capacity was probably in 1818, when he served as clerk at an election in Tuscarawas township, at which his father was one of the judges. In 1821 he was run by his friends for the office of auditor, and perhaps that time and once afterward, when he ran for a second term in Congress, were the only occasions in which he did not secure the coveted position. This work, under the heads of "County Officers" and "Relations to State and National Governments," will show the offices of public sort filled by him. Except a brief period in his youth spent in farming, and another in his maturer life spent in keeping a drug-store, his whole active life of more than fifty years was spent in public work. Never very exacting as to fees, and always free with his purse among his friends and fellow citizens, he left at the end of his days only a moderate portion. Many men with more of greed, or less honest or frugal in general habits, would have amassed great wealth with his opportunities. The affection of the large Virginia and Maryland elements in the population of the county for him was something worthy of study. The stock of which he came was the old Scotch-Irish, so largely prominent in the whole history of the country. His parents were Presbyterians, and his philosophy and faith partook of the old Covenanter cast. He always had some taste for military affairs, and was a major-general of the militia.

He was twice married—his first wife was Rebecca Price, and his second was Mrs. Alex. Hay. One of his sons was educated at West Point, and was during the war a brigadier-general, and another was clerk of the United States District Court of Iowa for some years. He had in all six sons and two daughters, and these with his widow survive him.

His latter days were rendered distressful by the nature of his disease—dropsy of the chest; but he continued, until within a few hours of his death, to transact at his home such of the business of his office (that of probate judge) as must receive his personal attention. Rising from his bed, and essaying to take a few steps, he sank to the floor, and in a moment was done with the burdens and honors of life, which he had received so largely and borne so bravely. He was a little more than a month beyond his seventy-fifth year.

John Burns was born in Waynesburg, Augusta county, Virginia, in the year 1807. He moved with his father's family to New Philadelphia, Tuscarawas county, in 1815, and in April, 1816, they moved to Coshocton county, as has been detailed in connection with the sketch of his brother, Joseph Burns. He remained with his father until 1828, when he went to Chillicothe as a clerk with his brother-in-law, John Smeltzer, and remained there one year. He then came to Roscoe, and clerked in the dry-goods store of John Smeltzer and his successors (Medbery & Ransom) until 1838, when he became a member of the firm, under the name of Medbery, Burns & Co. In 1840 he dissolved his connection with Medbery, and formed a connection with Samuel Moffitt for the sale of dry goods, under the firm name of Burns & Moffitt. He continued in said firm until 1845, when Moffitt retired, and the firm was changed to Burns & Retilley, and remained so until 1860, when he bought Retilley out, and continued in business in his own name until his death. He died July 31, 1871, aged sixty-four years.

His good sense and integrity were marked qualities. Thoroughly interested in public affairs, and always a zealous partisan, and ready to help his friends to office, he never had any desires in that direction for himself, and it is believed never held any official position. He was a painstaking and successful business and family man.

John Johnson was a prominent citizen of Coshocton county for nearly half a century. He was born in county Tyrone, Ireland; came to America in 1816, and to Coshocton about 1820. Under the direction of his stepfather, James Renfrew, and after the manner of his time, he learned the tanner's trade. He was a member of the well-known merchandising and banking firm, W. K. Johnson & Co. For some years, about 1840, he resided at Walhonding. He represented Coshocton district in the upper house of the Legislature, and was also a member of the lower house in Congress. He was a member of the State Constitutional Convention 1850–51. His health was not firm for some years before he died, and on this and other accounts he was not so much engaged with public affairs in his later years as in earlier ones. With limited education, his industry and native shrewdness and caution enabled him to achieve a considerable degree of business and political success. He was averse to display, and believed in "solid" things. He was a devout adherent of the Presbyterian church, in the faith of which he had been thoroughly trained. He died February 5, 1867. His wife was Miss Harriet Humrickhouse, and he died without issue.

William K. Johnson was born in County Tyrone in Ireland, and when only seven years of age was brought to America. The family, after a brief stay in Baltimore, came to Pittsburg, where a brother of Mrs. Johnson (Rev. Dr. Kerr) was living. About 1820 Mrs. Johnson was married to James Renfrew, then doing business in Coshocton, and the Johnson children thus and then came to Coshocton. At first a clerk, and then a partner in the mercantile business, and afterward in banking and in real estate operations. William K. Johnson was for many years regarded as a representative business man of the county. He had the confidence of the whole community, and his name was a synonym for integrity, sobriety, diligent application to business, and great prudence. By all the sons of the Emerald Isle, especially, he was looked to as a wise counselor. His approbation of any matter of town and county interest was regarded as quite important in order to its accomplishment. His views and actions have very largely shaped the social and business affairs of the region where for nearly forty years he lived and labored. He was for many years a member of the board of education and of the town council of Coshocton. He was postmaster for some fifteen years. He was connected with the Steubenville and Indiana railroad, as a director, from its organization until his death. He was one of the most regular attendants and spirited supporters of the Presbyterian Church. In the earlier years of its history, he superintended the Sabbath-school, and led the congregational singing. For a number of years he served the County Bible society as its treasurer and depository. While not uninterested in political affairs, he had little ambition in that line.

He married, in 1836, Miss Elizabeth Humrickhouse, who, with six children, survived him. His death occurred in comparatively early years, he being about fifty years old. He died Monday (having been in his place of business on Saturday), December 10, 1860.

Robert Hay was born in County Derry, Ireland, in February, 1801. He came to America in 1817, and was employed in stores in Pittsburg for two years, and then came to Coshocton in the employ of James Renfrew. After a clerkship of a few years, he became a partner with Mr. Renfrew, and subsequently with William Renfrew. For fifty years he was in business. He was in his store when taken with his last illness. No man ever stood higher in the community for truthfulness, honesty, promptitude, and careful application to business. Trained in the old school of merchants, he was a strict disciplinarian, and despised all trifling and trickery. He always was himself to be found at his business in business hours, and expected a conscientious devotion to his interest on the part of his employes, whom he always regarded with kindly interest. For the worthy poor he had always much sympathy, and was especially ready to help them to help themselves. He served the county for several years as county treasurer, but was never inclined to public station. In the regular prosecution of his business as a merchant and distiller, he steadily increased his worldly estate, and by the vast accretions in connection with the excise tax in the earlier part of the war, left at his death the largest estate ever administered upon in Coshocton county.

He married Miss Mary Corbin, of Granville, O., in 1858. She and one child preceded him to the grave, and two children survived him. He died, after a few days' illness, May 3, 1869, at the house of his brother James, which for some time he had made his home.

John Elliott, for many years commonly designated as "Deacon Elliott," belonged to a family of mark, all winning considerable fame, despite what would be accounted an unfavorable condition at the start. The family came from Ireland. The mother's piety seems to have been as strong a determining force in the children as the hard sense of the father. One of the sons, Samuel Elliott, was associate judge of the county; another, Charles, became a very prominent minister in the M. E. Church. The deacon was thrown, in early life, into Presbyterian surroundings, and, though not favorably affected at first, after thorough study, adopted that form of Christian faith, and held to it through all his life with notable pertinacity. He united with the church under Rev. Elisha McCurdy, of Western Pennsylvania. After learning thoroughly the carpenter's trade, he spent some time in erecting mission buildings—church, school-house, and dwellings—for the use of the Presbyterian missionaries among the Sandusky Indians. He was a citizen of Coshocton county about forty years. The first Presbyterian Church of Coshocton and the Methodist Episcopal Church of same place, and some others in the country, were built by him. About 1855 he went to Iowa, with the purpose of making that his home, but in a few years returned to Coshocton, and, after working a few years, ended his days in August, 1869. Strong sense and steadfast piety were characteristics of the man. Indifferent as to personal appearance, and exceedingly blunt in expression, he compelled the respect and regard of all who became to any extent acquainted with him. He was one of the two first chosen elders of the Presbyterian Church of Coshocton, and an almost never-failing attendant upon the church prayer-meetings, which he always found time to attend.

He married Miss Blythe, of Fayette county, Pa. She

lived only a few years, and left one son (John B. Elliott), at whose home the old deacon died, September 2, 1868, being sixty-eight years old.

Dea. Taliafero Vickers was a leading citizen in Washington township. He was born in Prince William's county, Virginia, on the 22d of September, 1789. He came to Coshocton county in 1827. Early in life, he identified himself with the Baptists, and he died in the Wakatomika Baptist Church on Sunday, February 19, 1863. He had gone to the church in his usual health, and his last utterance was an "amen" spoken while the minister was reading Rev. 1:18. A moment after, the attention of the congregation was drawn to him, and those going to him found him dead.

Wm. Brown was for eighteen years, from 1822 to 1840, a merchant and general business man in West Carlisle, of which town he was one of the original proprietors. He was born in Franklin county, Pennsylvania; spent a few years, before coming to Coshocton county, at St. Clairsville, Belmont county. His parents were from Germany, spelling their name Braun. His wife was Scotch-Irish. By the combination of the virtues of the two races, the Browns won for themselves great consideration in their neighborhood, and, though starting in their wedded life with very little, amassed quite a respectable fortune. Mr. Brown was for many years a justice of the peace and postmaster under Monroe, J. Q. Adams, Jackson, and Van Buren, although he was a very decided Adams and Clay man. He was an excellent horseman, and skilled in the use of the rifle, and these things helped him greatly in the state of society found in his day in the region of West Carlisle. In public movements and proper sports, he was never lacking, and was often recognized as a leader, and made the object of a good deal of "backwoods homage."

And yet, with all his activity in business and interest in the social life of the people, Mr. Brown is represented as having been a very earnest and faithful man in his religious duties. Family worship was on no excuse intermitted; the Sabbath was sacredly regarded; and when, as before and after a communion in the church, there was preaching, the store was shut, although he loved business, and avowed his intention to give himself steadily to it, and to make money for his family. His house was the "minister's hold," and he was one of the most active members of the Presbyterian church from its organization, contributing largely of his means to it, and especially in the erection of the building still in use by the congregation.

In 1840, he removed to Logansport, Indiana, and there died March 4, 1859. His wife, inheriting a considerable estate from her father, gave it all to foreign missions. One of the sons, Wm. L. Brown, Acting Brigadier-General of the Indiana Infantry, was killed at the second battle of Bull Run. Three sons became Presbyterian ministers. J. C., who died while pastor at Valparaiso, Indiana; Hugh A. was a missionary to China, and has been for many years pastor of a church in Virginia; and Frederick T. (the only child born in Coshocton county, and who even yet glories in being a Buckeye), who had charge of a church in Cleveland, then of one in Alexandria, D. C., then was in St. Paul, Minn., and is now at Ann Arbor, Mich.

Alexander Renfrew came from Union county, Pennsylvania, where he was born August 18, 1801, to Coshocton county in 1826, and remained therein until his death on his farm in Keene township, February 13, 1872. He married Miss Carnahan in 1833, who, with three children, survives him. Starting in life with little, he, by a life of industry and frugality, amassed a very considerable estate. Public life had little attractions, and his record is that of a quiet citizen, a successful farmer, and a busy man, manifesting the virtues of domestic and business life.

Eli Nichols was for forty years a well-known citizen of Coshocton county. He was for many years, ending with his death, the largest land-owner in the county, being in occupancy of the quarter township of New Castle, now held by his son, Lloyd Nichols. He came from Belmont county, Ohio.

His death occurred at his home, after an illness of only two days. His age was seventy-two years. His wife preceded him to the grave but a few months.

His interest in education, and especially his attachment to the public-school system, was often avowed.

He was born and reared in the Quaker church, but in after years disavowed the religious principles of that body, and repudiated the Bible as an infallible book. In early manhood, he took an active part in the operations of the Colonization Society, but soon abandoned it, and henceforward gloried in being an "Abolitionist."

His gentleness of nature made him patient amid whatever reproach he encountered in this, as in other lines of thought and action; and it is claimed for him that, whatever his antipathy to the system of slavery, and his sympathy with the oppressed, he was always wonderfully lenient toward the slave-holder.

In his later years, he became much interested in "Spiritualism," and much of his time in his declining years was given to study of this, and he became a full believer in it, continuing in this faith unto the last of earth.

Rev. Nathaniel Conklin was for many years a most zealous and successful minister of the Presbyterian Church in Coshocton county. He studied at Princeton, New Jersey; preached for some ten years at Frankfort, Sussex county, in that state, and came to this county about 1834. He labored at Coshocton, Keene, Clark (where he organized the church), West Carlisle, and near Warsaw (where he organized the church), in the days of the feebleness of all the churches in this region.

After leaving Coshocton county, about 1844, he labored for a time at Muskingum church, near Dresden. He then removed to Indiana, taking charge of the Covington church in that state. Broken by his missionary labor, he returned to his old home state, and, as he was able, supplied some churches there.

He died in 1866. His wife died in 1837, and lies in the Keene churchyard; and a son, born while he labored at Keene, Rev. N. W. Conklin, is now pastor of a large and vigorous church in New York city.

G. W. Silliman was the son of a lawyer (Willys Silliman) practicing at Zanesville, and a nephew of Lewis Cass. He pursued his academical studies at Ohio University, and afterward at the military academy at West Point. Having read law with his father in Zanesville, he was admitted, and soon thereafter came to Coshocton (about 1830). He was sent as bearer of dispatches to C. P. Van Ness, minister from the United States to Spain. He returned to Coshocton in 1833; was soon elected prosecuting attorney, and by re-election continued in the office for ten years. In 1843, he went on a voyage to Europe for his health, but was not greatly benefited, and on his return voyage grew rapidly worse, and died at sea. His remains were brought to New York, and interred in Greenwood Cemetery.

In 1834, he married Miss Ann Johnson, who survived him many years, dying in 1864. There was one child, Willys Cass Silliman, who survived the father only about two years. Mr. Silliman's reputation is that of genial, scholarly gentleman.

Robert M. Lamb was from Eastern Virginia. He came to Coshocton, and was employed as miller in the Coshocton Steam Mill, about 1834; afterward, as one of the Union Mill Co., was concerned with the building and running of the Union Mill, in lower Roscoe. He went to California in 1849, and died of cholera in San Francisco the next year, in the forty-first year of his age.

He married a daughter of Dr. S. Lee, and by her had three children, two of whom, Mrs. J. M. Thompson and Miss Emily, are residents of Coshocton; the third, Mrs. Barse, living at Michigan City, Indiana.

David Spangler was born at Sharpsburg, Md., December 24, 1796. In 1802, the family removed to Zanesville, Ohio

Here the father established himself in trade as a blacksmith, and David, as his age and strength admitted, was a helper, and continued at the forge and anvil for years, learning lessons of patient toil, and endurance, and self-reliance of vast advantage in later years. Subsequently, the father engaged in mercantile business, and in this, as in the other, David, as the eldest son, was his chief assistant. Study, however, was not neglected, and David profited diligently by his opportunities in that line, limited as they were.

When twenty-five years of age, he commenced the study of law with Alex. Harper, and was admitted to practice at a term of the Supreme Court of the State, held in Cleveland in 1824. He commenced practice in Zanesville. In 1830, he was nominated for representative for Muskingum county in the legislature, and polled far more than his (Whig) party vote, though not elected. In 1832 he came to Coshocton. Professional business poured upon him from the start, and beside he soon was taking a leading part in politics. In the fall of the same year in which he came into the county, he was nominated for representative from the Twelfth (then) Congressional District, and such was the esteem and popularity in which, as a lawyer riding the circuit, that he was elected by a round majority, although the district (composed of Coshocton, Knox, Holmes, and Tuscarawas counties) had been hitherto in the hands of the opposite party. He was re-elected by the same constituency in 1834, by a still more decisive vote. Mr. Spangler was thoroughly satisfied with the political experience thus had, and proclaimed his determination to give his whole attention thereafter to professional practice. In 1844, his party, then in the ascendancy in the state, nominated him, by convention assembled at Columbus, for Governor, but he declined the nomination, insisting upon his tastes for private life, and his need of attention to professional business, and the claims of his family, especially those of his two sons, then in course of education. While in Washington city in his first term as congressman he was admitted to practice in the United States Supreme Court, arguing a case carried up from Ohio, and prevailing for his client. From 1836 to 1856, in which year he died (October 18), his office and home, his neighbors and friends, received the whole of his time and attention. For some years before his death his health was far from vigorous. He was, it will be observed, about two months less than sixty years old.

His parents were members of the M. E. church, as was also the lady whom he married (December, 1829), Miss Elizabeth Grafton Etherington, of Baltimore, Md., and he was always awake to the interests of that body and exceedingly helpful to it, although never a member. In the heaviest of his business and height of his fame, he would give active aid in the Sabbath-school and in the musical department of the church.

He was initiated into the Masonic body about the time he attained his majority, and served in the capacity of Worshipful Master, Representative to Grand Lodge, of which he was S. G. Deacon, Grand Orator, and Deputy Grand Master. In 1846, the Lodge formerly established having become defunct, he, in connection with others, secured a dispensation for a new Lodge (No. 96), of which, for many years, he was W. M.

His sympathy and readiness to associate freely with the masses—his great industry and energy—and his keen insight of human nature and ready wit were qualities giving him his place and power in public life. And with this is our present concern. He used to joke with his friends about his growth in popularity when a candidate, stating that in one township he doubled his vote—the fact subsequently coming from him that the first time he ran he got in that township (a Democratic stronghold) *one* vote, and the second time *two*. A young lady came to his office to have him commence proceedings for " rape." After hearing the story, he said it was important he should know the case, and informed her that there was an offense called " rape," and one called " rapee," and that the latter covered the case of the mildest possible resistance. She concluded the latter was her case, as he keenly suspected from the first.

A minister of his church once undertook to deliver a learned controversial discourse, having very much to say about "the original." Coming out of church, he quietly observed to a prominent lawyer of the place, of another faith, "That was a remarkable discourse; remarkable, sir; remarkable, sir; and especially remarkable, because neither the preacher (as he knew) nor any of his hearers had any knowledge of that original language."

Peter Humrickhouse was only a few years a resident of Coshocton county, but as the paternal ancestor of one of the most prominent families of the county, may well find brief mention here. He was born in Germantown, Pa., August 26, 1783. His father soon after moved to Hagerstown, Md. After the manner of his time, he learned a trade, that of carriage-maker. In 1814, he removed to Brownsville, Pa. He came to Coshocton in 1834, and here died, August 23, 1839. He was the father of Thomas, and John, and Wm. Humrickhouse, and also of the wives of John Joseph K. and Wm. K. Johnson, of John G. Stewart, and James Irvine, all being resident in Coshocton. Mrs. Kincaid, of Greenfield, Ohio, is also his daughter.

Arnold Medberry was born in New Berlin, Chenango county, New York, March 24, 1806. He came to Roscoe in the fall of 1832, and remained a citizen of that place until his death, August 12, 1861. During this time he was one of the most prominent business men of the region. His farming, milling, merchandising, and connection with the public works, were features of the locality where carried on. Indomitable energy and ceaseless activity were his characteristics. He was undaunted before that which would have made many quail. He thought nothing of taking his buggy, riding thirty miles to Mt. Vernon, and then taking the cars, thus reaching Cleveland in a few hours. Losing two flour-mills by fire, he within a few hours had amtters all arranged for building yet a third. A zealous politician, he yet had little desire for office. He was, however, postmaster of Roscoe for many years, and was also county commissioner. When the public works of the state, with which from the first he had been thoroughly acquainted, were offered for lease, he was one of the principal lessees, and continued in that relation until his death. A single anecdote illustrates his keen discernment and disposition to have the best in every line attainable. A wagon-maker having built him a wagon, called for his inspection and acceptance of it. He discovered, by close examination, a few places stopped up and made to appear smooth and good by putty. The wagon-maker protested that there was no real defect; that in fact the parts where the putty was, were as strong as any, and would do just as good work. "Very good, then," said Medberry, with his accustomed twinkle of the eye, "just you keep this wagon, and make me another all out of putty, and we will then see whether putty is as strong as oak." Severe requirement was the rule with him in his relations to his employes, and what he thus demanded he was ready to yield to those having rightful claims.

His personal appearance was fine; his manner calm and stately, but withal kind.

His wife, who had been Miss Phœbe Denman, survived him several years, dying at the home of her daughter in Kansas. His two sons died in each case as they were approaching manhood. Two of his daughters are living in Kansas, the other in Columbus.

Matthew Scott was born in county Donegal, Ireland, in 1795. He came to America in 1816, but lived at Cumberland, Maryland, until 1833, when he came to Coshocton county, settling in Virginia township, near Adam's mills. As the owner and cultivator of a considerable body of land; as a man of diligence and integrity, of more than ordinary intelligence, and of fair education, Mr. Scott was long had in repute in the region where he dwelt. As an enthusiastic son of Erin, and a most earnest and liberal adherent of the Presbyterian church, he was known by thousands. In 1856, he made a visit to the old land. He was for several years a director of the Western Theological Seminary at Pittsburg. He was a member of the general assembly of the Presbyterian church, meeting in Peoria, Illinois, 1863. He was always a warm friend of the colored people, and was chiefly instrumental in establishing a school for the education of colored girls, called "Scotia Seminary," in North Carolina. Having no children, and his wife having died before him, he gave almost his whole estate—of some $25,000—for educational, missionary, and other benevolent purposes, in connection with the Presbyterian church, a large part going to the support of the little church in which he had long been an elder, and in which his kindred hold yet a large place. For some time before his death, Mr. Scott had been in poor health. Early on the morning of the 13th of September, 1872, the family of the brother with whom he had been staying for some days, were alarmed by his absence from the house and the appearance of his forsaken bedroom, and search having been made, his dead body was found, after some hours, in the Muskingum river, which flowed through his lands.

John Lockard died near Chili, September 20, 1868, in his eightieth year. He was a native of county Donegal, Ireland; emigrated to America in 1819; settled near Steubenville, but after a few years removed to Coshocton county.

Sharon Williams died at his residence in Keene township on the 19th of August, 1868. He emigrated from Virginia in 1812, and resided in the same vicinity until his death, being a period of fifty-six years.

Isaac Darling died at his residence in Jefferson township, March 26, 1869. He was born in Eastern Virginia in 1796, and emigrated with his parents to Ohio in 1806, settling at his manhood upon the place on which his early life was spent, and remaining there till his death. He was for many years a prominent member of the Jefferson Baptist church.

Matthew Trimble died at his home in Perry township, March 13, 1871. He was a native of Donegal, Ireland; had been many years in Coshocton county. He was sixty-six years of age. Was a devout member of the Protestant Episcopal church.

William Pancake died May 26, 1867, in Warsaw. He was born in Harrisburg, Pa., and in early life removed to Columbiana county, and thence, after a few years, to Coshocton county, where he married, and became a permanent resident. He was in his seventy-fifth year. Had been many years a member of the Methodist Episcopal church.

Reuben B. Whittaker, for more than forty years a resident of Coshocton county, died on his farm, in Jefferson township, on the 11th of April, 1868, in the sixty-eighth year of his age.

Rev. James W. Pigman was born near the town of Cresap, Allegheny county, Md., in 1806; settled in Coshocton in 1810. His connection with the Methodist Episcopal church commenced in 1837, and he continued as a local preacher until 1866, when he became a minister in the Christian Union church, and so continued until his death, which occurred in Perry township October 26, 1869.

Samuel Brilhart died at his home, in Monroe township, September 23, 1870, in his seventy-sixth year. He emigrated from the State of Virginia in 1836; was one of the pioneers of Monroe township. He was a member of the Nazarene Baptist church, and left quite a large family.

Matthew Ferguson, a well-known resident of Roscoe, died of apoplexy on March 4, 1871, in the eightieth year of his age. He was born in Pennsylvania in 1792, lived for a time in Zanesville, then ten years in Coshocton, passing thence to Roscoe, where was his home for thirty-seven years. He was a hatter by trade. He was several times elected a justice of the peace. He married Miss Mary Smeltzer in

1819, by whom he had twelve children. He was a "charter member of Coshocton Lodge of Masons."

John C. Tidball was born June 5, 1801, in what then was Allegheny county (now Lawrence), Pa. He graduated at Jefferson College; was ordained a minister in the Presbyterian church, in 1826, at Island Creek, O. He subsequently preached at Morrisville, Belmont county. His unquestionable ability was connected with a certain measure of eccentricity which frequently involved him in more or less of trouble, often leading to expostulations on the part of his brethren in the ministry, under which he grew somewhat restive. While in Belmont county, he became more and more dissatisfied with the position of his own and also of kindred churches upon the matter of slavery. Meanwhile his health was quite impaired. In this state of things, he turned to the law, and having read with Carlo C. Carroll, of Belmont county, was admitted to the bar, practically demitting the ministry. He came to Coshocton in 1848, and practiced more or less until his death. His keen insight and earnest and impassioned delivery were marked features in his practice; but calm investigation and cool judgment were not always so apparent, and his success in business was only moderate. His thorough classical education made him a valuable man in school matters, and to his efforts must, in some considerable amount, be attributed the deepened and enlarged interest in education apparent in the town of Coshocton soon after he came into it. He connected himself with first the one and then the other of the Presbyterian churches of Coshocton, and maintained his position as a Christian man unto the last. He had in earlier days paid no little attention to medical matters, and was ready on all occasions to visit the sick, and make himself useful in times of affliction. He was a very zealous politician—intensely anti-slavery. He had, however, little disposition to carry his partisanship into his social relations, and was in every way a kind neighbor and clever citizen. He had a large vein of humor, and keenly relished the ludicrous. His power of facial expression was wonderful—quite in the style of his friend, Sam Galloway, of Columbus.

In the summer of 1863, he got word of the serious illness of a son, then in the army at Vicksburg, and against the counsels of his friends he went to visit him. The son recovered before the father reached the place; but the old gentleman took sick, struggled back home, and died in a few days, on the 11th of August, 1863.

While preaching at Island Creek, he married Miss Hunter, who, with her children, N. R., Haddasah, and W. S. Tidball, still live in Coshocton. Theophilus Tidball, of Bedford township, is a foster-child, adopted when an infant.

Joseph B. Crowley was, as the son of an old citizen (John Crowley), much in public service, as a soldier in the Mexican war, and for his manly appearance and social habits very highly esteemed by a large circle of acquaintances. He was born October 24, 1837, and died in the prime of his manhood, being at the time of his death fairly entered upon his thirty-seventh year. He married, in 1855, Miss Louisa Williams, who, with one child, survived him.

Clark Johns was born in New Castle township, and died in Coshocton, in his young manhood, June 13, 1863. The "lot" having designated him for a soldier, he, taking his privilege, enlisted in one of the companies which had gone out from Coshocton, where his home and business had been for some time. He was soon promoted to be lieutenant; was taken sick, sent home, and died in a few days, on date above given. He married the daughter of John Burt, and left her and one child.

C. C. Nichols, son of Eli Nichols, of New Castle township, died in hospital at Clifton, Tennessee, January 14, 1865. He was forty-two years of age, and held the rank of captain in the 183d regiment of Ohio volunteers. His remains were finally placed in the home cemetery. "He was," says a friend, "the child of ups and downs." He was present at the first sack of Lawrence, Kansas, and gave his aid in making that state a free state. He afterward spent some time in Colorado, and took an interest in laying out St. Charles, which afterward became Denver City. He undertook the opening of an expensive gulch, and spent all he had on it, without avail. In the fall of 1863, he entered the military service, continuing therein till his death.

Wm. B. Glover was born in Clark township, April 26, 1832. While teaching school in Indiana he enlisted in the 21st Indiana regiment, and afterward became a lieutenant in heavy artillery service. While engaged in the siege of Port Hudson he was taken sick and placed in hospital. Thence he was brought by his father to his home in Coshocton county; and here, after being home some three weeks, died, on the 18th of June, 1864.

Joel Clark Glover, brother of the above, was born December 6, 1846; and, having enlisted in the army, died in September, 1864, at Wilson's Landing, near Richmond, Virginia.

Many noble young men like these fell, as they, during the late war of the rebellion, but few families have such a noticeable record as that of which they were members. At one time no less than six sons were in the military service, and two others were represented by substitutes.

Thomas Carroll, Jr., M. D., was born in Keene, in 1838. After attending medical lectures, he commenced practice in Philadelphia, Pennsylvania. Entering the medical department of the army, he was stationed in Washington City, and afterward in Philadelphia. He died while acting assistant surgeon at Jackson Barracks, New Orleans, Louisiana, April 23, 1867. His remains were brought to Keene.

Robert S. McCormick was the son of a substantial farmer in Keene township. In his twentieth year (1861) he enlisted in Capt. Wm. Marshall's company of the Eightieth regiment, O. V. I. He was wounded at Mission Ridge and captured, and for fourteen months suffered all the horrors of Andersonville, whereby he was made a mere skeleton, although when he enlisted being six feet two inches in height and weighing 200 pounds. At length being exchanged, he was brought to Savannah and there detained by military movements. He afterward laid sick for a month at Annapolis. In the summer of 1864 he reached his home, receiving an honorable discharge at end of term of enlistment. For many months he sought to recover his health, at his home and in a health institute in New York State, but in vain. He died at home, January 26, 1866. He was one of that great company of victims of the selfish ambition, greed, and cruelty which possessed the men who brought about the terrible " War of the Rebellion."

Asa G. Dimmock was well known to the people of Coshocton county, as being for ten years editor and publisher of the *Coshocton Democrat*. He was also, for two terms, prosecuting attorney of the county, and at that most important era in its history, the robbery of the county treasury, made his mark in that capacity. He was the son of a Baptist clergyman, was bred to the newspaper business, and was connected largely with the press, editing or publishing papers in Harrison, Holmes, Wayne, and Erie counties. He was in the Ohio State Senate as a member and also as clerk. He also served several years as warden of the Ohio penitentiary. In 1867 his health very seriously failed him, and on May 17, 1869, he died at the house of his sister, in Montrose, Penn., in the fifty-sixth year of his age. Of exceedingly pleasant manner, shrewd in management, and exceedingly self-sacrificing, he was always popular, commonly poor. He was twice married—had one child by first wife. His surviving widow resides at Millersburg.

M. C. McFarland was a son of one of the most substantial citizens of Bedford township. His youth was spent on the farm, at school, in teaching, and in reading law. He was for several years deputy clerk of the court and county school examiner. In 1863, he was elected probate judge, and subsequently re-elected, keeping, it is said, the records of the office in unusually neat and correct manner. Before his second term expired, his health was greatly impaired. Having spent some months in vain efforts to re-establish his health, he at length died at the house of his father-in-law in Newark, on the 12th of July, 1870, in the thirty-sixth year of his age.

He was a man of more than usual talent, literary taste, and social excellence. He married a daughter of Judge Wm. Sample, and by her had one son.

Samuel Ketchum died June 29, 1871, aged about forty-three years. His father was from the State of New York. With good common education, he entered upon active life. He was well known as the treasurer of Coshocton county, and from his difficulties growing out of that position he found relief only in death. Having plead guilty to the charge of embezzlement, he was sentenced to the penitentiary for five years, and became an inmate of that institution on the 1st of March, 1870. His health rapidly failed him, and in fifteen months he was pardoned, on representations made by the warden and physician, by Governor Hayes, and returned to his home. While in prison, he professed thorough penitence, and claimed to have little hope for the present life, and none for that to come, save by the mercy of God in Christ Jesus. In the hope of this mercy, he passed away —recognized by the world as a man of considerable refinement and of generous impulses, to be pitied, however much blamed. An aged, faithful mother, a wife true when all else failed, and two children bitterly lamented his death.

Samuel Morrison died in Coshocton on the 20th of August, 1871, in the seventy-third year of his age. He was born in Virginia; was brought to Coshocton county when only two years of age; he grew up with the county; held several offices of trust, among others that of sheriff. His death was the result of an apoplectic stroke. His wife died some time before he did. Of his children (seven daughters), Mrs. R. W. Thompson is dead; Mrs. Banks in Minnesota; Mrs. Marvin in Michigan; Mrs. Hankins in New York; Mrs. Rev. Robert Beer in Indiana; Mrs. Kepner in Columbiana county; and only Mrs. W. H. H. Price, of Coshocton, is in the county.

John Morgan died at his residence, a few miles east of Coshocton, September 14, 1866, in the seventy-ninth year of his age. He was born in New Jersey, October 9, 1789. He was among the earlier settlers of Coshocton county, cultivating a farm until old age and illness interfered. He was for twenty-five years a member of the White Eyes Baptist church.

Charles S. Barnes was born in Fayette county, Pennsylvania, in 1798. The family removed to Jefferson county, when Charles came to Coshocton county, settling as a farmer in Bedford township, and becoming one of its most highly esteemed citizens. He was probate judge from 1855–1858. He was for many years a class leader and steward in the Methodist Episcopal church. His death occurred on the 17th of May, 1866, at his home in West Bedford. Several of his children abide in the township.

William Henderson died at his residence, in New Castle township, in 1866, having been many years a farmer and stock-man in Coshocton county. He was in his seventy-first year; came from Pennsylvania; was married in 1837; connected by the marriage of his children with several of the prominent families in the west part of the county.

George Darling, youngest son of Isaac and Jane Darling, died at Holton, Kansas, October 30, 1870, aged twenty-five years. His mother had gone on a visit to a daughter in Kansas, and was there taken sick with typhoid fever. After a lingering illness, her recovery was despaired of, and her friends notified. George went to be with her in her last moments, and was himself smitten with the same dissease, and in one week died, the mother following in a few hours. The bodies were brought to the old home, near Warsaw. George had only been married a few months (to Miss Foster), and was a very popular young man, and the circumstances of the death made the event a notable one in his old neighborhood.

Samuel Squire, Sr., died on the 24th of November, 1874, at his residence in Jackson township, in the sixty-eighth year of his age. He was brought as a child to Coshocton county, in 1814, being then eight years of age. His parents came from Rutland county, Vermont. He took possession of the place where he died, in 1832. He was a deacon in the Regular Baptist church. He left children and a large circle of relatives.

Nicholas Bassett came from Mohawk valley, New York, and settled in Linton township, more than forty years ago. He died on the 11th of March, 1875, in the eighty-ninth year of his age. A friend says: " He was a very active and energetic man in the days of his strength; firm in purpose and vigorous in action; a man of noticeable sort in speech and movement. His politics and his religion (the one Democratic and the other Presbyterian) were two things never lost sight of."

Samuel H. Scott, brother of Matthew elsewhere mentioned, was for some forty years a citizen of Virginia township, engaged in farming. He had been out of health, was coming to his home from Adams' mills, walking on the railroad-track, was overtaken by a freight-train, and miscalculating as to time failed to get out of the way before the train, then "slowed" very much, struck him. The nervous shock in his enfeebled and diseased condition was too much for him, and he died in a few days, his death occurring March 5, 1875. He had been for many years a member and for a few years an elder in the Presbyterian church. His wife (Miss Jane Denny) survives him, without children.

Dr. W. H. Vickers died in Linton township on the 12th of February, 1875. On the evening of the 11th, he left his home, in Jacobsport, to visit a patient, Mr. M. B. Carr, one mile beyond Linton. He found Mr. Carr very low with pneumonia, who, also, as well as to administer medicine, asked the doctor to write his will. The doctor, after finishing the patient's will, conducted the evening devotions for the family, and was about to retire to bed, about eleven o'clock, when he complained to Mrs. Carr of feeling unwell, and asked for a little water and camphor, which were got for him, and after taking some he went to bed with one of Mrs. Carr's sons in an adjoining room. The next morning he was discovered to be seriously ill, and, having been removed to his home, died about four o'clock in the afternoon. He had established himself very thoroughly in the regards of the community, and was a prominent member of the Methodist Episcopal church.

Thompson Carnahan was born in White Eyes township, April 24, 1841, and died in Adams township (on a little farm which for some years had been to him a retreat after his work as a teacher was done), July 13, 1876. Obtaining the elements of a good education in the district school, he himself commenced to teach in 1860. In the summer of that year he attended the Normal School at Hopedale, in Harrison county, and having taught during the ensuing winter, took another term at Hopedale in 1862. In the fall of 1862, he went into the army, enlisting in the Ninth Ohio Volunteer Cavalry. He continued in service two years, and having been wounded at Big Shanty, Georgia, returned home and resumed his work as a teacher. In 1866, after attending one term, he graduated at the Poughkeepsie (New York) College. Having taught several of the most prominent of the country schools, and the one at Bakersville, he became the teacher of the grammar school in Coshocton in 1871. The next year he took charge of the Roscoe schools, and continued there until smitten by the disease (paralysis) that laid him low in death. Always somewhat out of health, his conscientious faithfulness led him to unduly tax himself with his professional work, and about a month before his year was up, and some two months before his death, he reluctantly ceased to teach. But the bow had been drawn too far, and the string was already virtually broken. Returning after the school year was closed (his wife having finished his work therein) to his farm near Bakersville, he for a time seemed to improve, but soon sank down in a peaceful death.

Conscientious and carefully trained in the principles of the holy Christian religion from his childhood, he made a profession of his faith in the Presbyterian church, at Bakersville, in 1870, and subsequently was an elder in the Presbyterian church of Roscoe.

With no special advantages of worldly sort and despite poor health he attained a scholarship that had merit above what his modesty disposed him to widely manifest, and showed what industry and conscientiousness may achieve even in comparatively early years. He married, in 1869, Miss Eliza J. Stonehocker, who, having herself been much engaged in teaching, proved a worthy help-meet in his school work, as otherwise.

INDEX

____, Bill 190
____, Sam 190
ADAMS, 59 101 Beal 18 Beall 36 Calvin 38 D 102 J Q 246 John 110 John M 92 Seth 85 Waldo 182
ADDY, 28 Hugh 18 Miss 29 Wm 18 46
AGNEW, Joab 96 187
AKEY, J B 224
ALBERT, John 43
ALDER, Dr 121
ALEN, B 195
ALEXANDER, Mr 132
ALLEN, Gov 65 76 J W 111 Wm 70
ALTMAN, Geo R 224
AMMERMAN, 196
ANDERSON, J 109 James 223 John 119 Sallie 137 T W 211
ANDRES, Father 202
ANDREWS, John 119 Professor 138
APPLESEED, Johnny 50
ARCHIBALD, Mcilroy 211
ARMORY, Elizabeth 18 George 18
ARNOLD, A W 195 197 198 199 Geo 24 45 George 143 180

ASH, David 45
ASHCRAFT, Daniel 18 32 Jonathan 32
AULT, Peter 33
AUSTIN, 214
AVERY, A W 125
AYRES, George 100
BAAD, 204
BABCOCK, 32 200 Daniel 31 Richard 31
BACHE, Mr 86
BACHELOR, Wm 89 188
BACHMAN, 55 109
BAGLEY, Wm 201
BAGNALL, 108 238 George 96 107 226
BAGNELL, 49
BAILEY, William 43
BAIRD, Dr 208 209 I N 207 208 Isaac N 211
BAKER, 17 47 111 217 Basil 29 C 110 Charles 28 29 46 Elizabeth 184 Esaias 28 29 46 239 Israel 19 John 5 19 28 46 70 143 217 Lane 28 Misses 110 R F 71 R L 67 Rezin 19 28 110 144 Sam 89 Zebedee 143 217
BALCH, C 96
BALDWIN, Joseph T 239 Mr 239

BALLANTINE, Hugh 18
BALLENTINE, Hugh 207 208
BANCROFT, 217 Wm 120
BANKS, Mrs 261 Rolla 219
BANTHAM, John 17 19 45 John M 143
BARCROFT, 80 D A 137 J B 137
BARCUS, 114 Mrs William 213 William 212
BARD, 110
BARGER, A E 201 Dr 118 G H 64 147 Gilbert H 80
BARNES, C S 76 Charles S 261 Dr 119 Elizabeth L 137 H B 137 Henry 130 M J 200 W S 198 199
BARNEY, 97 D N 96 F E 96 99 103 105 107 112 152 J A 105 John A 99
BARR, Thomas 221
BARRETT, Hugh 35
BARRICK, Frederick 203
BARSE, Mrs 249
BARTHOLOMEW, A N 203 A U 203 M 203
BARTLEY, Mordecai 70
BASSETT, 30 Chauncey 57 125 Nicholas 262
BATCHELOR, Wm 86
BEACH, 120 D C 110 H C 127 Joseph 31
BEAL, James 5 Jesse 37
BEALL, H 108 Hiram 93 112 152 Jas S 137 Liverton 222 Robert 59
BEAVER, 85 Geo 16 George 38
BEAZELL, B F 211
BEAZELLE, B F 205
BEBEE, J W 104
BECK, 97 111

BEEBE, 96 J W 97 James W 101
BEER, Mrs Robert 261 Robert 82
BEIBER, Lewis 102
BELL, Jno W 137
BENDER, T 201
BENNETT, E 57
BENTON, N H 37
BERRY, John 30
BIBLE, Geo 19 37 Mrs 32 Tipton 32
BIGGS, 214 William 182 Wm 19
BILLMAN, Andrew 30 Mr 203
BIRD, Wm 19
BIRKET, E 211
BLACK, R B 110
BLACKBURN, B C 70 92 117
BLACKMAN, N 119
BLANIPIED, 207
BLICKENSDERFER, Jacob 57
BLODGETT, William C 62
BLUCK, 86
BLUE, 98 Gilbert 211
BLYTHE, Miss 245
BODELLE, Araminta 132
BOES, Chas 102
BOGGS, John M 224 Thomas 180
BOLTON, John 183
BOMBERGER, C 221 222 226 Mr 223 Rev 223
BONAR, Matthew 143
BONNELL, L J 182
BONNET, 109
BONNETT, 98 Benjamin 65 Lewis 98 223
BOOKLESS, David 67
BOQUET, 9 12 13 16 52 Col 8
BORDEN, 19 Thomas 44

Index. 267

BOSTWICK, J 110 W 110
BOUQUET, Col 171
BOUTON, Enoch 222
BOWEN, J 109
BOWMAN, 85 A J 110 John 97
BOYD, 19 Calvin 93 Elizabeth 228 J C 229 James 229 James T 229 John 228 Kate 137 Nancy 228 R 106 108 Robert 34 63 227 228 Robert D 96 Robert Jr 227 Sam'l A 137 Samuel 228 Sarah 228 William 227 228
BRADFIELD, A 201
BRADSTREET, Gen 8 9
BRADY, E W 211 J W 120
BRAUN, 246
BRETSFORD, D 108
BREWER, Jacob 137
BRIDGEMAN, Wm 220
BRILHART, Samuel 255
BROADHEAD, 16 52 Gen 9 10
BROCKUNIER, S R 211 Samuel 206
BRODHEAD, Gen 167
BROOKS, Cyrus 211
BROOM, H 194 197 J W 197
BROWER, J C 120
BROWN, 189 207 A G 149 Ethan Allen 75 Ezra 211 Frederick T 247 Hugh A 247 J C 247 James M 65 112 188 190 Judge 56 Mr 40 98 246 Mrs Samuel 213 S W 135 Samuel 39 40 58 87 213 Wm 5 108 246 Wm L 247
BROWNER, Bennett 35
BROWNING, 217
BROWNLEE, W C 126
BRUSH, Daniel 239

BRYAN, Russell C 66 125
BRYANT, 200 Russell C 210
BUCHANAN, George 227 Sarah E 137
BUCK, John 225
BUCKALEW, 110 James 19 N 5 136 Nathan 68 Parker 41
BUCKINGHAM, E 131 Ebenezer 3 Mr 131 219 Rev E 219
BUCKLEW, James 143
BURBACKER, 110
BURGOYNE, 164
BURNET, Jacob 75
BURNS, 19 40 110 Gen 49 54 139 John 108 135 242 Jos 64 66 130 Joseph 64 70 71 76 240 242 Rebecca 241 Samuel 240 William 149
BURR, Dr 121
BURRELL, 88 96 110 Benjamin 19 Joseph 19 45 93 S C 92 Samuel 66 T H 92
BURT, 94 132 200 D W 180 Foght 57 104 186 J 106 J M 112 James M 4 5 48 53 69 70 74 92 112 186 John 4 93 133 186 257 Judge 92 Morris 98 102 104 R W 104 124 147 T H 104
BUSHONG, J W 211
BUTLER, 17 88 102 Demie 237 James 26 144 Joseph 18 41 Thomas 18 25 26 41 144
BUXTON, Francis 63 N W 55
CAIN, 139 Abel 19 39
CALDER, James 4 39 63 108 Jas 19
CALHOUN, H 130 132 137 138 220 225 Mr 138 226 N 120 Rev Mr 127

CALLAHAN, James 211
CAMP, 207 Rev Mr 215
CAMPBELL, 190 227 D 87 G
  E 135 Isa 137 J C 92 105 P
  S 135 Patrick Steele 46
  Thomas 67 76 78 80 94 112
  130 132 133 152 180
CANTWELL, 17 139 Barney
  19 39 H 64 110 133 James
  19 24 L L 80 92 107
  Thomas 39
CARHART, 200 H 98 110
  Henry 135 J 98 110 John
  96 135 237 L 136 Lewis 98
  Wm 5 42 96 130 Wm G 77
CARMAN, J H 110
CARNAHAN, Adam 34
  Andrew 34 Eliza 34 Eliza J
  264 Ellanor 34 Hugh 34
  James 34 John 34 180 Miss
  247 Mrs 137 Nancy 34
  Sarah 34 T 135 138 226
  Thomas 138 Thompson 34
  263 William 34
CARNES, James 57 146
CARPENTER, 14 16 62 63 Dr
  119 Geo 19 George 23 John
  166 Susannah 232
CARPER, Joseph 211
CARR, 110 Barney 17 19
  Henry 42 45 143 J H 42 92
  Joshua H 66 M B 263 Mr
  263 Mrs 263 S M 120 Thos
  210
CARROLL, C 79 Carlo C 256
  Edgar 137 Thomas Jr 258
CARTMILL, 179 William 178
CASE, Sabra 234
CASEY, Peter 19 72 74 75 88
CASS, A L 69 119 133 150 Dr
  117 G W 132 135 Joseph K
  135 Lewis 73 76 142 249

CASSINGHAM, 109 G F 66
  152 J W 105 112 John W
  101
CATON, 110
CHALFANT, 17 Mordecai 18
  27 63
CHAMBERLAIN, John 209
CHAMBERS, John 68
CHAPIN, Dennis 135
CHAPMAN, B W 120
CHAPPLES, 217
CHASE, S P 125 Salmon P 70
CHILD, Jonas 38
CHRISTIE, W B 207 Wm B
  209 211
CHRISTY, Albert 105 James
  203 Seth 92
CHURCH, A M 19 Aaron M
  76 B F 82 M E 131 M P 125
CHURCHILL, G W 194 J F
  194 199
CLARK, 110 139 Benton 182
  Gabriel 45 H 199 John 4 26
  45 Joshua 180 Payne 18 33
  Samuel 19 41 45 63 72 W R
  143 William 45
CLAY, 246
CLINGAN, John 210
CLOSE, H M 211
COBB, N 224
COCHRAN, Joshua 30 R 108
  W N 81
COE, Benj 68 Benjamin 200
COFFER, Mr 131
COFFEY, Addison 131 218 Mr
  218 219
COLBY, Lewis 116
COLEMAN, Austin 215
COLES, James 59
COLLIER, Mrs S H 10 T W 71
  125
COLLINS, 97 Perry 56

COLVER, John 18
COMPTON, A N 110 Elisha
  36 J M 81 94 133 R 138
CONANT, Geo 131 138
  George 43 Gov 134 Mrs 137
  138 Prof 138
CONDIT, 132 Timothy C 70
CONE, 97 A 222 E 92 117
  Edmund 86 Jared 116 117
CONKLIN, Mr 221 N 221 224
  N W 249 Nathaniel 218
  222 248
CONNER, James 44 John 44
CONNERTY, Farley 100
CONWAY, John 31
CONWELL, Brother 208
  George 98 George E 209
  210
COOLEY, 207
COOPER, D G 111
COPELAND, 143
CORBIN, Mary 245
CORBIT, Robert 46 144
CORNELL, Ezra 106
CORNING, 97
CORWIN, Tom 140
COSTON, Zarah H 211
COULTER, Wm 30 67
COWDERY, Mr 106
COX, David 18 26 J D 70
  Lewis V 111 137 Martin 18
  26 S 135 Wm 221
CRAGO, W 111
CRAIG, Andrew 17 James 18
  45 72 John 41 William 41
  Wm 224
CRARY, Isaac E 140
CRAWFORD, 110 Associate
  Judge 43 Col 13 James 149
  223 John 74 136 John T
  224 Nora 137 Oliver 182
  Robert 40 74 102 W H 222

CRAY, Jacob 27
CREIG, 39 Mr 40
CREIGHTON, A E 81 Eliza J
  137
CRESAP, 19
CRICHFIELD, S C 180
CRISMAN, John 211
CRISSMAN, Henry 18
CROOKS, James 146 William
  226
CROTHERS, Christopher 223
CROUCH, Robert 223 Wm
  223
CROUSE, S 211
CROWELL, W S 132 138 182
  Wm S 67
CROWLEY, 19 109 John 38
  57 66 69 257 Joseph 257
  Louisa 257 S B 144 Samuel
  B 66
CULBERTSON, James 221
  Robert 143 S W 76
CUNNINGHAM, James 218
  220 222 Mr 222 Wm 211
DARLING, 17 109 183 Demie
  237 George 261 Isaac 63
  254 261 Jane 261 Marion
  92 Mr 184 Robert 18 25 41
  51 63 96 Thomas 42 63 87
  92 236 Wellington 92
DARNES, Peter 61 Peter H 61
DARR, 97
DAUGHERTY, 227 Andrew
  61 C 219 John 38 Rob't 225
DAVENPORT, J W 55
DAVIDSON, O 18 Obadiah 24
  T 211 William 24
DAVIS, E 63 208 H 133 Henry
  133 John 92 93 99 217
  John C 120
DAY, George 118 Sherman
  171

DECKER, L F 109 Nancy 209
DELAMATER, 4 Dr 118
DELANO, 71
DELAY, Jacob 211
DEMOSS, John 39 40 L 103
  Lewis 40 65 92 96 99 Mr 94
DENMAN, 16 108 A D 73 92
  220 Caroline 132 D F 133
  149 J M 92 Martin 73
  Matthias 73 Mr 101 Mrs C
  13 Mrs Samuel 132 Phoebe
  253
DENMEAD, 133 E 59
DENNIS, R B 59
DENNY, Jane 263
DESCHWEINITZ, Bishop 170
  171 Dr 170 Francis 171
  Mier 171
DESTCHAULEPINKOFF,
  Serge 202
DEWEY, Mrs Geo 132 Sallie
  132
DEWITT, Sol 110 Vincent 46
DICKENSON, Joseph 92
DICKERSON, Robert 135
DILLON, Israel 30 64 John 19
  209 Peter 30 William 30
DIMMOCK, A G 190 Asa G 67
  81 126 259
DINSMORE, Alex 92
DISNEY, 121 L 151 L E 109
  Rev Mr 215
DIXON, W L 211 William 210
DOAK, 43 111 203 Robert 182
  Wm 63
DODD, John 63 135 Lucy 137
DODDRIDGE, 159 160 172
  Philip 168
DOEPKEN, G 204
DOHERTY, John 230
DOLBY, J 217
DONLEY, 96 Stephen 180

DONOHEW, James H 102
DORSEY, C 184
DOUGHERTY, Jno L 149
DOUGLAS, David 18
DOUGLASS, James 223
DOWNING, C F 74
DOYLE, J W 146
DRAPER, Isaac 18 44
DRONE, Burkit E 123
DRYDEN, 109 Jas 71 132 133
DUDLEY, T 105
DULING, D 111
DUNCAN, M 26 Matthew 18
  T D 134 224
DUNN, J W 196
DURBAN, Wm 44
DWYER, J W 49 71 86 87 93
  99 109 125 Joseph W 92 Mr
  94 Thomas 26 68
E____t, Christ 191 Deacon
  190
EATON, 228
ECKERT, Charles 109
EDGAR, William 221
EDWARDS, Dr 149 J T 120
  Wm 7
EICHMIER, Andrew 203
ELDER, Cyrus 42 223 John 17
  19 42 223 Matthew 223
  Miss 132 Sallie 132
ELDRIDGE, 5 62
ELI, John 26
ELLIOT, 127 Matthew 163
ELLIOTT, 93 110 200 Andrew
  38 Charles 46 206 215 245
  Chas 130 Deacon 245
  Elisha 38 J B 91 J S 92
  Jacob 218 John 61 90 210
  218 222 228 245 John B
  246 Joseph 102 150 Kate
  137 Martha 228 Mr 94 Nat
  149 Sam'l 180 Samuel 74

ELLIOTT (Continued)
   245 Thomas 31 209 Thos
   97 Tip 137
ELLIS, Eph 138 M 211
   Simeon 91
ELLSON, Archibald 19
ELSON, Archibald 18 Samuel
   143
EMERSON, C 137 Jacob 38
   221 T 238 Timothy 38 221
   222 William 116 117
ENDSLEY, James Jr 224
ENOCH, J 110
EPT, 182 Frank 181
ESTINGHAUSEN, 200
ETHERINGTON, Elizabeth
   Grafton 251
EVANS, 99 Anthony 43
   Gabriel 63 Henry 18 28
   Isaac 5 16 18 28 51 72 74
   95 101 114 142 185 193 Jos
   185 Nathan 35 Owen 63
   Phebe 185 T 196 200 Wm
   18
EVERHART, 43 Frederick 203
FACTOR, Geo 92
FAIR, Daniel 182
FAMILTON, T 111 T H 136
FARMER, F H 146
FARQUHAR, Benjamin 26 Dr
   121 O C 147 Samuel 30
FARWELL, 5 37 200 Charles
   222 Robert 38 89
FAULKNER, F S 109
FELLER, Gotlieb 98
FELLOWS, Dr 117 I N 118 J
   N 70
FERGUSON, A 56 Andrew 46
   48 63 69 180 C 110 Col 47
   139 M 102 Mary 255
   Matthew 255

FERNSLER, John 5 43 Philip
   43 Samuel 5
FERRELL, J M 110
FETROW, Daniel 43 Jeremiah
   43
FIELDS, Henry 57
FINDLEY, John 70 Sam'l 227
FINLAY, 121
FINLEY, A 110 John M 136
   138 Moses 182 W B 110
FISHER, G W 225 J C 59
   John C 69 71 126
FISK, Jonathan 102
FISKE, Ezra 218 Jonathan
   218
FLAGG, T W 125 Thomas W
   78 124
FOLLETT, C 81
FORD, George 227-229 Sarah
   227
FORKER, 109 Daniel 33 63
   180 Samuel 33 64 W R 64
   92 131 Wm R 33
FORNEY, C 134 William 63
   Wm 110
FORSYTHE, Robert 106
FORT, J 225
FOSTER, Andrew 39 Benja-
   min 39 David 39 Eldredge
   225 Jas 110 Miss 262
   Moses 39 Nancy 227 Pryor
   183 Samuel 39 Thomas 19
   143 William 39
FOUTS, W R 211
FOWLER, 29 R 28 Richard 19
   128 144
FOX, Eli 41 63
FOY, John 223 Mr 223 Rev
   223
FREDERICK, J C 68 S W 195
   196 197 198 199

FREEMAN, John 101
FRENCH, Zeba 73
FREW, C W 103 David 209
   210 John 57 58 59 64 71 90
   96 97 108 123 133 Joseph
   151 Maj 139 W C 120 132
FREY, E 195 198 J Jr 195 197
   J Sr 195
FRITCHEY, A H 71 74 149 F
   X 108 109
FRITZ, A 103
FROCK, 203 Elizabeth 34
   Michael 34
FRY, Benjamin 17 18 45 72
FULKS, John M 67 Wm 137
FULTON, J 23 John 28 Miss
   233
FUNK, 227
FUNSTON, John 179
GAGE, Gen 8
GALBRAITH, A V 211
GALLOWAY, Sam 257
GAMBLE, G R 110 James 57
   70 97 Levi 67
GARBER, A H 120
GARDINER, Juliet 135
   Samuel 58 68 92
GARDNER, Juliet W 137
GAULT, 19 Adam 33 95 223
   W R 81 126 132
GAUMER, Daniel 203
GEARHART, 181 John 180
GIBBS, Elisha 54
GIFFIN, Robert 4 18 25
GILBERT, J W 211 John W
   211 L 194-197
GILES, John 134
GILLESPIE, Jane 171
GILRUTH, James 206 Jas 211
GIRTY, 164 Simon 12 13 163
GIST, Christopher 163

GIVEN, 42 J W 111 James
   214 Josiah 81 146 William
   214
GLAZE, Samuel 210 Zachariah 203
GLEASON, 101
GLENN, 30 John 224 225
GLOVER, J 94 103 109 151
   Joel 41 180 222 Joel Clark
   258 Josiah 152 220 Wm B
   258
GODDARD, Chas B 66
GONSER, John 5
GOOF, 207
GORDON, Mr 224
GORHAM, Mary 137 Wm 26
GORSELINE, Wm 136
GORSLINE, Wm 137 138
GOTSHALL, George 43 William 43
GOUGH, Abner 213
GRAHAM, Alexander 32
   William 33
GRANGER, Ebenezer 76
GRAVES, John 36 Wesley 36
GRAY, Jane 171 John 171 172
   Oliver 78
GREEN, Wm M 57
GREENWALD, E 202 Mr 202
GRIER, T W 196
GRIFFITH, C S W 135 William 43
GRILL, Michael 203
GRIM, Andrew 130
GRIMES, Charles 208
GRIMM, David 32 129 Henry
   31 32 203
GUILD, H 123 124
GUINTHUR, Joseph 132
GUNBY, John 225
GUTHRIE, Thomas 224

HACK, P 110 Peter 146
HACKINSON, 183 Miss 47 R
　M 66 109
HAGGERTY, B 55 J 55
HAIGHT, E C 182
HAINES, Henry 35 John 35
HALDEMAN, Dr 131
HALL, William 106
HAMILTON, Claudius 229
　Joseph 217 Samuel 228
　Thomas 227
HAMMOND, 108 Edwin 86
HAND, Gen 164 165
HANKINS, Mrs 261 Louise
　Morrison 127 T 18
HANLON, Alex 76 John A 67
　92 107 Wm 63 86 92 100
HANNA, A 221 Daniel W 101
　S 224 Samuel 221 224
　Thompson 101
HARBAUGH, H W 136 S 109
HARDESTY, 16 Edmund 27
　John 27 Samuel 72 Thomas
　27
HARGER, 17 Jacob 201
HARMON, Gen 86 Rev Mr
　170
HAROLD, S 62
HARPER, 74 Alex 66 250
　Alexander 73 76 77
HARRIS, Asa L 71 125 Dr 131
　J 102 132 138 138 Joseph
　19 Josiah 74 118 130 138
　M C 211 Mary 163 Timothy
　234
HARRISON, 110 Gen 142 239
　J C 135 John 72
HART, Asa 24 Asher 19 60
　Capt 144 Joshua B 89 Mr
　89 Reuben 40
HARVEY, A D 101 Samuel
　211 T W 138 Wm 223

HASTINGS, J F 137
HAWK, Leonard 46 Richard
　19 144 Robert 25
HAWLEY, John 68 Mrs E 109
HAY, 96 109 Aunty 186 Delia
　132 George 133 H 103 109
　112 Houston 57 99 103 112
　150 Jackson 101 108 112
　James 54 57 99 245 Jos H
　109 Kirk 99 Mary 245 Miss
　110 Mr 47 101 Mrs Alex
　241 Mrs Houston 132 R
　109 Robert 54 65 97 99 108
　128 130 233 244 William G
　106
HAYES, Gov 260 R B 70
HAYS, James 201 Mrs 36
　Nancy 36
HAZLETT, Wm 130
HEADINGTON, Laban 182
HEATON, Micajah 5 Michael
　35
HECKEWELDER, 162 John 7
　164
HEDGES, 108
HENDERSON, A M 120
　George 33 90 James 211
　James M 228 John 33 220
　Mr 228 Rev 225 William
　261 Wm 5 86
HENKLE, M 211 Professor
　138
HENNIGH, H K 219
HENRIGH, Mr 132
HENRY, William 14
HERBIG, H C 112
HERKETT, 30
HERSHMAN, Elizabeth 184
　John 19 184 Philip 24 25
HESKET, Capt 146 John 55
　66 190 Wm 92
HESKETT, J 71

HESLIP, 19 28 I V 82 J V 96
147 James B 182 Joseph 29
96 Thomas 116 117 Wm 69
HIBITS, John 23
HICKMAN, S M 132 211
HIGBEE, Joseph C 47
HILDRETH, S P 226
HILL, 139 Benjamin 37 116
Calvin 30 Geo 138 Geo D
137 James 135 220 226
HILLYER, A R 125 132 219
HILYER, A R 78
HIMEBAUGH, 43 Wm 34 64
HIRT, 99 Matthew 44 William 44
HITCHCOCK, P 75
HITCHENS, Jos 68
HOAGLAND, Isaac 17 41 143
HOBAN, John 100
HOGLE, Charlotte 137 H
Misses 137 138 John 92
Langdon 57 214 Michael 45
HOGUE, R 135 R S 211
HOLDEN, W L 59
HOLLOWAY, Isaac 18
HOLMES, C A 211 Samuel 108
HOLT, 204 John 44
HOOK, John 214
HOOPER, Jas 211
HORD, Kellis 91
HORN, Ellen 137
HORTON, Ezra 18 35 L F 82
Mr 102 Thomas 18 35
HOSELTON, 110
HOSMER, S R 57
HOUTS, Dr 119
HOWARD, L 118
HOWE, 86
HOY, C 190 Charles 67 80 82 135
HUBBARD, Wm B 129

HUFF, J 102
HUGHES, A J 120
HULL, 142 Edith 25
HUMPHREY, Mr 38 Squire 26 63 69 Wm 44
HUMPHRIES, 86 Gen 85
HUMRICKHOUSE, 109
Elizabeth 244 Harriet 243
John 92 252 Joseph K 252
Peter 252 T S 5 59 67 78 86
87 90 92 130 132 219 220
Thomas 81 252 William 81
Wm 252
HUNT, Mr 219 W E 103 132
William E 94 221 Wm E 88
104 112 134 138 152 162
170 219 220
HUNTER, Miss 257
HUSTON, Robert 224
HUTCHINS, 184 Lyda 137
HUTCHINSON, Eliza 135 137
J H 66 John H 53 Mrs 40
Samuel 135 209
INDIAN, Eagle Feather 163
Gelelemend 7 165 Killbuck
7 14 165 Killbuck Jr 14
Monsey 13 Netawatwees 7
8 14 Pekilon 10 Samuel
Nanticoke 162 White Eyes
7 12 14 163 164 Wolf 13
INGRAHAM, Charles 135 J B
112 119
IRVINE, Capt 144 James 79
80 132 145 147 190 252
John 228 229 John E 80
132 137 S 228 Samuel 228
IRWIN, John 103 W W 75
JACK, Geo 146
JACKSON, 130 246 Gen 125
Jacob 18 24
JACOB, E 211 E P 210 P H
132 Prosper H 219

Index. 275

JACOBS, Dr 121 P H 226
JACQUET, Father 202 John M 202
JAMES, 19 190 Ann 30 Dr 118 E W 81 Elias 3 35 Mrs E W 127
JAMIESON, Mrs 235
JEFFRIES, 103 Jas 19 Wm 68
JEWETT, S W 86
JOHN, 17 David 18 26 Thomas 18 26
JOHNS, Clark 257
JOHNSON, 40 178 179 Adam 24 37 66 71 142 Ann 249 Anna 136 C H 71 190 Charles 24 D 223 David 111 J K 91 111 J R 132 135 151 James 228 James R 219 220 Jane 24 John 69 70 71 89 98 111 182 219 233 242 John H 111 John M 68 208 Jos K 219 233 Joseph 111 Joseph K 59 91 98 148 219 Judge 206 M 37 129 135 233 Margaret 239 Maro 135 Matthew 24 88 Mr 101 Mrs 233 243 Richard 143 239 Robert 208 239 240 Sarah 239 T H 133 135 Thomas 4 28 29 54 74 95 101 143 206 238 Thomas H 107 Valentine 24 W A 71 W K 57 63 104 108 111 130 185 243 William 239 William K 54 61 218 243 Wm 233 Wm A 24 Wm K 5 59 92 132 219 252 Wm N 123
JOHNSTON, 17 110 Adam 19 54 60 62 64 72 73 142 C H 57 64 92 133 Catharine 18 Charles H 57 Ella 137 Gen 139 J Hugh 111 M 61 62

JOHNSTON (Continued) Maro 118 Matthew 92 142 Mrs R 114 Thomas 54 56 98 Thos 108 Valentine 18 W A 125 William 18 Wm A 124 232
JONES, 81 166 Abraham T 180 David 165 Ellis D 114 James 46 225 Jas 68 Nannie 137 T G 195 Thomas 111 Thos 66 Wm 46
JUNKIN, John 28
JUNKINS, John 18
KALOG, 207
KAMMERER, S 203
KARR, John 228 Robert 228
KAUFMAN, A 110
KEIM, Joseph 63
KENNY, Wesley 210
KEPNER, Mrs 261
KERR, Dr 233 John P 224 Joseph 227 Moses 227 Rev 227 Rev Dr 243
KETCHUM, 5 188 189 Mr 187 S 59 Samuel 65 190 260
KIDD, Professor 138
KILPATRICK, W S 137
KIMBALL, Abner 34
KIMBERLY, Ira 45
KINCAID, Mrs 252
KING, 103 Henry 98 99
KINKEAD, Joseph 210
KINNEY, John 146
KINSEY, Lemuel 64 67
KIRK, Edward 99
KITTREDGE, A E 106
KLOSSEN, J H 109 John G 107 K 102
KNAVAL, H K 137
KNIGHT, Jonathan 98
KNISELY, Professor 138

KNOTT, J W 221
KNOX, William 210
KORS, John 146
KORTZ, Dr 119
KREMLER, 133
LAMB, 4 Emily 249 R M 96 108 Robert M 235 249
LAMBERSON, S 96 Samuel 63 65 108
LANDIS, Felix 209
LANING, Richard 81
LANNING, David 92 Linda 137 Richard 66 67 146
LASALLE, 6
LASH, Peter 18 27
LATHAM, T P 67 111 136
LAUGHEAD, Wm 219
LAUGHLIN, D E 68 223
LAWRENCE, G V 108
LAWSON, 110 D L 149 David 119
LAWYER, Jas P 137
LEAR, J 106
LEAVENGOOD, 102
LEAVITT, H 77
LEE, 81 94 B S 79 80 Dr 117 234 235 236 E G 30 116 117 Rev Mr 134 S 17 76 96 116 117 120 129 143 249 S H 4 71 93 105 109 120 149 220 234 Sabra 234 Sam'l 19 Samuel 24 54 64 69 116 118 218 219 221 234
LEGGETT, Beall 111 James 222
LEIGHNINGER, B F 149 Geo 17 67 Lewis 136
LEIGNINGER, George 28
LEMERT, 19 Joshua 33
LENHART, J 110 John 136 Jonathan 137 Peter 120
LENNON, 88 John 66

LEONARD, 82 C 79 Finley 214
LERETILLEY, 108 James 74 135 180 209 213 238 Jos 96 Rachel 213
LEWIS, B W 135 Butler T 66 Mr 135 T Butler 5 Thomas Butler 57
LEWTON, Lewis 78
LEYBRAND, Charles C 211
LINCOLN, 145
LINEBAUGH, J K 199 N 110
LITCHFIELD, Chancery 38
LITTICK, 217 Geo 24
LIVINGSTON, William 38
LOCKARD, John 254 Wm 19 67
LOCKHART, R W 197
LODER, 200 Isaac 137 John 228 Wm 219
LOHR, M 201
LONG, 109 Mr 161 Robert 96 Wm H 13
LOOSE, Geo 17 George 28 Mr 29
LOOZE, 217 George 18
LORENTZ, 43 109 John 110
LORRAIN, Alfred M 211
LOVE, 30 96 J M 70 78 144 J S 79 Jos 93 M J 120 Sam'l 97 T 97 Thos 97 Wm 225
LOWE, B I 221
LOWELL, 207
LOWEN, 43
LOWERY, Thomas 223
LUCAS, Robert 70
LUCCOCK, T S 211
LUKE, 19 Jacob 43 John 43
LUMSDEN, Wm 224
LYBARGER, 17 111 Andrew 19 24 98 143 E L 24 44 70
LYNCH, 207

LYNDE, E F 110
LYONS, A H 223 John 223 Robert 225
MADDEN, James 129
MAGAW, J G 109 151
MAGINITY, J C 98 114 Jos C 66 Joseph C 132
MAGNESS, 217 B 114 Elizabeth 137 Geo 19 George 28 29 144 James 136 Levi 19 144
MALTBY, A F 109
MANNER, Alex 103
MAPLE, Johnston 111
MARKLEY, 17 139 Adam 45 73 Barbara 45 D 106 David 45 215 Frederick 143 John 45 179 180 Wm 45
MARKS, C 102
MARQUAND, Peter 96 207
MARQUARD, Chas E 108
MARQUIS, R W 222 224
MARSH, J K 102 Professor 138
MARSHALL, D W 146 George 228 Joseph 227 Sarah 34 William 228 Wm 146 259
MARTIN, John 164 Thomas 182
MARVIN, J W 201 Mrs 261
MASSA, Emma 137
MAST, David 18
MASTON, 217
MATTHEW, C H 232
MATTHEWS, 80 Alex 63 Alex Jr 225 Alex Sr 225 C H 147 J 222 224 James 69 70 71 77 78 90 124 125 130 180 John 3 89 Rev 223
MAXWELL, Dr 123
MAYER, C 102 J 102 L 102
MAYHUGH, W C 82

MAYNARD, Isaac 86
MCANNALLY, Thomas 68
MCBANES, 217
MCBRIAR, James 68
MCBRIDE, H C 226 Walter 27
MCCARTNEY, A 150 Andrew 229 T J 111
MCCASKEY, George 34
MCCLAIN, Andrew 143
MCCLEANS, Samuel Hindman 228
MCCLEARY, G A 25 James T 68 Mrs George A 25
MCCLINTOCK, Wilson 100
MCCLOSKEY, Charles 145
MCCLUGGAGE, John 223 226
MCCLURE, Robert 222
MCCONNELL, Daniel 182 Mr 229 Thomas 92 W A 229 William A 229
MCCORMIC, Robert 130
MCCORMICK, Robert S 258 William 91
MCCOY, Edward 35 Joseph 18 36 Nancy 36 Wm 68 92
MCCULLOUGH, Geo 17 24 George 143 Wm 223
MCCUNE, 28 29 Geo 18 68 James 18 John 18
MCCURDY, Daniel 35 Elisha 245 James 35
MCDONALD, 109 E 103 Geo W 137 Mrs G A 110
MCDOWELL, 207
MCELROY, Hugh 101
MCELWEE, A 119 David 119 S 119 Samuel 119
MCFADDEN, 227 Hugh 91 92
MCFARLAND, John 182 Joseph 143 M C 76 82 132 138 259 Wm 62 209

MCFARLANE, Andrew 18
　Ezekiel 18 Samuel 18
MCFARLIN, Andrew 28
　Ezekiel 28 Samuel 28
MCFETRIDGE, Mr 90
MCGAW, J E 211
MCGILL, 110
MCGONAGLE, J 126
MCGOWAN, 62 A M 64 Alex
　24 60 130 Alexander 121
　Wilson 24 60 69 71 114 200
MCGUIRE, 88 Francis 17 18
　46 73 92 Frank 87 Mr 47
MCHENRY, David 30
MCILVAINE, Bishop 230
MCINTOSH, Gen 14
MCKEAN, John 143
MCKEE, Alexander 163 Geo
　70 223 George 211 Jas 223
　Joseph 228 Thomas 63 223
　W A 134 Wm 109 Wm A
　137
MCKENNAN, T M T 78
MCKENZIE, James 229
MCLAIN, 17 19 28 29 Isaac 47
　James 47 N 147 R W 47
　145 146 Richard W 66 Seth
　47 108 150 Thomas 18 47
MCLEARY, Thomas 211
MCMAHON, James 211
MCMANUS, P 110
MCMASTER, E D 227 Gilbert
　227
MCMORRIS, C W 67
MCNABB, 19 John 35
MCNARRY, Isaac 104
MCNAUGHTON, M W 109
MCNEAL, A 66 126
MCPHERSON, John 34
MCSUITT, J 138
MCVEY, 98 J S 96 111 Joseph
　S 63

MEAD, Wm E 57
MEANS, Isaac 57 Thomas 19
MEARS, Wm 195 196
MEDBERRY, 95 Arnold 87 96
　135 252 Phoebe 253
MEDBERY, 242 A 96 Arnold
　63 108 Mrs P W 226 Sylvester 57
MEDILL, Joseph 123 Wm 70
MEED, H 109
MEEK, H 108
MEGGS, Joseph 214
MEHAFFEY, S 223
MEIGS, Return J 70 142
MELISHE, Mr 113
MELSHEIMER, E 203
MENDENHALL, Professor
　138
MEREDITH, 17 26 Abner 41
　Gen 139 Isaac 142 144
　Jesse 70 Jesse H 144 John
　125 Obed 18 Stephen 41
MERRIHEW, John 45
MESKIMENS, 17 28 55
　James 18 29 51 63 86 John
　87 92 William 89
METHAM, Pren 146
MILHOLLAND, A S 224
MILLER, 97 200 A 71 Abraham 41 143 C S 100 Chas
　66 69 72 143 Daniel 87 143
　David G 225 Edward 143
　Geo 67 92 George 46
　George Sr 18 Henry 18 72
　117 Isaac G 143 Isaac M
　143 Isaac W 68 John 225
　John G 143 John H 143
　John M 143 Jonathan 117
　L R 110 Levi P 211 Michael
　24 49 72 95 143 Michael Sr
　18 24 Mr 94 Nicholas 16 17
　23 O 111 P 110

MILLER (Contined)
  Patrick 18 51 Saul 92 201
  Wendell 46 Windle 72 143
MILLIGAN, T V 134
MILLS, John 18 28 73
MILNER, A N 109 133
MIRISE, 103 Jas 98 John 57
MITCHELL, 17 32 D P 211
  John 63 74 205 210 230
  William 72 74 Wm 19
MIX, A 195 Amos 193 195
MOFFAT, S 100 Samuel 100
MOFFIT, W J 151
MOFFITT, 121 S 57 Samuel 242
MONROE, 246 J F 95
MONTEUR, 167
MONTGOMERY, Mr 106
MOODE, Richard 63 90 130
MOORE, 17 42 88 110 217
  Allen 143 Commissioner 23
  J T 138 James 70 180 214
  James Sr 214 John 120 214
  223 225 226 John D 17 23
  143 Peter 19 23 143 Philip
  92 Robert 86 214 S H 56
  Samuel 7 63 87 92 Thomas
  31 William 214
MORELAND, J W 198
MORGAN, 148 G W 70 John
  261 Moses 28 114
MORRIS, Bishop 205 Thomas
  A 209 Thos A 211
MORRISON, B M 197 Sam'l
  19 Saml 66 Samuel 16 23
  45 53 66 114 143 260
  William 16 23 142 Wm 19
  45 114
MORROW, J B 221 Jeremiah 70
MORTON, G R 116 Geo R 130
  George R 117

MOSSMAN, 19
MULATT, Isaac 183
MULFORD, 19 H S 137
MULLIGAN, J 110 John 92 102 182
MULVAIN, 108 Jas 18 John
  18 28 Joseph 28 William 28
  Wm 18
MUNHALL, William 217
MUNRO, Joseph F 89
MUNROE, 97 E B 76
MURPHY, F M 137
MUSSEY, Rev 220
MYERS, J W 203
MYSER, 46 J F 137 Jacob 203
  Jennie M 137
NANTICOKE, Samuel 162
NEAL, Moses L 114
NEEL, Moses 129
NEELEY, A 81
NEFF, 17 Joseph 19 24 63 143
  Peter 107
NEIGH, J 211
NELDON, 19
NELSON, Elijah 18
NEWCUM, 139 Elijah 19 144
NICHOLAS, 81 82 190 J D 79
  150 Jennie 135 John D 67
  80 145 146 149 182 W 138
NICHOLS, C 146 147 257 Eli
  26 247 257 Lloyd 248 Loyd
  26 Willard 182
NOBLE, David 219 John 18 23
NOLAND, Pierce 33
NORDMEYER, Father 202
NORMAN, Benjamin 18
NORRIS, 17 19 Daniel 36
  Elder 193 M L 93 96 186
  206 Nancy 36 S 193
  Samuel 36 Stephen 193
  194 Thos Sr 35 Wm 36 46

NORTHRUP, Thomas J 43
NORWOOD, David 227
NUNEMACHER, J D 230 Rev Mr 134
O'HARA, 123
O'LEARY, Mrs 186
O'NEIL, Thomas 130
ODELL, Sherry 101
ODER, 200 A W 135 193
ODOR, A W 194 195 196 197 198
OGILVIE, F M 137
OGLESBY, James 16 19 37 144 Mr 38
OLIVER, John 125
ONSPAUGH, George 18
ORR, Joseph 136 Matthew 18
OSBORNE, S 111
OTIS, E 195
OVERTURF, Wm 201
PALM, 99
PANCAKE, William 214 255
PARKER, Ezekiel 19 James 43 Leonard 215 Mr 56 Sarah 239
PATTON, John D 57 John G 146
PECK, J B 111 215
PEIRPONT, Wm 18
PENN, Wm 11
PEPPER, G W 146 149
PERKINS, 207 Samuel 33
PERRY, John 57
PERSHING, H 211
PETERS, E 201
PEW, James 37
PHILIPPE, Louis 174
PHILLIPS, 217 Jas D 137 Maggie S 137 Theophilus 40 114 185 209 213
PIEFFER, G A 103
PIERSON, John 70
PIFFER, Adam 92
PIGMAN, 17 J G 19 J W 19 James W 255 John G 24 26 63 143 John H 108 Joseph W 30 69 74 212
PIPE, Capt 7 14 163 165
PLATT, T J 111 Thomas 66 68
POCOCK, 109 111 E J 92 216
POE, Lt 149
POMERENE, 81 J C 80 112
POMRENE, J C 132 133
POMREUE, J C 59
PORTER, John 218
PORTEUS, 217
POWELL, F W 182 Thomas 46
POWELSON, 19 162 S V 217
POWERS, W R 131 134 Wm R 132 137
PRENTISS, E P 87
PRICE, 185 Geo W 66 Mrs W H 261 Rebecca 241 S 194 W H 66 114 William H 57
PRIMER, 204
PRITCHARD, 194 John 30 200
PROSSER, E 94 105 Edward 104
PROUDFIT, David 227
PUGH, Ida 137 138 Ida A 138
PURCELL, J B 202
PURDY, Wm 200
QUIGLEY, John 63
RABB, B 201
RADER, H W 211
RAHAUSER, H 64
RALSTON, Dr 111 T 120
RAMPHEY, Thomas J 40
RAMSEY, Henry 38
RANCH, Father 202
RANDLES, Abraham 40 41 John 41

Index. 281

RANKIN, Mr 239 Sheriff 190
RANSOM, 4 95 242 Alonzo 57
   Leander 57
RAVENSCRAFT, 19 129 Col
   139 James 34 67 69 128
   Jas 63 67 William 34
RAYMER, Cassie 137
REA, 65 John 64 Samuel 64
   77 128 130
RECK, J B 202
RECTOR, N 96
REED, D F 227 J W 195 196
   Jacob 18 James 183 Judge
   183 William 74 80 Wm 182
REID, D F 228
REMICK, Chas K 64
RENFREW, 19 Alexander 247
   James 54 57 64 96 108 218
   221 233 243 244 James Jr
   233 John 242 Mr 233 244
   Mrs Alex 34 Nancy 34
   William 54 244 Wm 56 92
   97 98 108 233 Wm Sr 85
RENNER, 110
RETILLEY, 49 107 110 242 E
   L 138
RHINEHEART, L 194
RICE, Lewis 89 Sedgewick
   200
RICH, 126 John D 211 Mr 107
   Samuel 71
RICHARDS, Abraham 61
   John 145 Joseph K 179
   Mrs 178 Wm 35
RICHARDSON, John 93
RICHASON, David 208
RICHESON, John 68
RICHIE, Richard 228 229
   William 228 229
RICHISON, Theophilus 217
RICHMOND, J 111 John 47
   215

RICKETT, 4 233
RICKETTS, 19 23 Baxter 111
   Benjamin 54 63 108 114
   237 G W 105 109 Josephus
   67 78 Mr 237 Mrs 131 T C
   99 107 108 109 111 112 186
   208 219 220 T H 81
   Thomas C 208 209
RIDGELY, G 59
RIENNECKE, Dr 171 Mr 170
   Rev Mr 170
RINE, Henry 35 John 33
RIRIE, Jas 149
ROBE, R 219 Robert 224
ROBERTS, Delia 132 Dr 40
   Martin 121
ROBINSON, 16 89 183 184
   Benjamin 18 24 51 E L 92
   James 18 24 25 69 74 128
   208 209 236 James E 63 92
   John 24 Judge 87 207 Maj
   85 139 W H 62 W H Jr 101
   102 W H 133 151 219 220
   Wm 18 Wm J 24
RODAHAVER, D 150 David
   66
RODERICK, 19 139 Lewis 24
   Louis 25
ROOT, L 66 194 195 196 197
   198 199
ROSCOE, Wm 4
ROSE, 98 D 109 149
ROSECRANS, J H 202
ROSS, Geo 58 152 John 58
   Ninian 58
ROW, Lewis 68
RUE, 5 109 J L 92 J W 58 59
   64 65 130 179 186 Joseph
   210 233 Joseph W 89 233 T
   L 179 Thomas 63 Thomas
   L 24 72 143 232 Thos L 19
RUSSELL, Dr 119 120

RYAN, Charles 44
S_____h, Christ 191
SALSBURY, Daniel 43
SAMPLE, S 137 William 74 79
    80 81 94 180 220 Wm 67 70
    78 79 130 132 133 182 190
    219 260
SAMPSON, H 195 196 198
SAMSON, S 203
SANGSTER, C F 68 70 92
SAPP, 79 E 119 121 151
    Enoch 118 Silas 118
SAUNDERS, William C 91
SAWYER, J 59 Joseph 145
SAYER, H 194 197 Stephen D 68
SAYRE, S 226
SCARBOROUGH, W B 225
SCHAUMEEKER, 204
SCHEBOSH, 164
SCHLEGLE, 204
SCHLEICH, Geo 103
SCHMELZ, 204
SCHMESER, Henry 25
SCHMIDT, 204
SCHMUESER, Henry 63 182
SCHOTT, N 96 102 Nicholas 68
SCHREID, Fred 97
SCHWEIKER, C 109
SCOTT, Gen 145 Jane 263
    John P 229 Jos 18 Joseph
    18 24 Matthew 104 253 262
    Mr 253 254 Samuel H 262
    Thomas 70
SEARL, C W 74
SEARS, Dr 118
SEDGEWICK, Geo C 200
SEEVERS, Henry 67 Robert 90
SEITZER, John 182
SELDENRIGHT, Elizabeth 34

SELLS, 19 47 Abraham 68
    209 233 234 B F 64 102 147
    234 James 66 James M 147
    190
SENTER, E B 194 196 197 198
SEVERNS, 17 Joseph 25 26
    Samuel 26 William 26
SEWARD, F 91 Mr 102 O M 137
SHAFER, 30 N 108
SHAFFER, A 225 Abraham 63
    E 147 John 18
SHAMBAUGH, Isaac 19 25
    144 217
SHANBAUGH, Isaac 24
SHANNON, 46 I N 222 John
    32 152 Nathan 222 Thomas
    224 Wm 225
SHAW, Araminta 132 B 112 B
    R 64 74 109 114 133 180
    209 210 Benjamin R 74 209
    H 110 H N 71 98 99 103
    104 108 109 133 Henrietta
    209 Henry N 182 Hiram 99
    Joseph 211 Mrs N H 132
    Robert 5 Velzer 136
SHELDON, H O 213
SHEPHERD, Col 9
SHEPLON, 32
SHERNAN, Charles R 75
SHERROD, John 101
SHIELDS, John 103
SHIPMAN, J W 55 James W 99
SHITZ, Mr 91
SHOEMAKER, 105 Joseph 213
SHOFFNER, 108
SHRAKE, John 55
SHREVE, C R 137 138
    Charles R 135 Mr 138

SHURICK, N M 121
SIBLE, 39
SIBLEY, 30 A 225 Alonzo 136
SILLIMAN, Ann 249 G W 5
  67 78 88 174 249 Geo
  Willys 77 Mr 249 W 66
  Willys 249 Willys Cass 249
  Wyllis 76
SIMMONS, 183 C W 42 135
  Charles W 69 John T 67 76
  79 118 137 Maj 85 R 118
  Wm 42
SIMONS, Wm 68
SIMPSON, Bell 137
SINCLAIR, Robert 101
SINSABAUGH, H 211
SKILLMAN, Isaac 223
SKINNER, C 102 Geo 18 J C
  195 196
SLAUGHTER, 17 19 Alex 36
  Dr 36 Henry 36
SLAVE, Letty Thomas 183
  184
SLAYTON, A H 59
SLEUTZ, J S 203
SMAILES, G W 147 Thomas
  182
SMELTZER, John 66 69 108
  178 186 242 Mary 255
SMITH, 29 227 E 196 E B 195
  Edward 35 Francis 143
  Geo 18 George 27 28 H O
  152 J G 132 J M 92 120 Jas
  M 63 John 30 43 203 Maro
  J 110 R N 135 Solomon 30
  Thomas 35 W 121 William
  239 Wm 120
SNEETHEN, N 217
SNYDER, S 110 S P 137
SOUTHARD, Rev Mr 47
SOVERNS, Joseph 144
SPALDING, Rufus P 75

SPANGLER, 4 A H 74 80 105
  133 David 66 71 77 79 80
  180 209 249 E T 59 70 79
  112 190 Elizabeth 209
  Elizabeth Grafton 251 Mr
  101 250 Mrs D 153 Mrs
  David 208 Mrs E T 127
  Sister 208
SPARKS, David 203
SPEAKS, Wm 45
SPENCER, Nathan 90 Robert
  O 209 W K 137 William
  194 Wm 193 200
SPRAGUE, 98 200 John 38 W
  110
SPRINGER, C 211 Cornelius
  211 217
SQUIRE, Samuel Sr 262
SQUIRES, 19 Bradley 27 130
STACKHOUSE, Amos 18
STAFFORD, 17 19 F A 114
  Francis 27 Frank 92 Mr
  102
STALL, William 43 203
STAMFORD, C W 110
STANBERRY, Jonas 43
STANFORD, C W 66
STANLEY, Capt 146
STANTON, Dr 117 William
  118 Wm 69 98 101
STARKEY, Wm 40
STEEL, 204
STEENBERG, B Van 103
STEERMAN, John 143
STEPHENS, H 135
STEVENS, W D 211
STEVENSON, B 110 J B 225
  J V 223 Mr 131 Peter 92
STEWART, Caroline 132 J G
  111 112 133 James 74 John
  G 39 87 103 108 111 252
  Matthew 56 89

STILLWELL, A H 81 Richard 66 74 180
STOCKTON, Commodore 187
STONE, 80 Sam'l 38 Wm 115
STONEHOCKER, Eliza J 264 Jacob 33 34 John M 33 Melissa 137 Michael 33 34
STORKEY, J E 211
STORM, Nicholas 203
STOVER, A J 149
STRINGER, Geo 18
STRINGFELLOW, Geo 182
STROME, C 110
STROUSE, J 110
STUART, E P 120
STURGIS, Mr 131 Rev Mr 131
STURGISS, C 230
SWAYNE, 4 N H 69 78 130 Noah H 66 77 129
SWAYZE, John J 209 211
SWEENY, John M 57
SWENEY, John M 67
SWIGERT, Col 139 Lewis 63
SWORMSTEDT, Leroy 211
SYPHERT, Addison 68
TAIRARE, Andrew 29
TALMADGE, Mr 102
TANNER, Capt 142 James 18 24 25
TAPPAN, Professor 138
TAYLOR, 133 Edward 208 211 Gen 144 Hiram 187 James 101 John 63 98 152 T J 219 William 24 Wm 18
TEMPLETON, S M 224
THATCHER, Isaac 44 Rev Mr 214
THAYER, Bartholomew 37 Ephraim 56
THOMAS, A E 216 Letty 183 184 Lucy 209 W C 138 Wm C 137

THOMPSON, 17 19 42 108 110 Abraham 18 24 James 5 35 214 John 18 Moses 31 Mrs J M 249 Patrick 70 R W 182 261 S T 31 85 Thomas W 111 Wm 5 214
THOMSON, A H 109 110
THORNHILL, F W 69 70 76 108 186 Judge 86
THRAPP, Israel 217
TIDBALL, Haddasah 257 J C 132 133 180 John C 79 256 Mr 185 Mrs N R 110 N R 145 149 257 Nicholas 152 Theophilus 257 W S 152 257 William 185 Wm 114
TIDRICK, Robert 228
TILTON, Joseph 36 Richard 18
TIMMONS, John 71
TINGLE, 7
TIPTON, 19 William 43
TIRALLA, Joseph 110
TIVIS, John 210
TODD, David 70
TOLAND, J W 211
TORREY, Albert 45
TRAVIS, M 135
TRAXLER, J F 219
TREADAWAY, Thomas 214
TREDAWAY, 42
TREGO, Rebecca J 137
TRIMBLE, Allen 70 Matthew 255 Wm 18
TRIPLETT, 4 D L 89 92 96 105 112 184
TRUBIT, John 221
TRUEMAN, D 211
TRUMAN, D 217
TURBIT, Mr 224
TURNER, James 72 John B 64 Walter 27

TUSSING, S C 195 196
TUTTLE, Phineas 220
VAIL, J D 211 Joseph 19
　Lewis 18 19 74 Solomon 5
　31 56
VANALLEN, 103
VANBUREN, 246
VANCE, John 91
VANEMAN, M D 136
VANKIRK, 139 C 66 233 C P
　19 Cornelius 24 72
VANNESS, C P 77 249
VICKARS, W H 119
VICKERS, Taliafero 246 W H
　263
VONRUEDEGISH, Dr 121
VOORHEES, R M 71 80 94
　145 182 190
VOORHES, R M 67
W, 181
WADDELL, Dr 121
WADDLE, John 57
WADE, Matilda 180 Mrs 180
WAGGONER, David 217
　Harrison 133 J 109 Jacob 5
　95 132 133 239 John 66 92
　Philip 17 18 28 72 Phillip
　217
WAGNER, John 137
WAGONER, Phebe 185
WAGSTAFF, Mr 125
WAIT, Dr 121 Joshua W 229
WALKER, Mrs W 109 W 133
　Wm 64
WALLACE, 166 Adam 209 C
　W 132 150 220 226 Martha
　209 Mary 209 Rev 225
WALLING, A T 117 125 Dr
　121
WALMSLEY, John 24
WALMSLY, John 18

WALTERS, 46 David 225
WARD, 179 188 Charles J 57
WARING, 183 184
WARNER, Geo 218 George
　221 Wright 19 66 76
WARREN, 227 Robert C 229
WASHBURN, D 224 Mr 224
WASHINGTON, George 163
WATERMAN, John 210
WATKINS, Dr 119
WATTS, Dr 87
WAYNE, Anthony 34
WEATHERWAT, Andrew 41
WEATHERWAX, Abraham
　182 Andrew 214 George
　224 John 149 Wm 224
WEAVER, J W 211
WEBER, John 203
WEEKS, Mr 125
WEISER, Martin 101 147
　Pauline 137
WELCH, 200 Jacob 57 James
　18 William 62
WELKER, 79 Judge 74
　Martin 74
WELLING, Mr 103
WELLS, Chester 220 W 210
WERNETT, 121
WERTHEIMER, 183 Abra-
　ham 181 Isaac 181 182 J
　110
WERTZ, John 203
WEST, S 195 198
WESTLAKE, Burnis 211
WETZEL, Lewis 10
WHEATON, 126
WHEELER, Caleb 149 H T
　137 Henry 63 68 Samuel
　219 Wm 5 Wm P 65
WHITAKER, J G 194 196 198
　R 195-198

WHITE, Augustine 33 114 B
  195-197 200 Elder 196
  Perry 111 Professor 138 T
  H S 211
WHITHAM, John D 221
WHITMORE, Samuel 70
WHITTAKER, 214 James 180
  Reuben B 255
WHITTEMORE, 200 D G 110
  Henry 215
WHITTEN, 17 William 184
  Wm 19 24 60 64
WICKHAM, S 197
WIGGINS, Jane 18 Jonathan
  111 Thomas 16 46 68
WILCOX, Charles 209
WILCOXEN, G F 109
WILEY, James 144 Samuel 37
WILKIN, A J 81 133 Andrew
  J 70 J 109
WILKINS, Andrew 98
WILLETTS, Dr 118
WILLIAMS, 4 17 53 62 63 81
  102 109 114 139 175 A M
  64 80 Addison M 101 B F
  100 Charles 16 18 23 24 28
  32 51 60-63 69 72 73 112
  142 143 232 Chas 66 Col 76
  88 89 108 174 Dr 70 117 H
  92 Heslip 70 92 118 J M
  137 J S 152 James 27 144
  John 16 19 32 227 John F
  66 Joseph 32 49 70 Louisa
  257 Matthew 143 Professor
  138 Sharon 254 Susannah
  232 W H 120 Wilber G 137
  Wm G 32 65 67 125
WILLIAMSON, 169 170 Col
  166 167 168 John 228 229
  Piatt 41
WILLIS, James 19 John 149

WILSON, 108 109 Dr 121 J S
  112 133 John P 3 31 Judge
  72 73 Thomas 100 Wm 72
WIMMER, A 62 M W 66 138
WINDERS, James 24 143
WINKLEPLECK, 19 A 203
  Samuel 63 180
WINKLPLECK, 43
WINN, J M 195 197 200
WINSLOW, J W 120
WIRICK, Rev Mr 126
WOLF, 88 102 Francis 92
  Frank 214 G W 92 Geo 87
  98 George 63 86 Jacob 222
  John 17 18 26 L B 149
  Philip 18 28 Wm 64
WOLFE, Wash C 126 Wm 98
WOLLFE, 171
WOOD, A G 56 89 Col 105
  William 238
WOODWARD, S P 136 137
WOOLFORD, 17 Frederick 18
  27
WORK, Joseph 147
WORKMAN, 17 Benj 143 Gen
  139 Isaac 18 72 J 24 J D 63
  Jas 182 Jesse 24 Jos D 144
WORTHINGTON, Thomas 70
WRIGHT, 17 200 Darius 103
  F C 196 Highland 182
  Hiram 116 J W 109 120
  John C 75 John W 201
  Joseph 18 36 Thomas 36 W
  110 Willis 36 Wm 130
WYLIE, J S 221 Joseph S 218
  Mr 221
WYRICK, C 211
YOCUM, Rev Mr 214
YOUNG, David 207 209 211
  Jacob 209 Wm 211
YUNGE, E C 202

ZEISBERGER, 160 162 165   ZUGSCHWERT, C 109
  David 7

www.ingramcontent.com/pod-product-compliance
Lightning Source LLC
Chambersburg PA
CBHW071422150426
43191CB00008B/1013